SEATTLE TOTEMS

On the Cover: Seattle Totems center Gerry Leonard attempts to fight his way past the goaltender while being checked by defenseman Sandy Hucul during a game against the Victoria Maple Leafs in the mid-1960s. Primarily known for his play on Seattle's checking lines, Leonard also had a good scoring touch, averaging just over 13 goals per season with the Totems. (Photograph by Bob Carver.)

On the Back Cover: The Seattle Totems hosted the Russian national team in an exhibition at the Seattle Coliseum in 1974. The Russians were the defending world champions at the time and featured arguably the best goaltender in the game, Vladislav Tretiak. The Totems shocked the hockey world with an 8-4 upset, the only loss the Russians suffered in eight games against WHL opponents.

SEATTLE TOTEMS

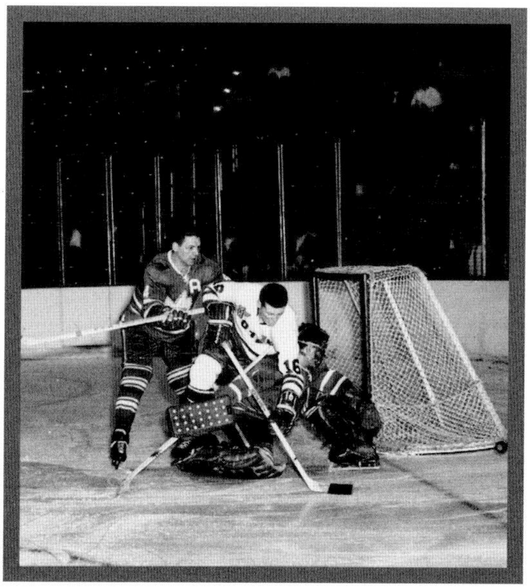

Jeff Obermeyer

ARCADIA PUBLISHING

ISBN 978-1-14671-3360-9

Published by Arcadia Publishing
Charleston, South Carolina

Printed in the United States of America

Library of Congress Control Number: 2015930976

For all general information, please contact Arcadia Publishing:
Telephone 843-853-2070
Fax 843-853-0044
E-mail sales@arcadiapublishing.com
For customer service and orders:
Toll-Free 1-888-313-2665

Visit us on the Internet at www.arcadiapublishing.com

To all those who laced up their skates and gave it their all

CONTENTS

FOREWORD

Seattle, Washington, together with Vancouver and Victoria, Canada, and Portland, Oregon, comprised one of the first professional ice hockey leagues in North America. Players from the prairies and Eastern Canada came west in 1911 to form the league. This league, the Pacific Coast Hockey Association, competed for and won the Stanley Cup several times from 1914 until 1924. New and larger buildings were built in New York, Boston, Detroit, and Chicago. The four Northwest teams moved to those cities to form the NHL, together with teams from Toronto and Montreal.

There is something magical about the game of ice hockey. Watching an ice hockey game is a memorable experience for people of all ages. The atmosphere is more vivid and exciting than any other sporting event.

The history of the Seattle Totems is unique in that the Totems provided Seattle a tremendous surge to become a major-league city. As a professional hockey team, the Totems played at the highest level in defeating the Toronto Maple Leafs and Chicago Blackhawks of the NHL and the national teams from Czechoslovakia and Russia in exhibition games.

When the Totems were formed in 1958, Seattle entered into an agreement with the Detroit Red Wings and later the Montreal Canadiens to acquire surplus players to complete the roster. The Totems won the championship that year. Since that beginning, Seattle was continuously frustrated by the deceit and dishonest dealings of the NHL.

From 1958 to 1975, the Totems played well enough to win three championships and play before more people than several NHL teams. Three players, namely Rudy Filion, Bill MacFarland, and Guyle Fielder, were better than the majority of the NHL players. Their performances as Totems were spectacular in comparison.

This book provides the details of the Totems performance, how the WHL disappeared, and why Seattle has been without professional hockey since 1975.

—Vince Abbey
February 2015

Vince Abbey passed away on June 15, 2015, shortly before *Seattle Totems* was published. His passing was a loss for his family, friends, and the Seattle hockey community as a whole, a community he was so much a part of for so many years. It was an honor and privilege to have known him, and a joy to have talked hockey with him. I will cherish those memories.

—Jeff Obermeyer
June 2015

ACKNOWLEDGMENTS

While the author gets the honor of seeing his or her name on the cover, there are always a number of people who helped along the way. This book simply would not have been possible without Dave Eskenazi, who gave me complete and total access to his archive of old Seattle hockey photographs and memorabilia. The *Seattle Post-Intelligencer* Collection from Seattle's Museum of History and Industry was also a valuable source of images, thanks in large part to the efforts of librarian Carolyn Marr. The family of the late Rudy Filion was very generous with their time and photographs, and I cannot thank them enough for the enjoyable evening I spent with Ron and his family talking about Rudy's career and, more importantly, his character as a man. Former team photographer Jerry Berg shared his photograph archive with me, as did the family of the late Bob Carver, who shot Totems games in the 1960s and whose work is well known in Seattle. I also dug deep into my own collection of Seattle hockey photographs and memorabilia as well, and any uncredited images originated from my own collection.

David Zimmerman and Louis Chirillo have been keeping the memories of the Seattle Totems alive through the Seattle Totems Hockey Club (1958–1975) Facebook page, as well as Chirillo's own Seattle Totems website: seattletotems.org. Longtime Totems owner Vince Abbey was very generous with his time, and I was honored that he agreed to write the foreword to this book. I also received support from fellow historians and friends Alan Anderson, Tim Winegard, and Hoko Shodee. Thanks, too, to Arcadia acquisitions editor Matthew Todd for giving me this opportunity and for supporting the project.

Last, but certainly not least, thanks to my wife of 21 years, Holly, who has always shown tremendous patience with my crazy research and writing projects. Without her in my life I would not be where I am today.

INTRODUCTION

Before major-league sports came to Seattle, fans made do with the minors. In the summer, the city followed baseball's Seattle Rainiers of the Pacific Coast League. But when the days got shorter and colder, when the constant drizzle that defines three of the city's four seasons started, the fans turned in other directions. On a half dozen fall Saturdays, it was University of Washington football that commanded their attention. But when it got really cold, and dark, and wet, when you thought you would never have dry shoes again, there was only one game in town. Seattle Totems hockey.

Seattle has a long and illustrious hockey history dating all the way back to 1915 and the founding of the Metropolitans, a team that in just its second season became the first American club to win the oldest and most prestigious trophy in North American sports, the Stanley Cup. Whether it was professional or amateur, hockey drew in Seattle's sports fans, giving them a place to dry off and work out some aggression by cheering on the home club as they battled and fought, sometimes quite literally, in pursuit of frozen glory.

Seattle Totems is a celebration of our hockey past, a recognition of the 200-plus men who laced 'em up, put on the uniform, and gave it their all every night. Sure, they got paid to play. But almost all of them held jobs in the off-season—they had to; there was not much difference in the pay of a minor-league hockey player and what the fan in the stands earned at his job. In the summers, they worked as electricians and plumbers, salesmen and craftsmen. They were part of our community, and many of them put down roots and stayed in the Seattle area after their playing careers ended.

Whether *Seattle Totems* is an opportunity for you to learn more about the city's hockey past or a trip down memory lane to relive your own experiences as a Totems fan, I hope you enjoy reading it as much as I enjoyed writing it.

1

Before the Totems

The Totems were not the first hockey team in Seattle. Far from it. In fact, the city's history with the winter sport predated the Totems by four decades, with the establishment of the Seattle Metropolitans in 1915. The Mets, as they were known, took their name from the Metropolitan Building Company, the conglomerate transforming Seattle's downtown into a modern city, a process that included the construction of one of the nation's very first indoor ice arenas. The team quickly became the darlings of the city, and within two years Seattle became the center of the hockey world, hosting the 1917 Stanley Cup Finals between the hometown Mets and the Montreal Canadiens. Perhaps because they were so sure of an easy victory over their West Coast rivals, the Canadiens did not even bring the vaunted cup with them, so when the final whistle sounded to end the fourth game of the series, the Mets were world champs—but did not have a trophy for their celebration.

The Mets only survived for nine seasons, folding in 1924 and seeing their beloved arena converted to a parking garage. But the city had other plans for hockey, and the completion of the Civic Arena in 1928 gave the game its new home, one that would host countless amateur and professional games over the next seven decades. From the amateur City League and the University of Washington, to professional and semiprofessional teams such as the Eskimos, Seahawks, Olympics, Ironmen, and eventually the Totems, generations of Seattle hockey fans and players called the Civic Arena home, its cozy confines and tight corners dictating a tough style of play that ensured excitement.

To understand the relationship between the Totems, their fans, and the city, one needs to go back in time to hockey's origin and development in Seattle. So, get a ticket and find a seat for this journey back to Seattle's rich hockey past.

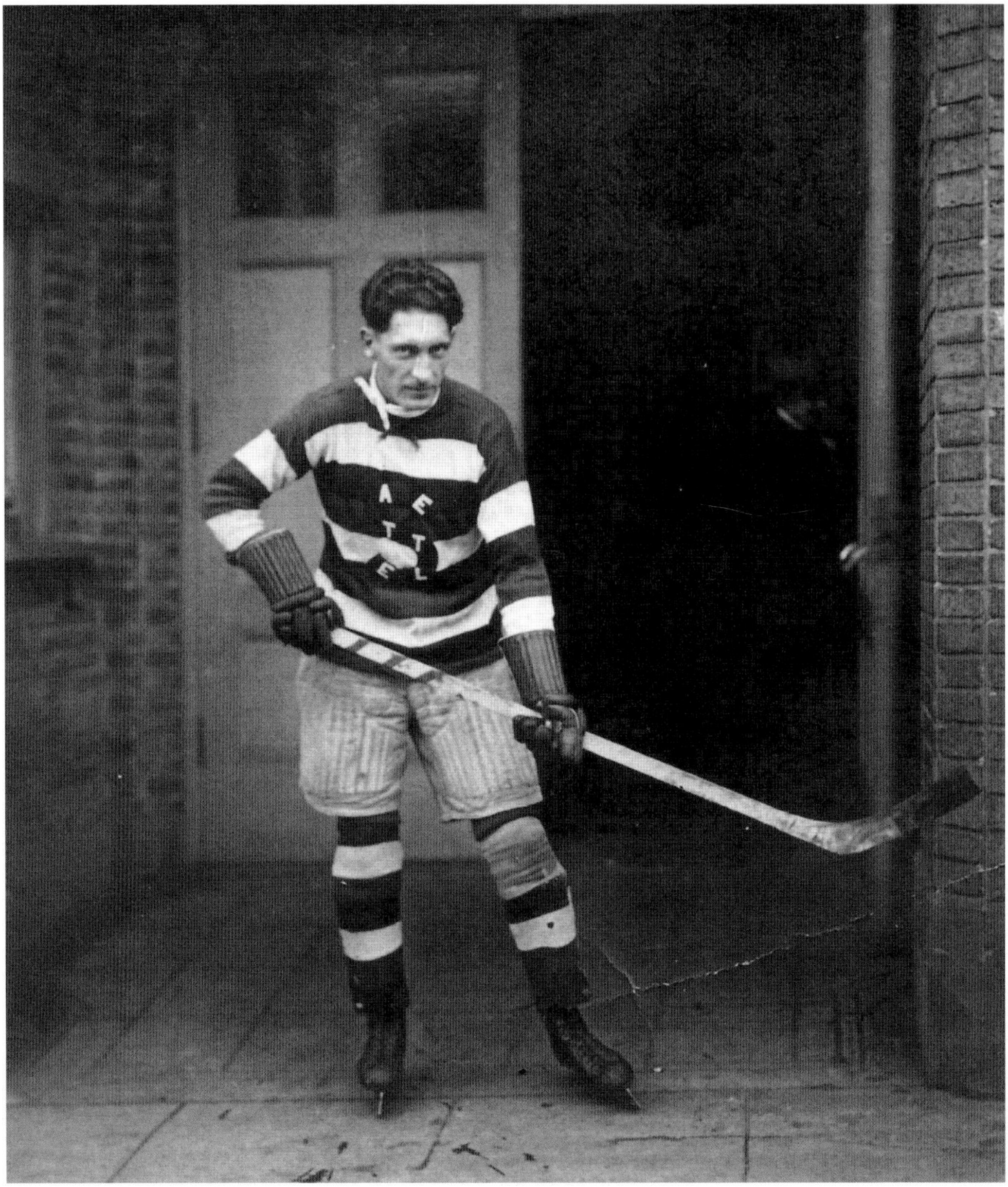

Brothers Frank and Lester Patrick were responsible for hockey making its way to the West Coast, financing the construction of new indoor hockey arenas in Vancouver and Victoria, British Columbia, and founding the three-team Pacific Coast Hockey Association in 1911. The brothers were not just fans and financiers though—both were also accomplished players in their own rights. When the Metropolitans found themselves without a coach due to Pete Muldoon heading south to take over the reins of the Portland Rosebuds for 1917–1918, Lester (shown) agreed to move from Victoria to Seattle to coach the Mets and suit up as an occasional substitute. Patrick led the Mets to a first-place regular-season finish on the strength of a 11-7 record, but the club fell to Vancouver in a two-game playoff, preventing them from traveling East to defend their Stanley Cup title against the NHL champions from Toronto. (Courtesy of Dave Eskenazi.)

Jack Walker had already won a Stanley Cup with Toronto in 1914 prior to heading West to join the newly formed Seattle Metropolitans in 1915. Despite missing most of the 1917–1918 season due to military commitments, Walker still skated in every Mets season, winning the Cup with them in 1917. He later played for the Seattle Eskimos and was a referee in various West Coast leagues. (Courtesy of Dave Eskenazi.)

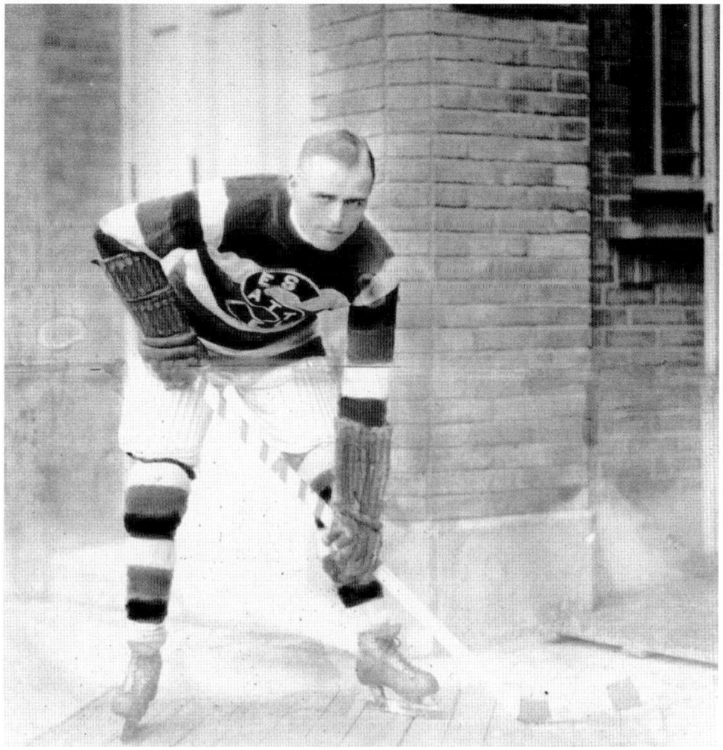

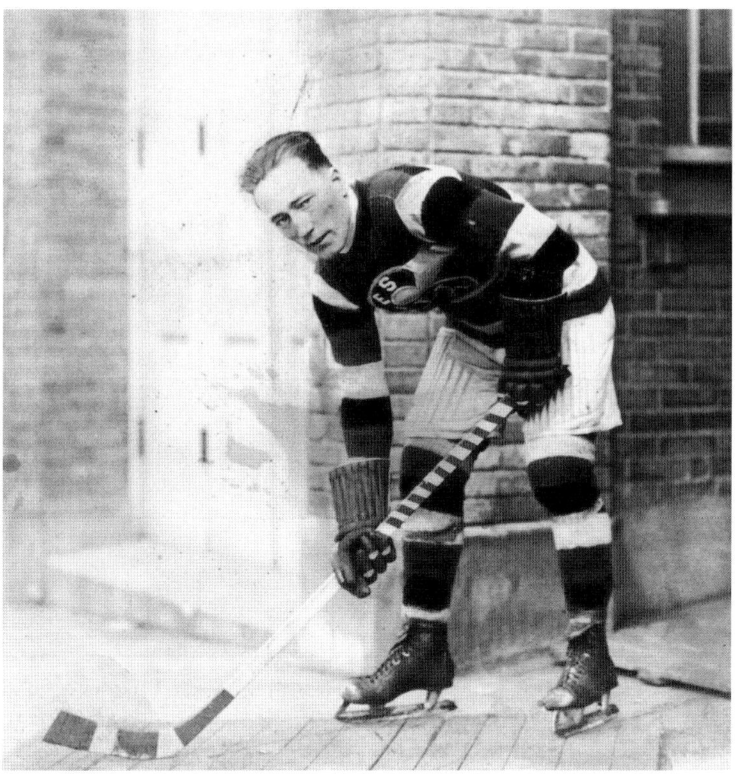

Bernie Morris was the most potent scoring threat on the Metropolitans, leading the team in goals four times and scoring 221 points in 155 career games. He almost single-handedly crushed the Canadiens in the 1917 Stanley Cup Finals, scoring an astounding 14 goals in the series, six of which came in the decisive fourth game. (Courtesy of Dave Eskenazi.)

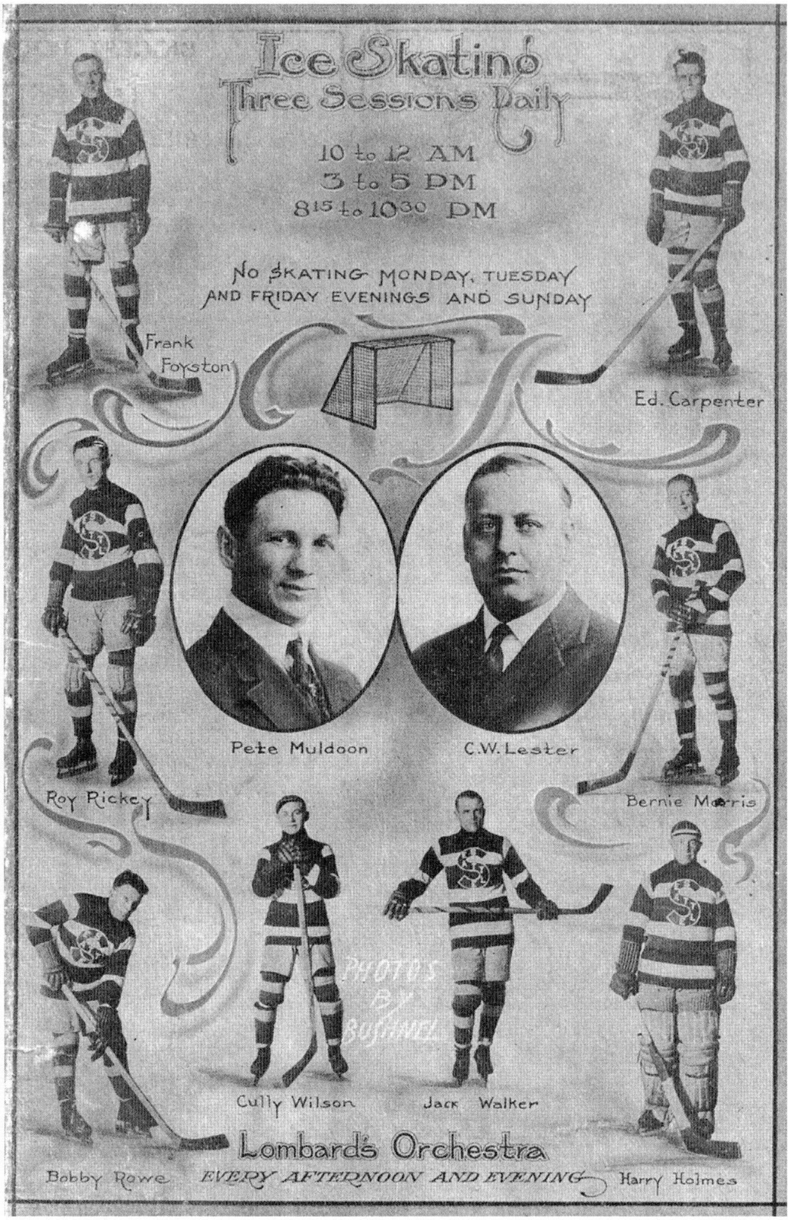

The Metropolitans finished the 1916–1917 PCHA regular season atop the standings with a 16-8 record, earning the right to host the NHA champion Montreal Canadiens in the best-of-five Stanley Cup Finals. The series may have represented the greatest collection of hockey players ever to skate on Seattle ice at one time. The Mets had an incredibly deep roster, one that included three future Hall of Famers: Frank Foyston, Harry "Happy" Holmes, and Jack Walker. The Canadiens, however, were not to be outdone and brought four Hall of Famers of their own to Seattle for the series: Georges Vezina, Newsy Lalonde, Didier Pitre, and Jack Laviolette. In the end, the Metropolitans proved to be too strong for Montreal, outscoring the Canadiens 23-11 and winning three of the four games to become the first American team to win the Stanley Cup. (Courtesy of Dave Eskenazi.)

While small of stature at five feet six inches tall, defenseman Bobby Rowe packed a wallop on the ice. Over the course of nine seasons with the Metropolitans, he racked up 297 penalty minutes, the most of anyone in franchise history. When he was not punishing the opposition, Rowe could sometimes be found coaching the University of Washington hockey club. (Courtesy of Dave Eskenazi.)

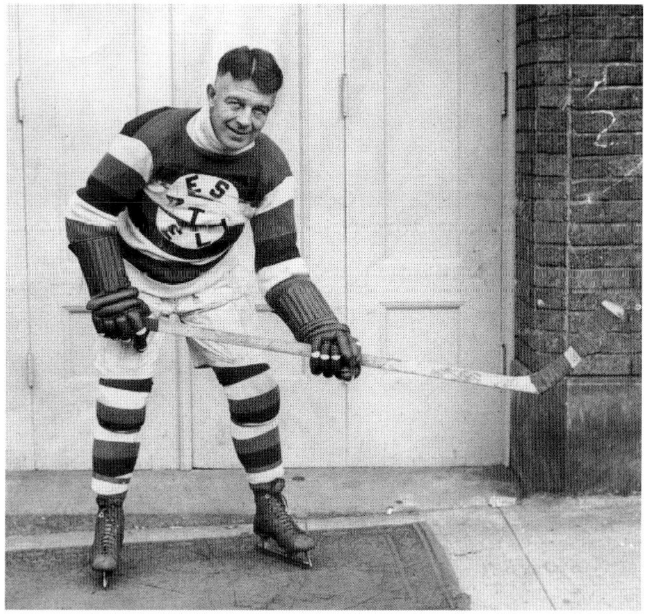

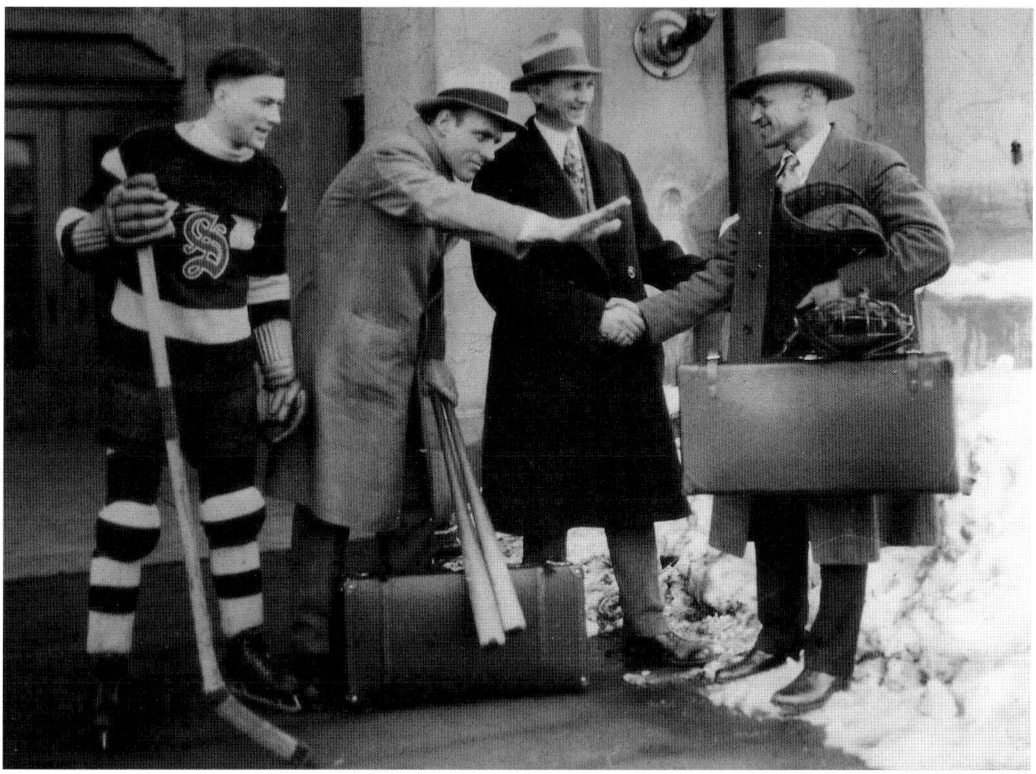

Pete Muldoon (second from right), a former professional boxer and lacrosse player, spent eight years behind the bench as the coach of the Seattle Metropolitans. Here, he says goodbye to athletic trainer Ad Schacht (far right), who was switching duties from hockey to baseball. This photograph was taken shortly before Muldoon's passing in March 1929. (Courtesy of Dave Eskenazi.)

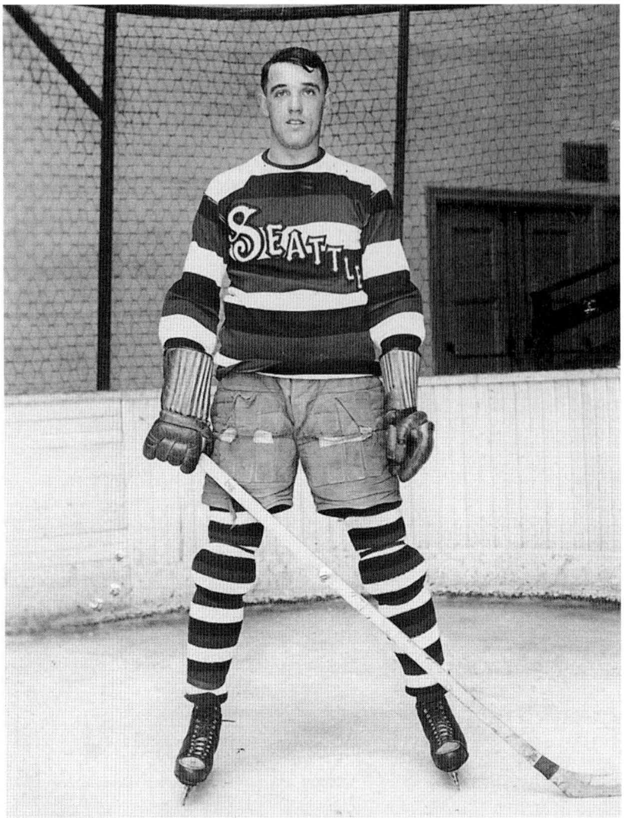

Big John Houbregs was a mainstay on Seattle ice throughout the 1930s and into the 1940s, imposing his will upon the opposition. He won a North West Hockey League (NWHL) championship with the Seattle Seahawks in 1936, scoring six goals and appearing in all 40 games. He was the father of Basketball Hall of Famer Bob Houbregs. (Courtesy of Dave Eskenazi.)

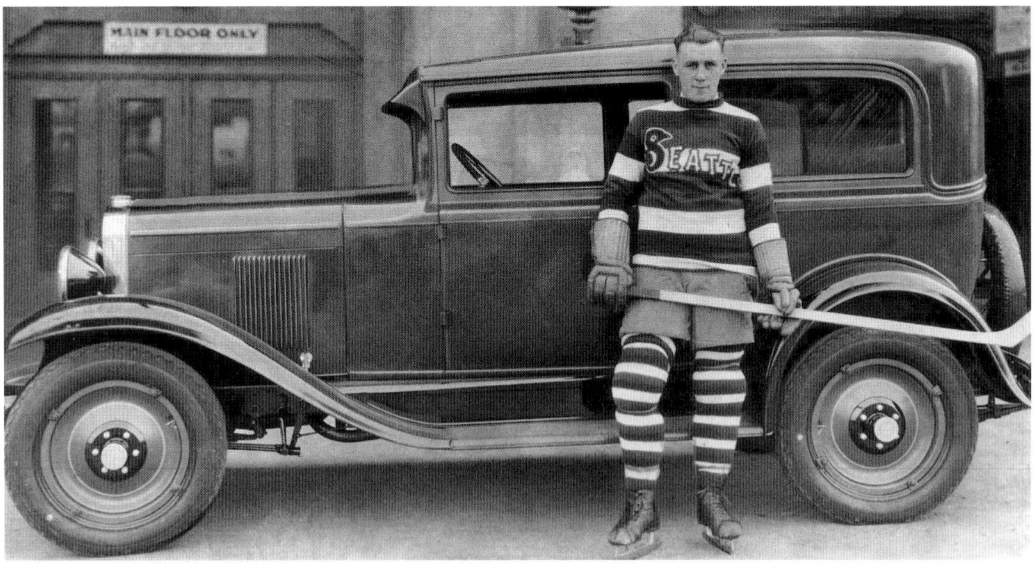

The Seattle Eskimos were the first team to form after the Metropolitans disbanded, playing three seasons in the Civic Arena between 1928 and 1931. Though they never had a losing record, they simply could not get past Vancouver in the playoffs. Following the Eskimos' demise in 1931, Seattle found itself without professional hockey for the next two seasons.

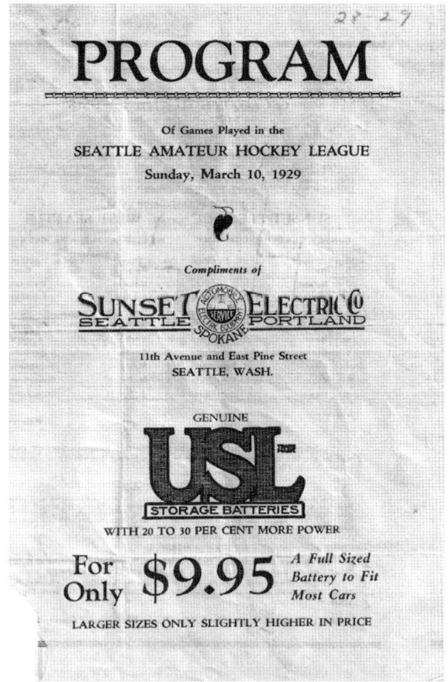
PROGRAM

Of Games Played in the
SEATTLE AMATEUR HOCKEY LEAGUE
Sunday, March 10, 1929

Compliments of

SUNSET ELECTRIC Co
SEATTLE PORTLAND SPOKANE

11th Avenue and East Pine Street
SEATTLE, WASH.

GENUINE
USL
STORAGE BATTERIES
WITH 20 TO 30 PER CENT MORE POWER

For Only $9.95 A Full Sized Battery to Fit Most Cars

LARGER SIZES ONLY SLIGHTLY HIGHER IN PRICE

The brand-new ice surface of the Civic Arena barely had time to freeze before the earliest amateur leagues formed to take advantage of the new facility. The first of these was the Seattle Amateur Hockey League, though generally the assorted amateur circuits were referred to locally as the City League. (Courtesy of Dave Eskenazi.)

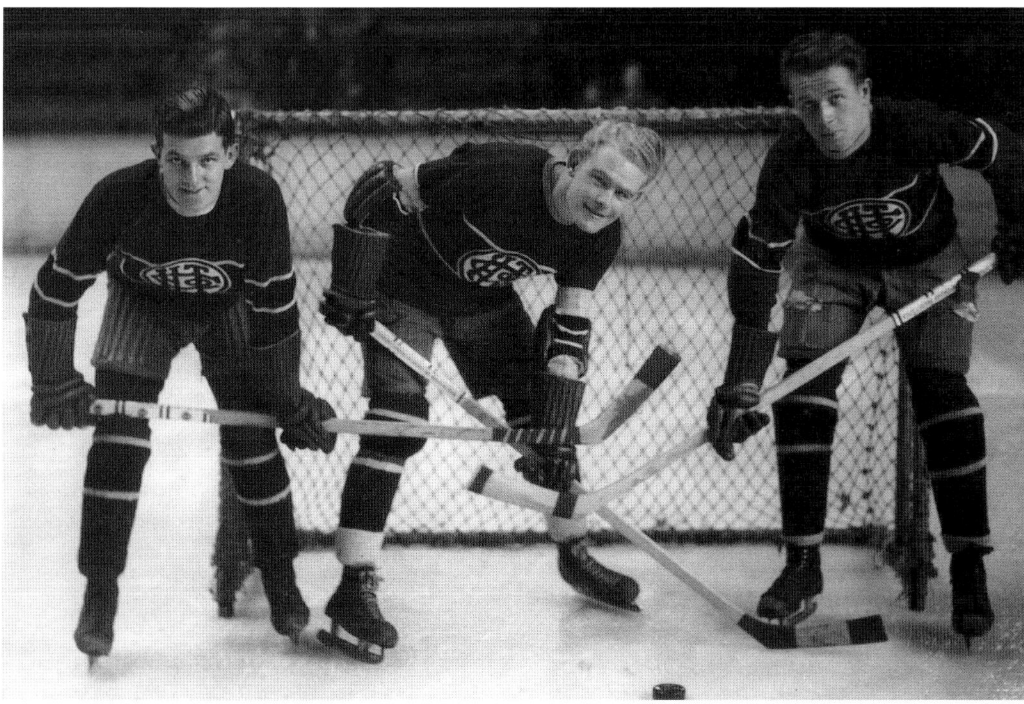

The City League was generally comprised of four teams, each tied either to a local community or a corporate sponsor. The three players shown here skated for the Hullin club around 1932–1934. The league usually limited its schedule to Friday- or Saturday-night double-headers, with all four teams in action. The Hullin squad won the league title in both 1933 and 1934.

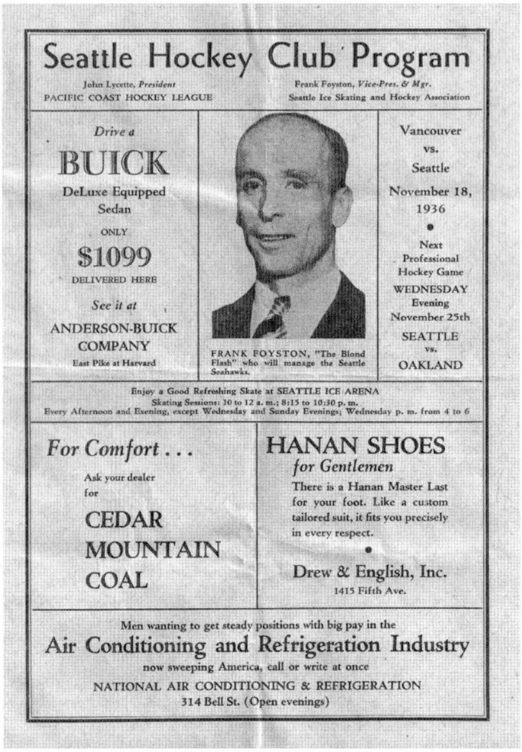

Seattle Hockey Club Program

John Lycette, *President*
PACIFIC COAST HOCKEY LEAGUE

Frank Foyston, *Vice-Pres. & Mgr.*
Seattle Ice Skating and Hockey Association

Drive a
BUICK
DeLuxe Equipped Sedan
ONLY
$1099
DELIVERED HERE
See it at
ANDERSON-BUICK COMPANY
East Pike at Harvard

FRANK FOYSTON, "The Blond Flash" who will manage the Seattle Seahawks.

Vancouver vs. Seattle
November 18, 1936
•
Next Professional Hockey Game
WEDNESDAY Evening November 25th
SEATTLE vs. OAKLAND

Enjoy a Good Refreshing Skate at SEATTLE ICE ARENA
Skating Sessions: 10 to 12 a. m.; 8:15 to 10:30 p. m.
Every Afternoon and Evening, except Wednesday and Sunday Evenings; Wednesday p. m. from 4 to 6

For Comfort . . .
Ask your dealer for
CEDAR MOUNTAIN COAL

HANAN SHOES
for Gentlemen
There is a Hanan Master Last for your foot. Like a custom tailored suit, it fits you precisely in every respect.
•
Drew & English, Inc.
1415 Fifth Ave.

Men wanting to get steady positions with big pay in the
Air Conditioning and Refrigeration Industry
now sweeping America, call or write at once
NATIONAL AIR CONDITIONING & REFRIGERATION
314 Bell St. (Open evenings)

The Seahawks were Seattle's professional hockey team from 1933 to 1940, playing in the North West Hockey League (NWHL) and Pacific Coast Hockey League (PCHL). They had some success, finishing atop the standings three times and winning a championship in 1936. They were coached during their first four seasons by Hall of Famer and former Metropolitan Frank Foyston.

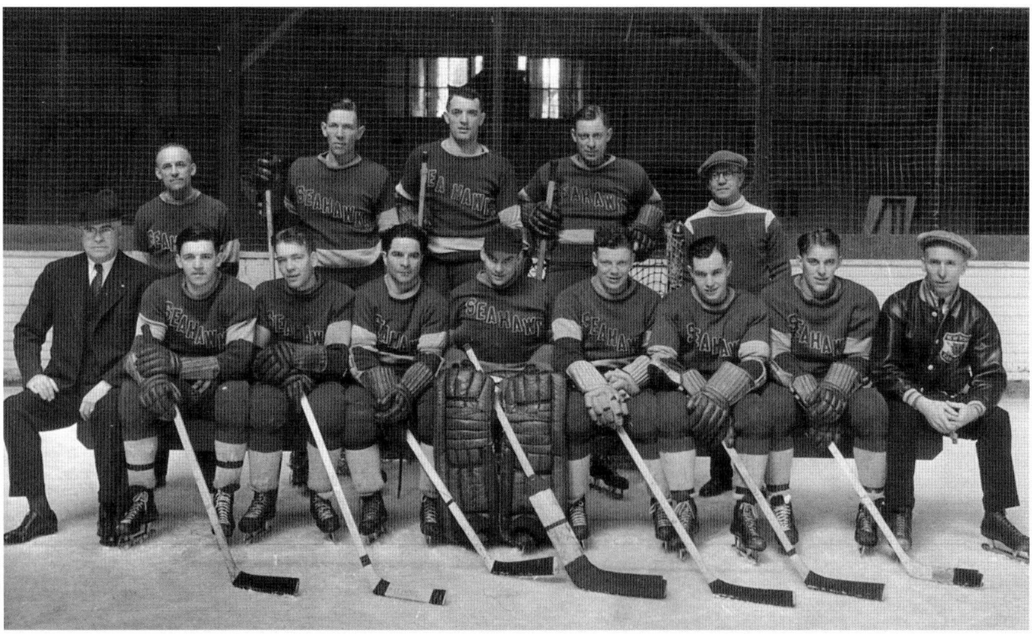

Former Metropolitan Frank Foyston (seated, far right) was fired from his coaching role prior to the start of the 1935–1936 NWHL season, but he was brought back after the team got off to a 3-7 start. The Seahawks went 16-7-6 over the remainder of the schedule and finally broke the Vancouver jinx, defeating the Lions to win the championship. (Courtesy of Dave Eskenazi.)

The Seahawks were sold after the 1939–1940 season, and the new owners rechristened the club the Olympics for 1940–1941. They also acquired the services of young 19-year-old defenseman Vic Lofvendahl, who made his presence felt by leading the team in penalty minutes with 83. Lofvendahl was even pressed into service as a goalie on one occasion when regular netminder Paul Gauthier was knocked unconscious during a game.

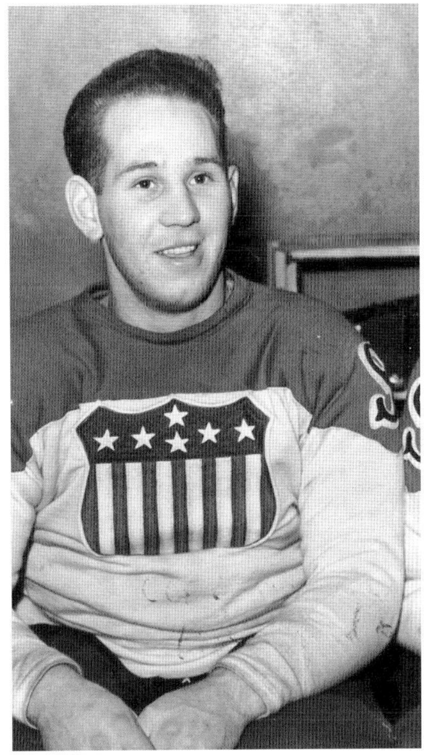

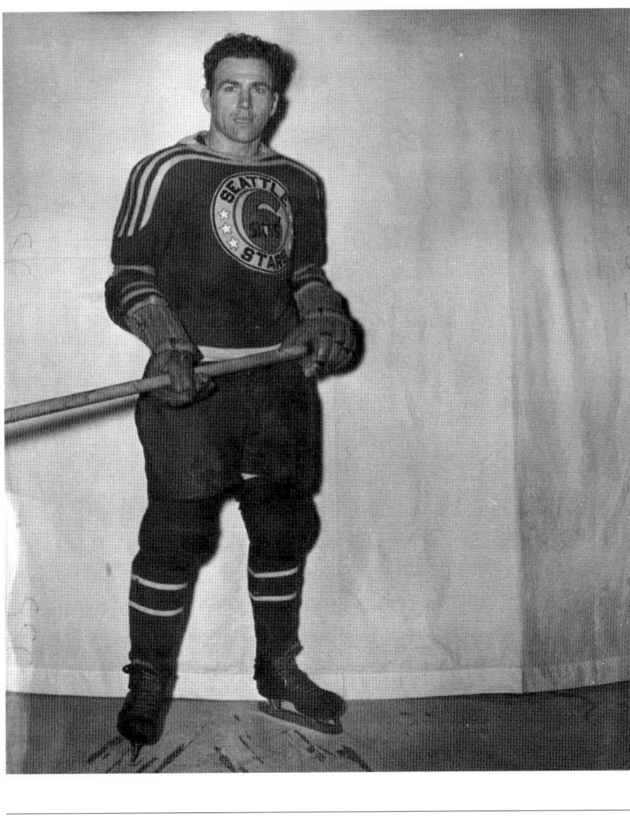

World War II put a temporary end to professional hockey in Seattle, but the amateur game played on. In 1944–1945 the new amateur Pacific Coast Hockey League (PCHL) formed, the forefather of the professional Western Hockey League (WHL) that later included the Totems. Among the league's 10 teams in that first season were two from Seattle, including Sick's Stars, led by player and coach Roger Jenkins.

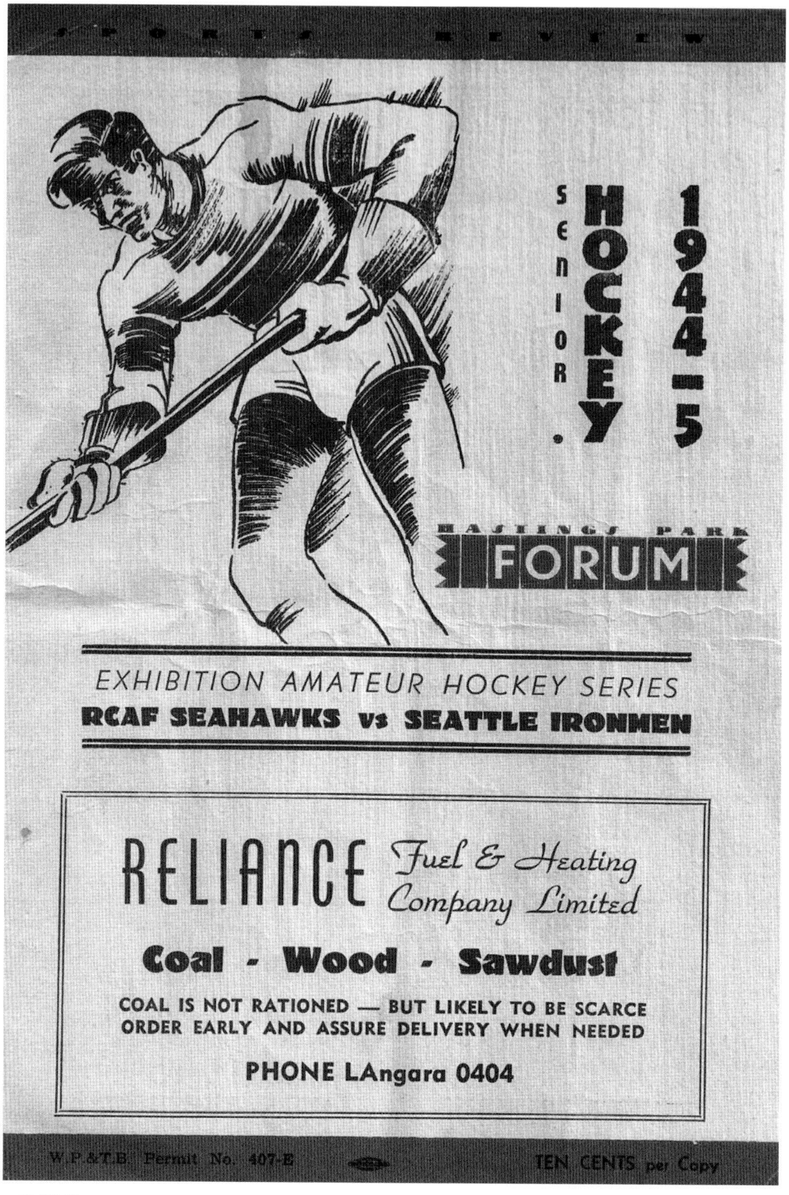

Seattle's other PCHL team in 1944–1945 was the Isaacson Ironmen, named for the Isaacson Iron Works construction and shipbuilding company. Established in 1943, the Ironmen began as an amateur team before later going professional, eventually becoming the Totems in 1958 (after periods as the Bombers and Americans). During World War II men poured into Seattle from all over the country to take advantage of wartime shipbuilding jobs, and many of them were hockey players, ensuring the city of a steady supply of skaters. That season, the Ironmen won the PCHL's Northern Division, though the series with the Southern Division champs was cancelled due to unspecified "player difficulties." Instead, the Ironmen played the Boston Olympics of the Eastern Hockey League for the Amateur Hockey Association championship, defeating their Beantown opponents in a six-game series to be crowned the amateur hockey champions of the United States.

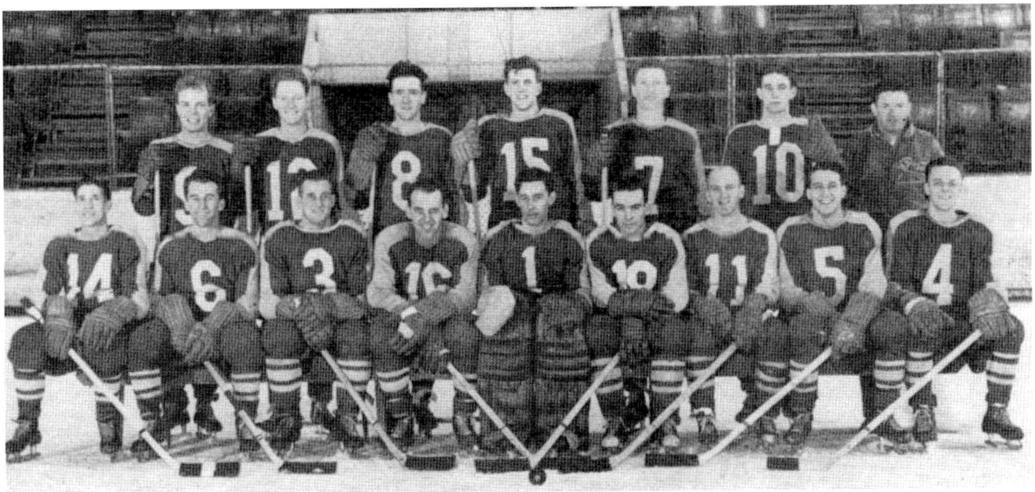

The 1947–1948 season was the PCHL's last as an amateur circuit, with the league turning professional the following year. Ironmen team members are, from left to right, (first row) Wyatt "Scoop" Bentley, Eddie Dartnell, Maurice "Butch" Marchant, Fred Ferens, Ron Pickell, Al McFadzen, Dutch Evers, Bill Robinson, and Walt Dorohoy; (second row) Maurice Duffy, Bill "Red" Tilson, Roy McBride, Ralph Toohy, Gordy Kerr, Cy Rouse, and Paul Kinney.

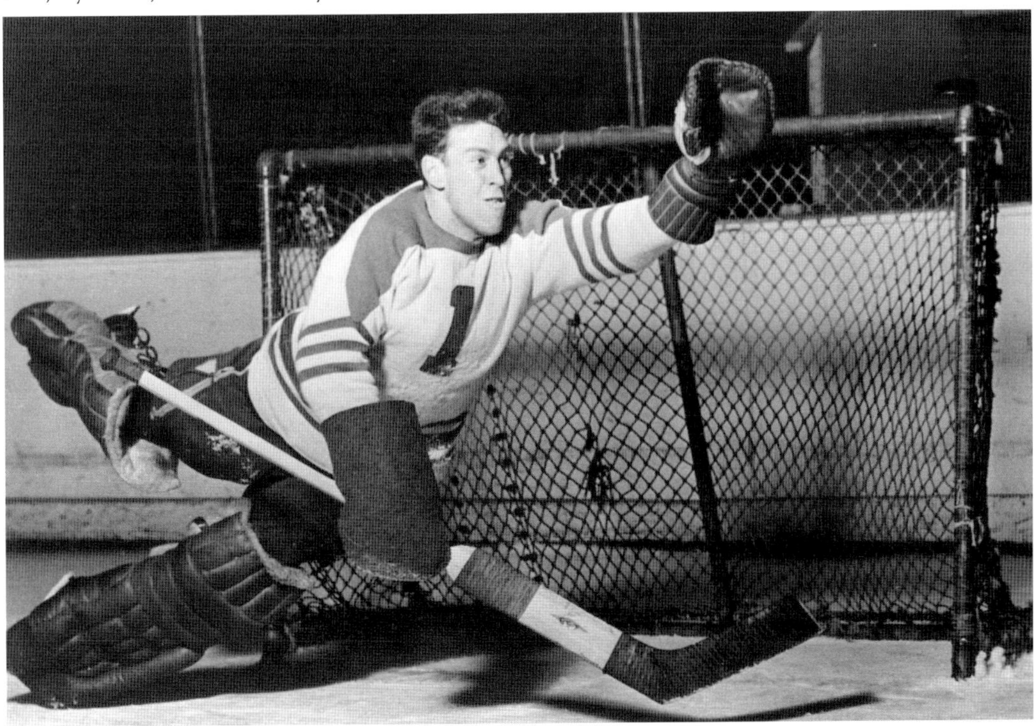

Many players, like goaltender Jerry Cotnoir, stayed with the PCHL when it transitioned from an amateur to a professional league. Cotnoir did, however, move teams during that period, heading north from Tacoma to join the Seattle Ironmen in 1948–1949. He played 95 games in Seattle, earning a 39-48-8 record. (Courtesy of Dave Eskenazi.)

The PCHL changed its name to the Western Hockey League (WHL) before the start of the 1952–1953 season. Not to be outdone, the Ironmen too opted for a new name, becoming known as the Bombers, a moniker they kept for only two seasons before financial difficulties forced them to sit out the 1954–1955 season.

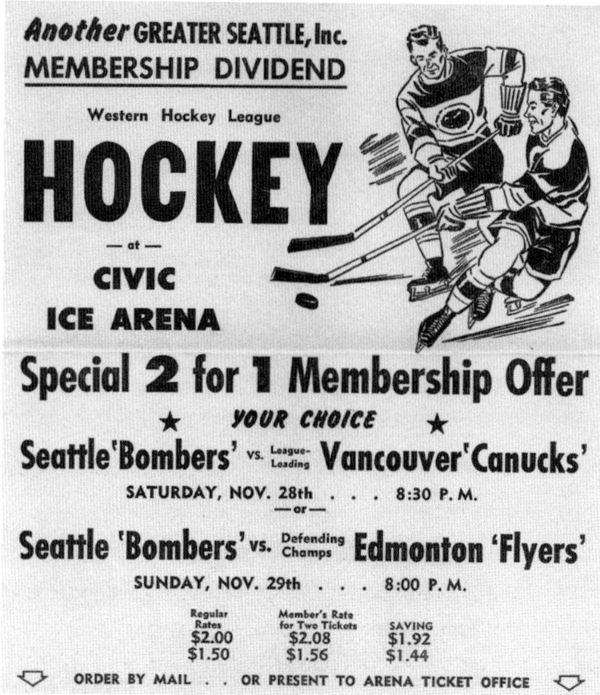

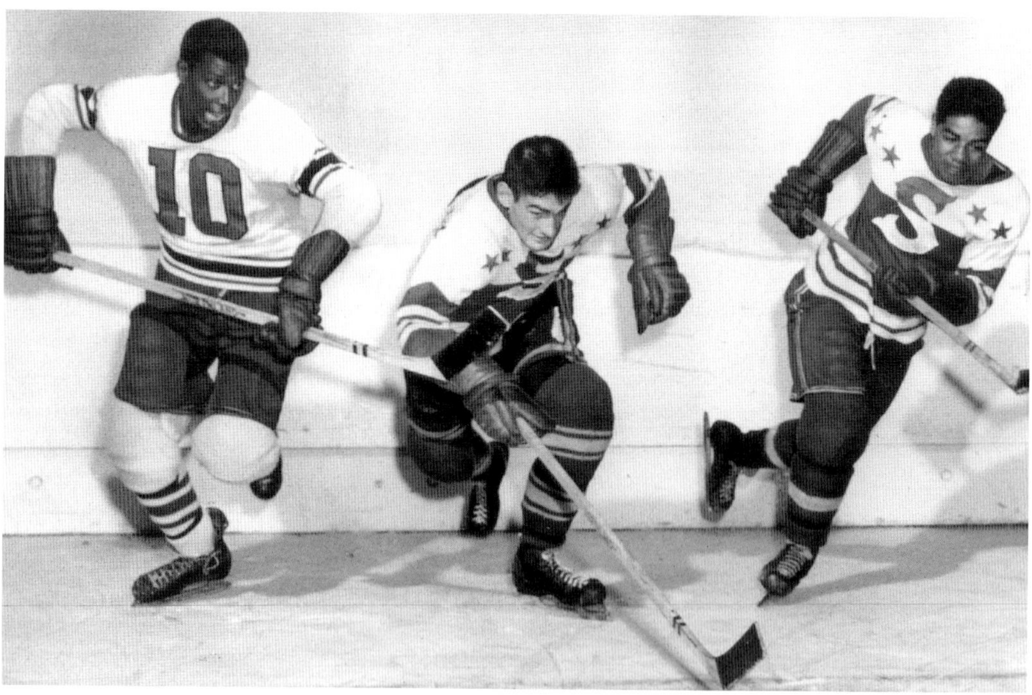

Frank Dotten raised some eyebrows when he invited Alf Lewsey (left) and Bill Geary (right) to camp prior to the 1953–1954 season. It was not due to their age or talent, but their race—both were black in an era of mostly segregated professional sports. While they appeared in preseason games, neither made the team. (Courtesy of the *Seattle Post-Intelligencer* Collection, Museum of History and Industry.)

2

Rudy Filion

A capacity crowd filled the Civic Arena on March 11, 1960. Sure, they were there to see their second-place Seattle Totems take on their cross-state rivals, the Spokane Comets. But more importantly, they were there to honor one of their own hometown heroes, the only man who played for the Ironmen, Bombers, Americans, and Totems, the one constant in a sea of changing players—Rudy Filion. Rudy Filion Night celebrated the career of one of Seattle's great hockey players and gentlemen, with gifts presented by fans and teams across the league and congratulatory telegrams coming in from politicians and hockey luminaries. In an ironic twist of fate, on the night for one of the game's cleanest players, Seattle and Spokane fought like a pack of dogs, racking up 33 penalties. Rudy, however, stayed out of the box and put the icing on his own cake by scoring a hat trick in the 4-3 win.

Rudy Filion played 14 seasons in a Seattle uniform between 1948 and 1963, the last five of which were with the Totems. In considering the entirety of his Seattle career, the results are impressive—Filion is second all-time among all Seattle players from the 1915–1975 era in regular season games played (887), goals (316), assists (553), and points (869), trailing only Guyle Fielder in all four areas. He succeeded due to his puck handling and a style of play that kept him on the ice and out of the penalty box, earning a paltry 82 penalty minutes during his entire Seattle career.

Filion was one of the classiest players in the game during a rough-and-tumble era, when stick-fights and bench-clearing brawls were still common. That class extended off the ice as well—a consummate family man, Rudy remained married to his wife, Ethel, for 63 years, raising three children and seven grandchildren. He passed away in 2011 at the age of 83.

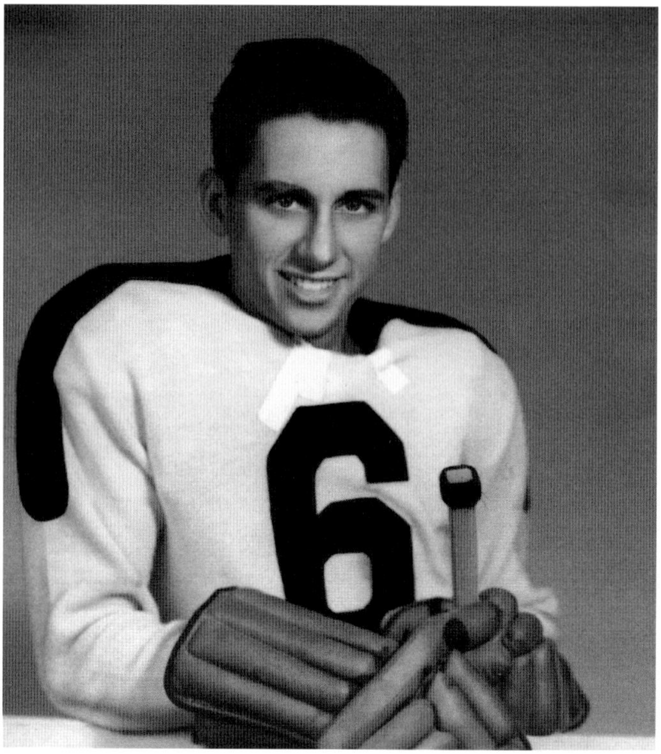

Rudy Filion's PCHL career started in the league's final year as an amateur circuit in 1947–1948, playing with the Tacoma Rockets (shown here). When the league turned professional the following year, Rudy headed north to Seattle, where he became a mainstay for the next 14 seasons. (Courtesy of the Filion family.)

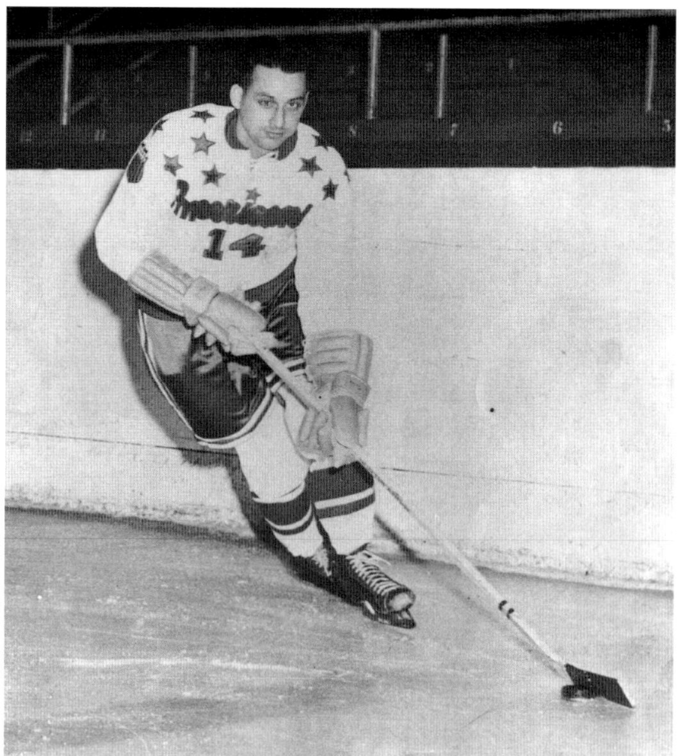

When the Seattle Bombers took a one-year hiatus from WHL play in 1954–1955, many of the players scattered to other teams. Filion, however, remained in Seattle, and when the team re-formed and returned to the league in the fall of 1955, he put the uniform back on to skate for the newly minted Seattle Americans.

Rudy Filion, shown here in action with the Seattle Americans (bottom, with puck, wearing No. 6), was a consistent offensive threat, one whom defenses needed to take seriously even when he was not among the team's top scorers. He scored 47 goals and picked up 67 assists during his three seasons with the Americans.

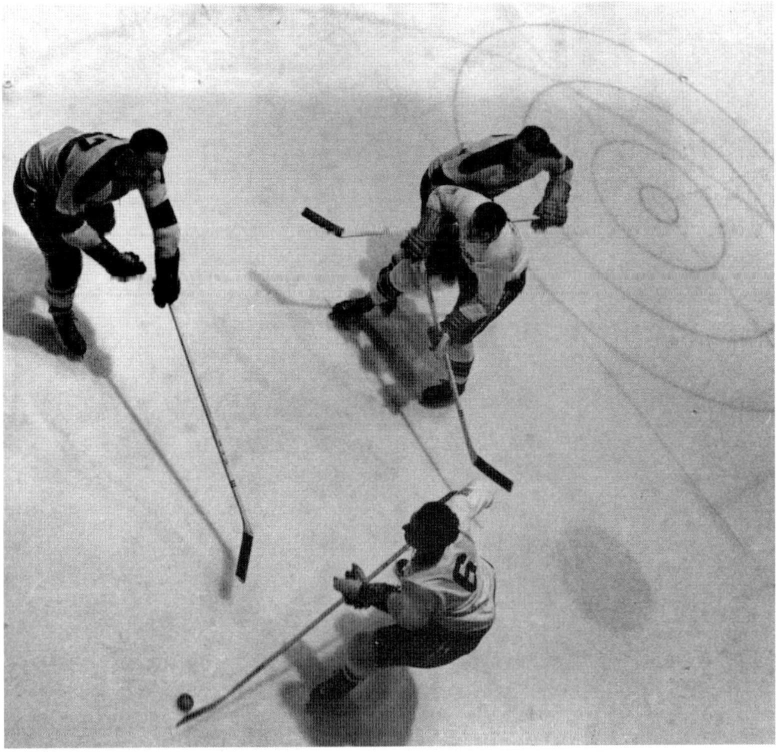

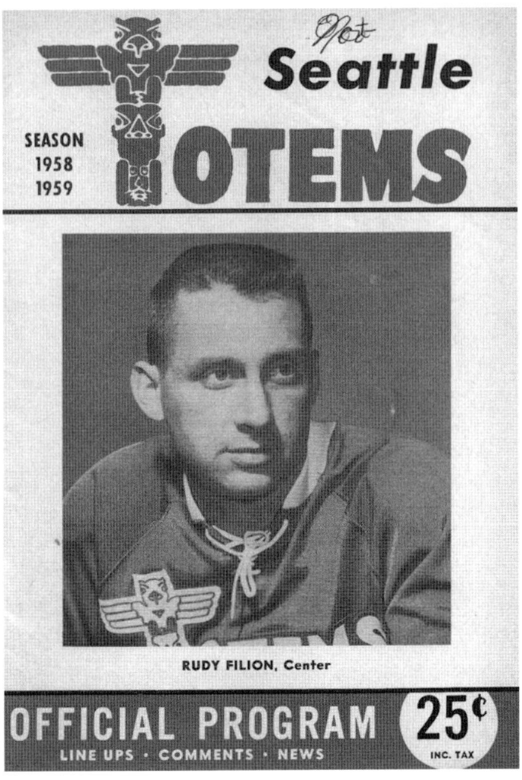

Filion was a key part of the Seattle Totems 1959 championship squad, finishing third on the team in goals (30) and fourth in points (67). He led the Totems in scoring during the playoffs with seven goals and 11 assists to help the club to its first of three WHL titles. It was Filion's only championship with Seattle.

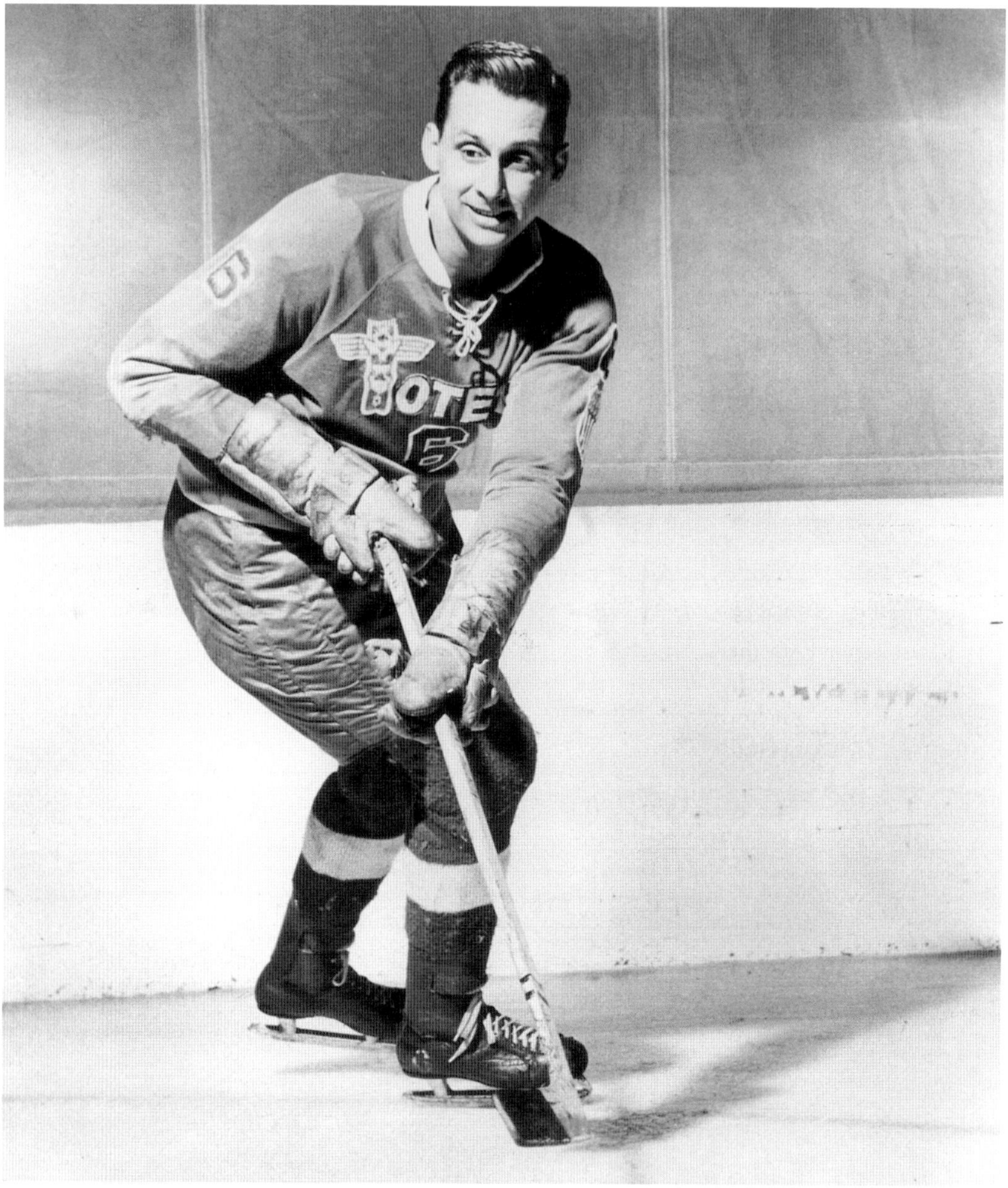

On every team he played for, Rudy Filion was regularly among the top offensive threats. Over the course of his 14 seasons in Seattle, he led his clubs in goals twice and assists and total points four times each. While his five seasons with the Totems came at the tail end of his career, they were arguably his most productive. He scored 30 or more goals in each of his first three seasons as a Totem and led the team in overall scoring in 1960–1961 and 1961–1962. He holds the distinction of being the only Seattle teammate of Guyle Fielder to ever earn more assists than Fielder in a single season, picking up 63 helpers in 1961–1962 compared to Fielder's 52. His 96 points in 1960–1961 is the fifth highest single-season total in Totems history, and he was one of only four men (along with Guyle Fielder, Bill MacFarland, and Rob Walton) to score more than 90 points in a season for the club. (Courtesy of Dave Eskenazi.)

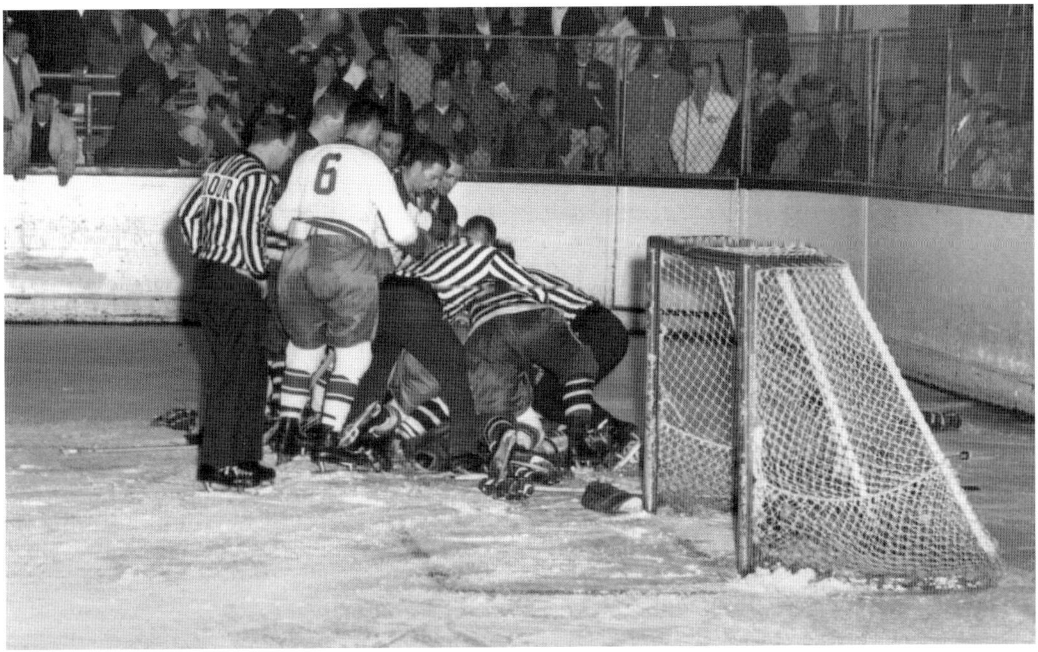

Fights were common in the WHL, though Filion (No. 6 in white) generally kept out of the fray. At least once, though, Filion lost his cool, and he engaged in a three-minute brawl with Hartley McLeod on January 6, 1952, a fight that continued in the penalty box. (Courtesy of the *Seattle Post-Intelligencer* Collection, Museum of History and Industry.)

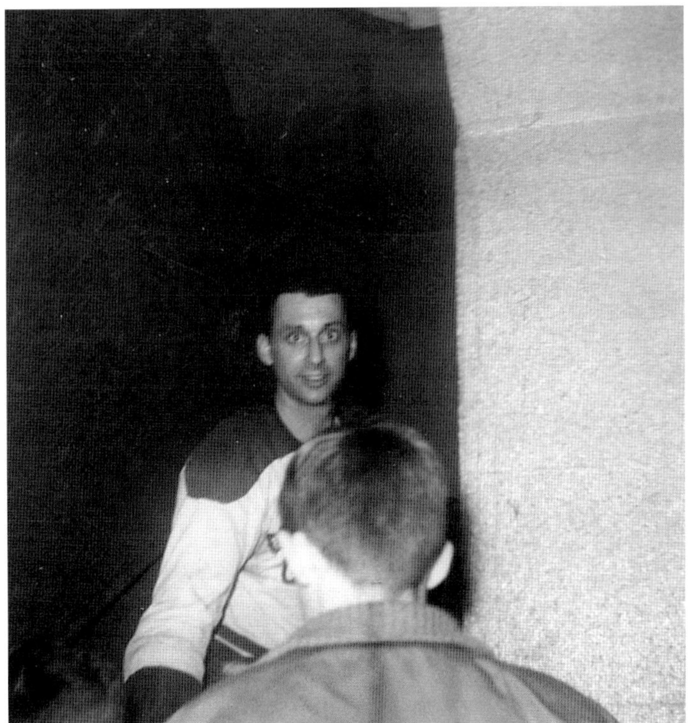

Professional-sports contracts were heavily weighted in favor of the teams until the 1970s, when the balance began to shift ever so slightly. Rudy Filion was a critic of the power owners held over the players and had the rare courage to hold out for better contracts a number of times early in his career with the Ironmen and Bombers. (Courtesy of Dave Eskenazi.)

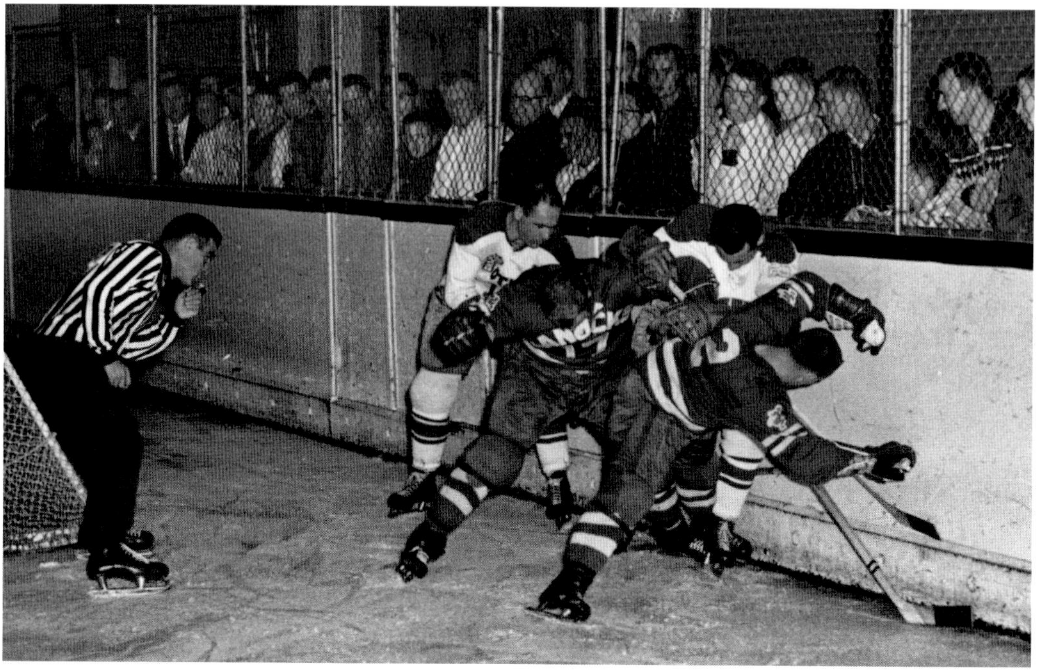

Filion, here pinned up against the boards by two Vancouver opponents, was often paired with Bill MacFarland, (left side of the action in white), a tough guy with a great scoring touch. The duo complemented one another well with their abilities, and MacFarland helped ensure no one took liberties with his linemate. (Photograph by Bob Carver, courtesy of Dave Eskenazi.)

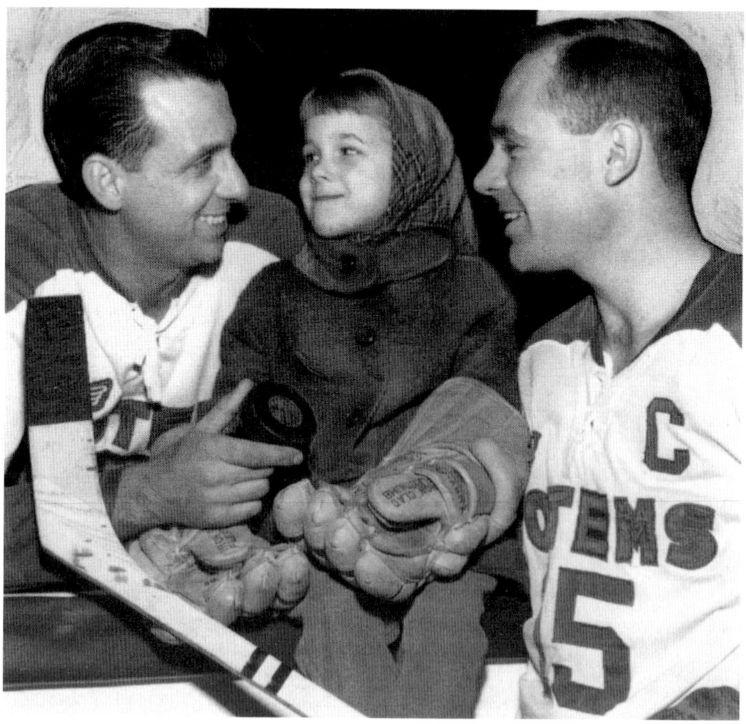

Filion was a gentleman both on and off the ice. Shown here (left) with teammate Bill MacFarland (right), he spends some time with six-year-old Jamie Keller, who suffered from cystic fibrosis. The players were helping publicize the upcoming cystic-fibrosis benefit game played in Seattle on February 1, 1963. (Courtesy of the *Seattle Post-Intelligencer* Collection, Museum of History and Industry.)

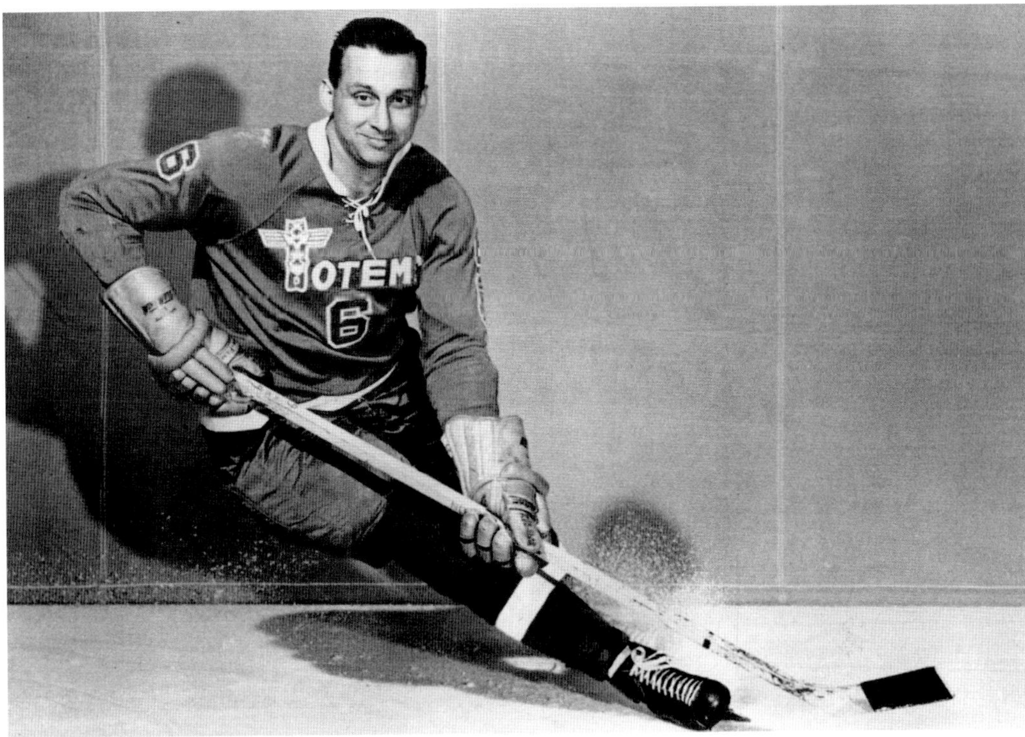

Filion's scoring prowess was not limited to the regular season. He also appeared in 67 playoff games in a Seattle uniform, scoring 23 goals and 60 points. His 11 assists and 18 points in the 1958–1959 playoffs led the Totems, who went 11-1 and swept the Calgary Stampeders in the finals, to win their first WHL title.

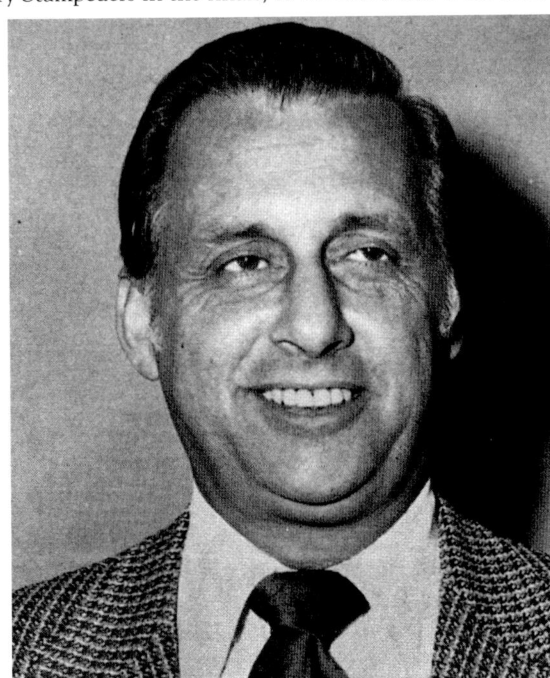

Rudy Filion played three seasons in the EHL before returning home to fill a number of front-office roles with the Totems. He was pressed into service behind the bench in January 1974 to take over for head coach Phil Maloney, who was called up to the Vancouver Canucks of the NHL. The injury-riddled Totems only managed 11 wins during the 35 games of Filion's tenure. (Photograph by Jerry Berg.)

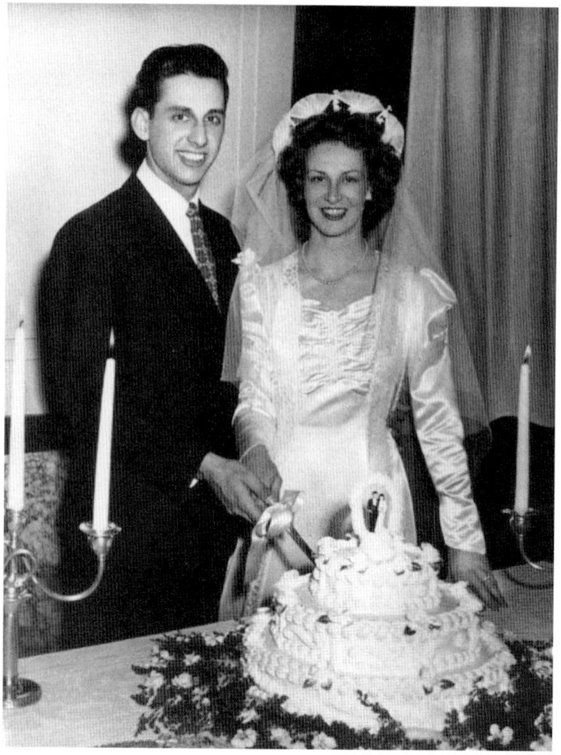

Filion met his wife, Ethel Gunnette, while in Tacoma playing hockey with the Rockets. The pair quickly fell in love and married, sharing their lives together for 63 years. They remained in the area following Rudy's retirement from hockey, raising their three children and spending time with their seven grandchildren. (Courtesy of the Filion family.)

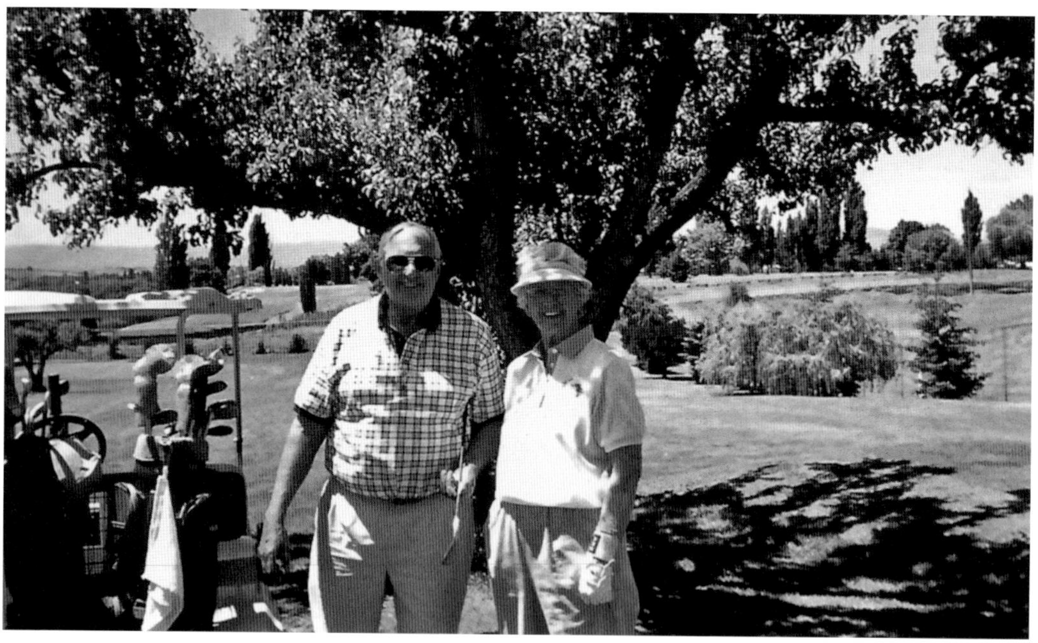

Rudy and his wife, Ethel, were avid golfers, both playing the game into their 80s and even working in the golf industry for a bit during the off-seasons in the 1950s, when they managed the restaurant at Meadowbrook Golf Course. Golf was a family pursuit, one that at times saw three generations of Filions playing together. (Courtesy of the Filion family.)

3

The Birth of the Totems

When the Totems' train arrived at King Street Station, they were greeted by their fan club. The team had just taken the first two games of the 1959 WHL Finals, both on the road, and they were flying high. And a few nights later, after completing the four-game sweep over Calgary with a 5-1 win, it got really crazy. Coach Keith Allen, trainer Dick Bielous, and part owner Vince Abbey all found themselves doused in the locker room showers, sticks were passed as souvenirs to the fans who surrounded the rink, and the Lester Patrick Cup was filled with beer, champagne, and whatever else was at hand. It was Seattle's first professional hockey championship since 1936.

The road to the championship had not been an easy one. A string of lackluster seasons in the late 1940s and into the early 1950s saw attendance drop to the point that the franchise was barely sustainable. When the Bombers were granted a one-year leave-of-absence from the WHL for the 1954–1955 season, few thought that professional hockey would be back in Seattle. Fortunately, one man had faith—Al Leader, the president of the WHL—who helped put together a new ownership group for the franchise. While the reborn Seattle Americans stumbled out of the gate to a last-place finish in the league's Coast Division in 1955–1956 (31-37-2), the following year found them atop the standings, the first of seven consecutive years at .500 or better. Seattle hockey was entering its golden age.

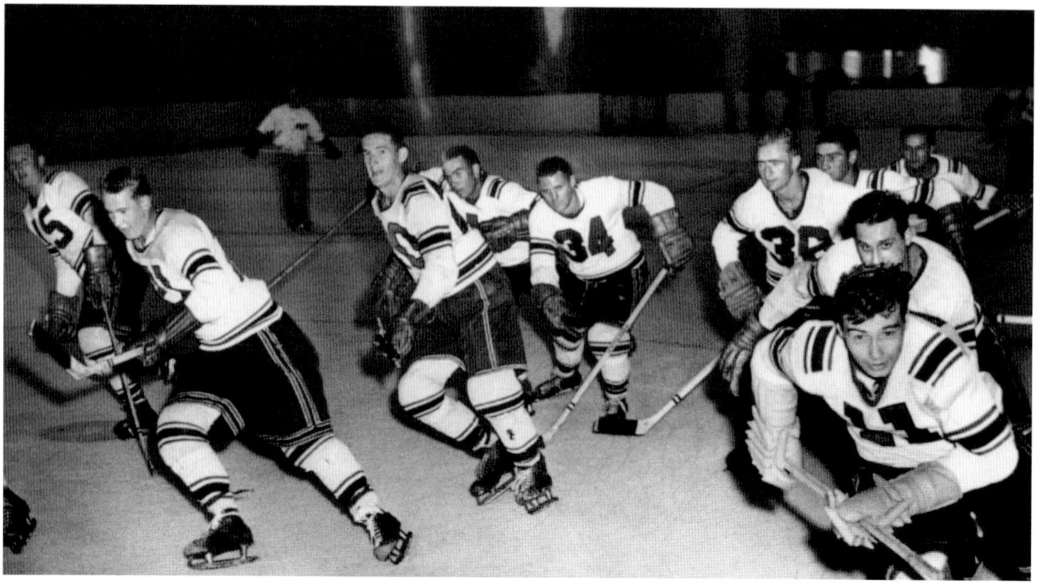

Professional hockey returned to Seattle in 1955–1956 with the re-formed and renamed Americans, though at the club's first practice players had to use recycled Bombers jerseys for the session. In what was a pivotal move, former Bomber Guyle Fielder (far right, No. 11) returned to the new Seattle franchise after playing the previous season in New Westminster. (Courtesy of the *Seattle Post-Intelligencer* Collection, Museum of History and Industry.)

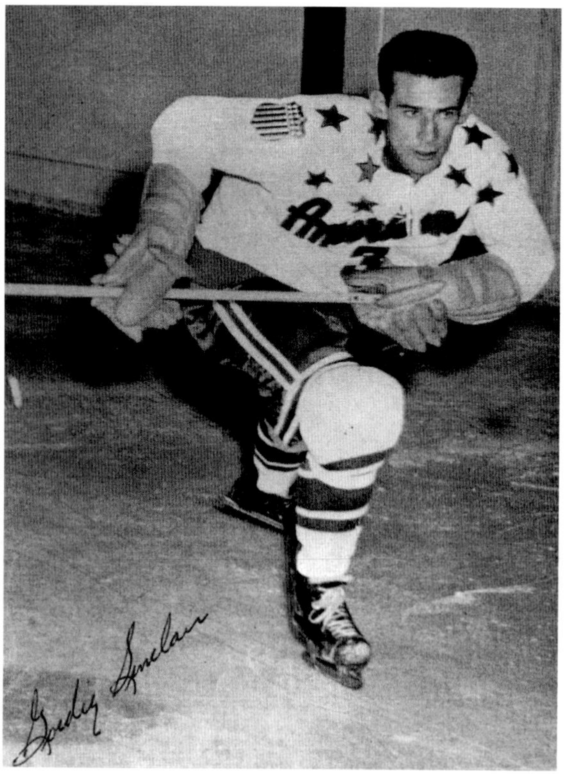

In addition to getting back a number of former Bombers, the Americans also added some new players to the roster who later proved essential to their success. One of the new arrivals was two-way defenseman Gordie Sinclair, who anchored the blue line for the Americans and Totems for the next 11 seasons.

The Americans played a rough brand of hockey during their first season, which actually helped attendance. They averaged roughly 2,000 fans a game until a pair of January contests that got out of hand and resulted in suspensions to Pat Coburn and Lloyd "Pete" Durham, after which attendance jumped by 50 percent. The 77,570 fans that season were a significant improvement over the 46,178 drawn by the Bombers in 1953–1954.

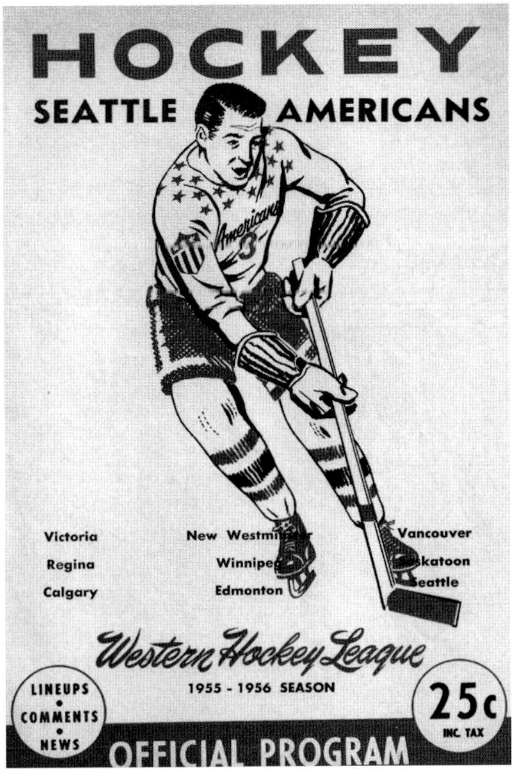

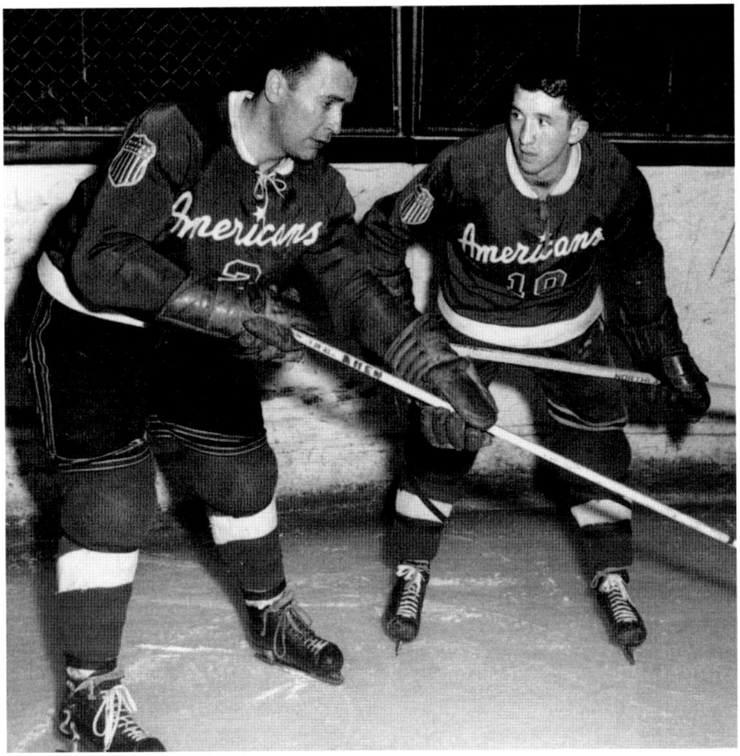

Veteran defenseman Keith Allen was brought to Seattle to serve as a player and coach for the 1956–1957 season. Allen (No. 2), shown here working with young rookie Norm Lenardon (No. 10), transitioned to full-time head coach in 1957–1958, a position he held through the 1964–1965 season. After several seasons in the general manager role, he left Seattle to be the coach and general manager of the NHL Philadelphia Flyers.

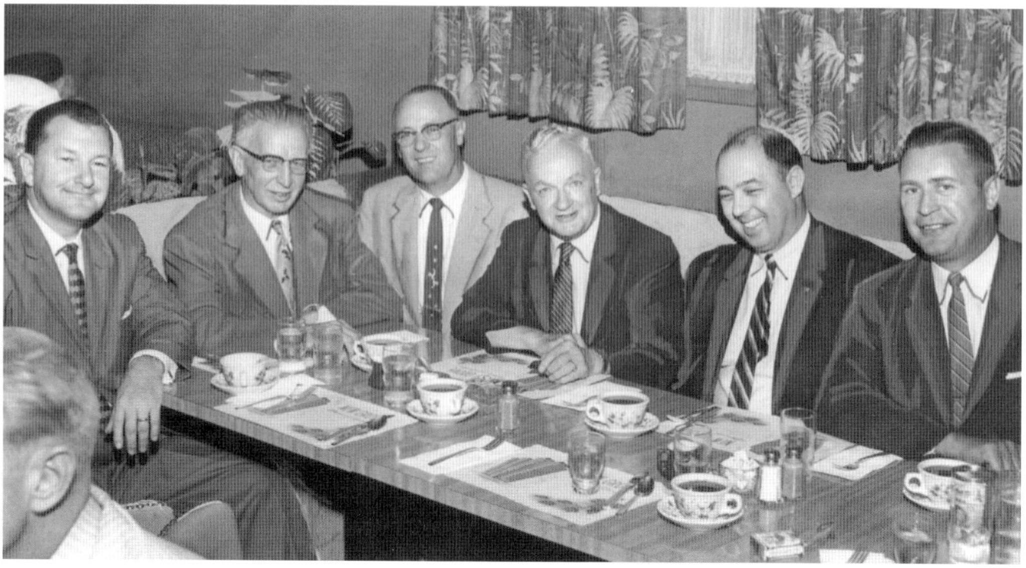

A new 12-person ownership group took over the franchise in 1958. Shown here are some of the key members of the new organization; from left to right are Marvin Burke (president), Leo Lassen (director), Al Leader (WHL president), Frank Hixon (vice president), Vince Abbey (secretary-treasurer), and Keith Allen (coach). (Courtesy of the *Seattle Post-Intelligencer* Collection, Museum of History and Industry.)

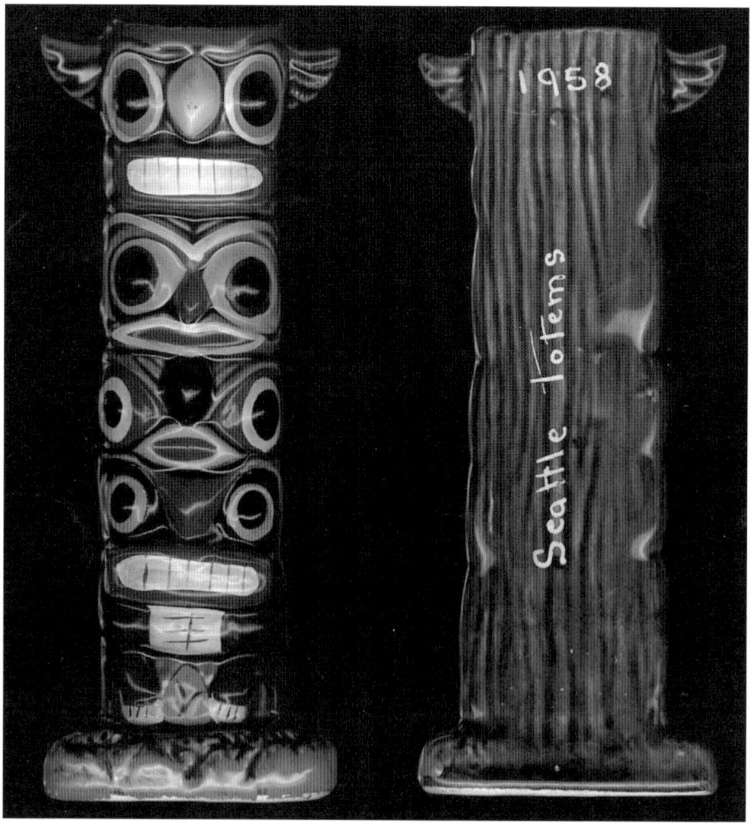

The new ownership group wanted a new name for the team that better reflected the city. The original choice was the Seattle Jets, but sportswriter Hy Zimmerman suggested the name Totems to honor the region's Native American heritage, and it stuck. The ownership group had ceramic totem poles made to commemorate the new name. (Courtesy of Dave Eskenazi.)

The Totems got off to a quick start in 1958–1959, winning 10 of their first 12 games en route to a first-place finish in the WHL's Coast Division. The team's 40 wins remain the professional franchise record, only surpassed by the 42 wins of the amateur Seattle Ironmen in 1947–1948.

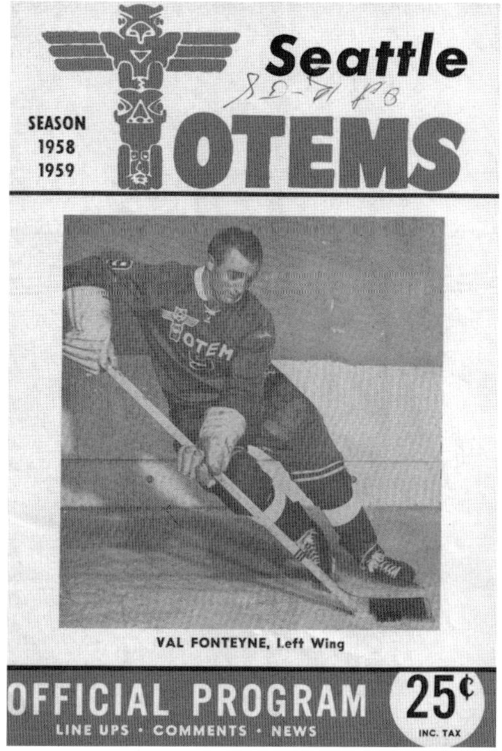

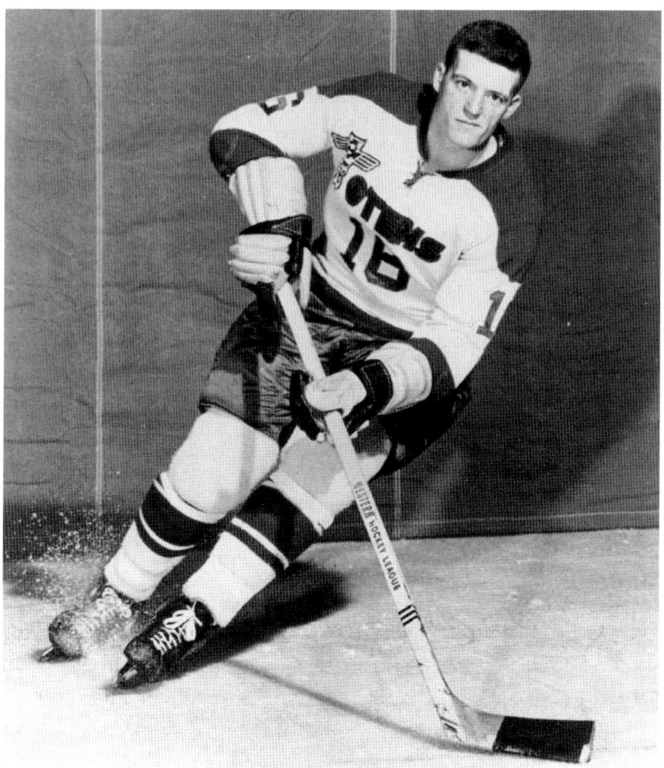

One of the unsung heroes of the 1958–1959 Totems was their new 22-year-old center Gerry Leonard. He was not a flashy offensive player, but he made up for it in grit and physical play. Leonard racked up 109 penalty minutes, second most on the team and over double that of the next closest forward, and earned nine fighting majors on the season.

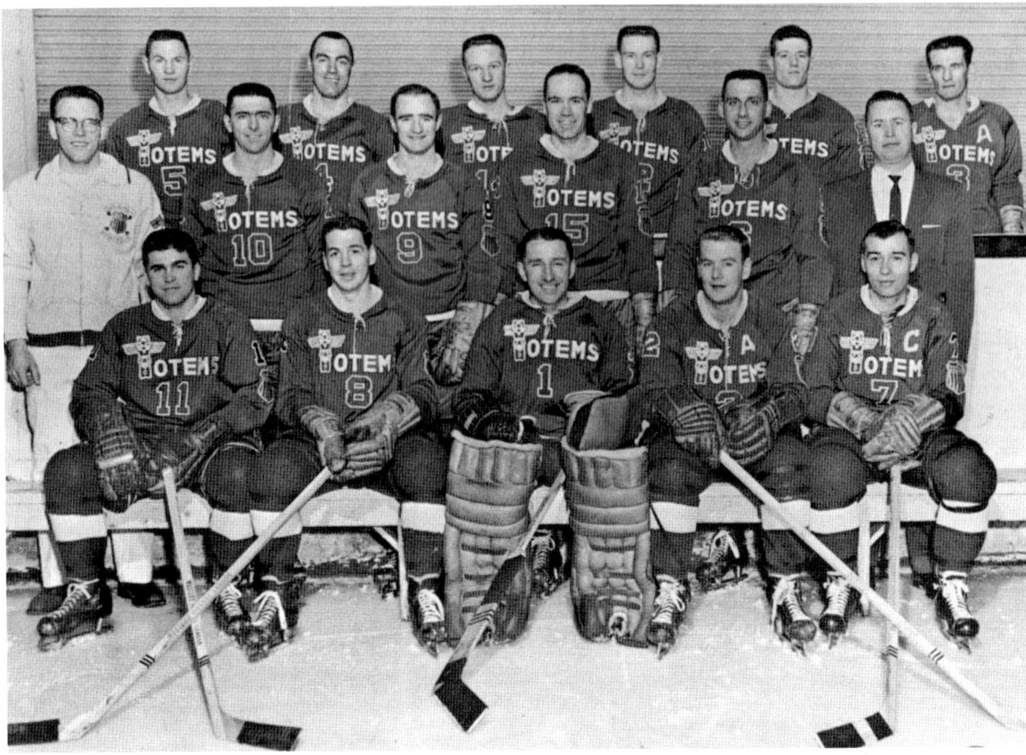

The 1958–1959 Seattle Totems were, from left to right, (first row) Dave Rimstad, Tom McVie, Bev Bentley, Les Hunt, and Guyle Fielder; (second row) Dick Bielous (trainer), Marc Boileau, Val Fonteyne, Bill MacFarland, Rudy Filion, and Keith Allen (coach); (third row) Bill Davidson, Frank Arnett, Don Chiupka, Jim Powers, Gerry Leonard, and Gordie Sinclair. Not shown are Cummy Burton, Gerry Goyer, Alex Kuzma, and Bill Tibbs.

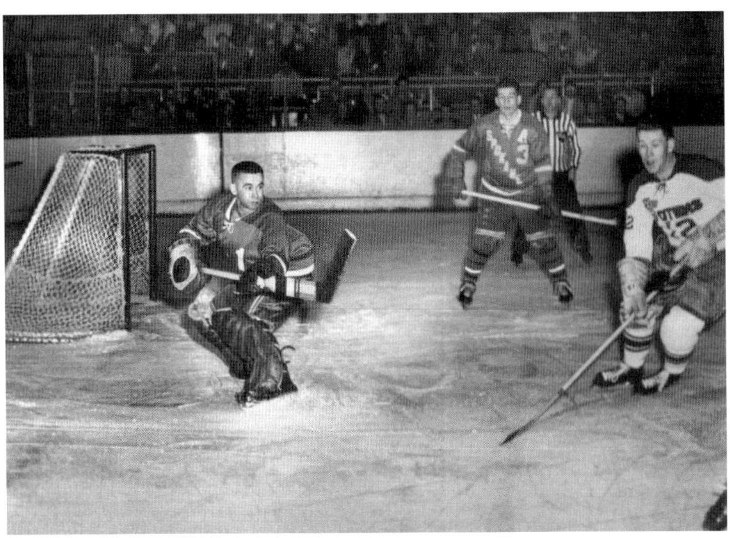

Future Hockey Hall of Famer and Spokane Spokes goaltender Emile "The Cat" Francis clears the puck from the front of his net while Totem Jim Powers turns in pursuit during this home game in 1958–1959. Francis played in 68 games with the Americans in 1956–1957 and got between the pipes one more time for the Totems as a substitute in 1959–1960.

Defenseman Frank Arnett only knew how to play the game one way—hard. In 1958–1959, he led the WHL in penalty minutes with 210, though still managed to earn 25 assists. His rampage through the league was punctuated by not one, but two stick fights, one of which left him bloodied and escorted from the ice with a match penalty.

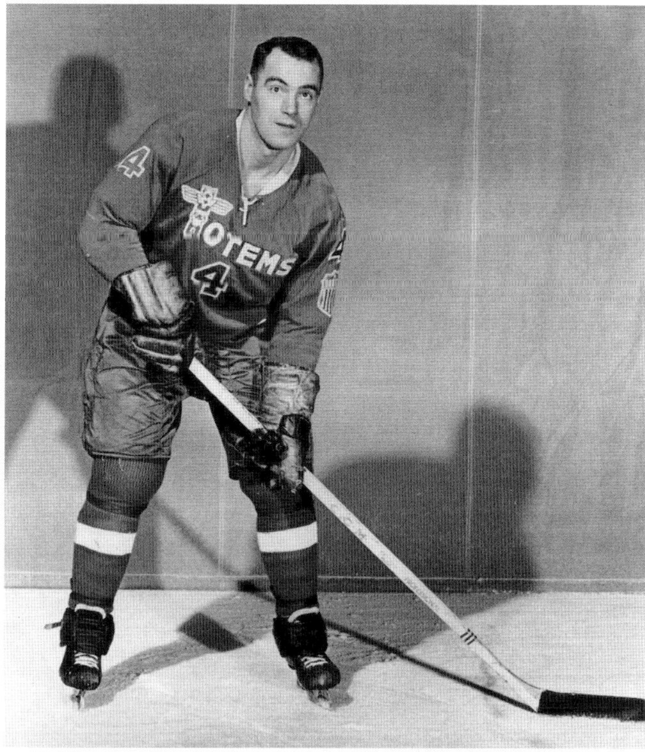

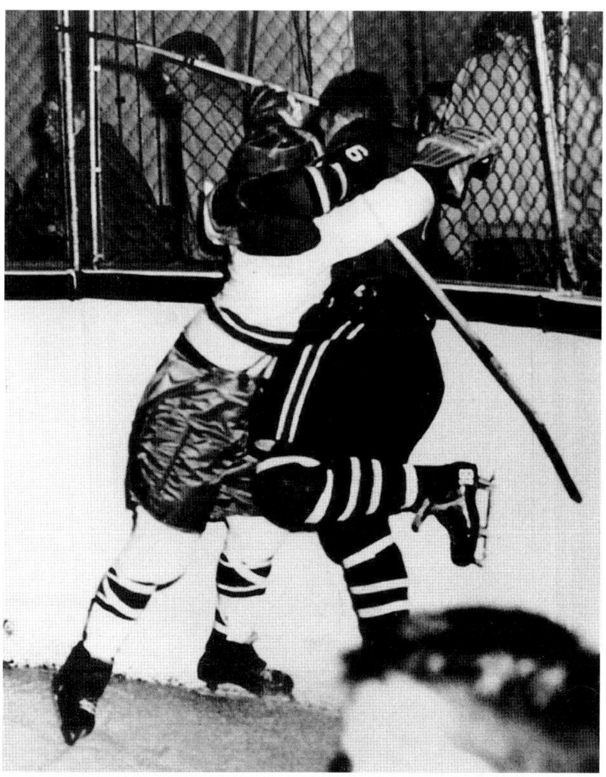

Frank Arnett delivers a driving check to an opponent in the corner of the Civic Arena. Arnett led the WHL in penalty minutes in back-to-back seasons from 1958 to 1960 and was at times unpredictable. His striking of linesman Pete Wywrot during a game in 1961 contributed to the end of his time in Seattle. (Photograph by Bob Carver, courtesy of Dave Eskenazi.)

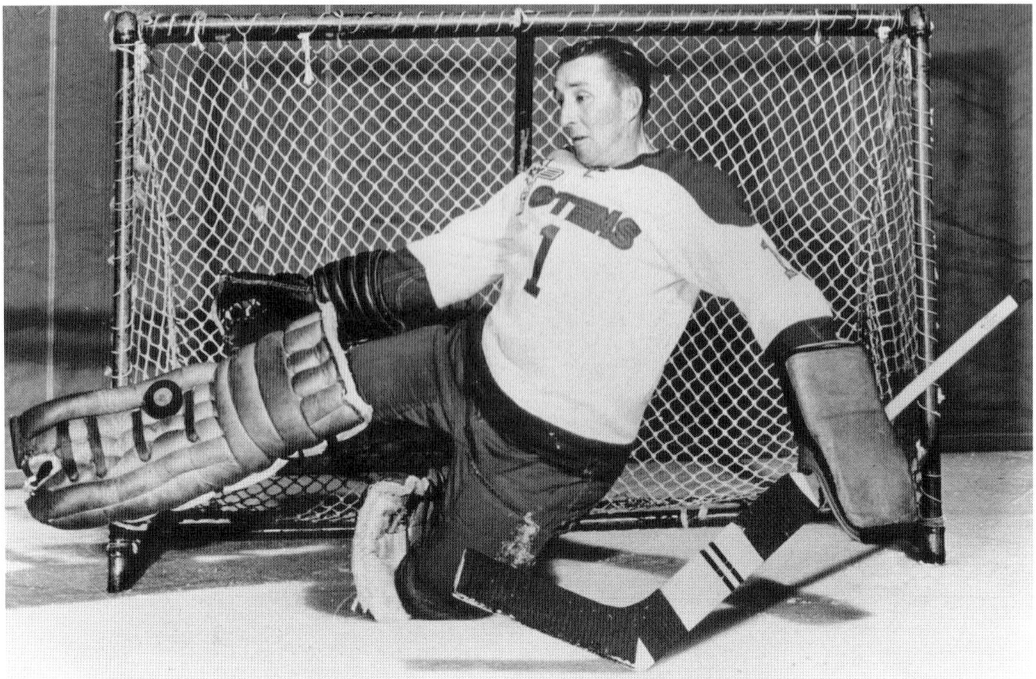

Goaltender Bill Tibbs started the first six games of the 1958–1959 season for the Totems, posting a 5-1 record. However, coach Keith Allen was not enamored with his play, so he acquired Bev Bentley, shown here, from New Westminster to take over between the pipes. And take over he did, playing all 64 of the remaining games and posting a 35-26-3 record.

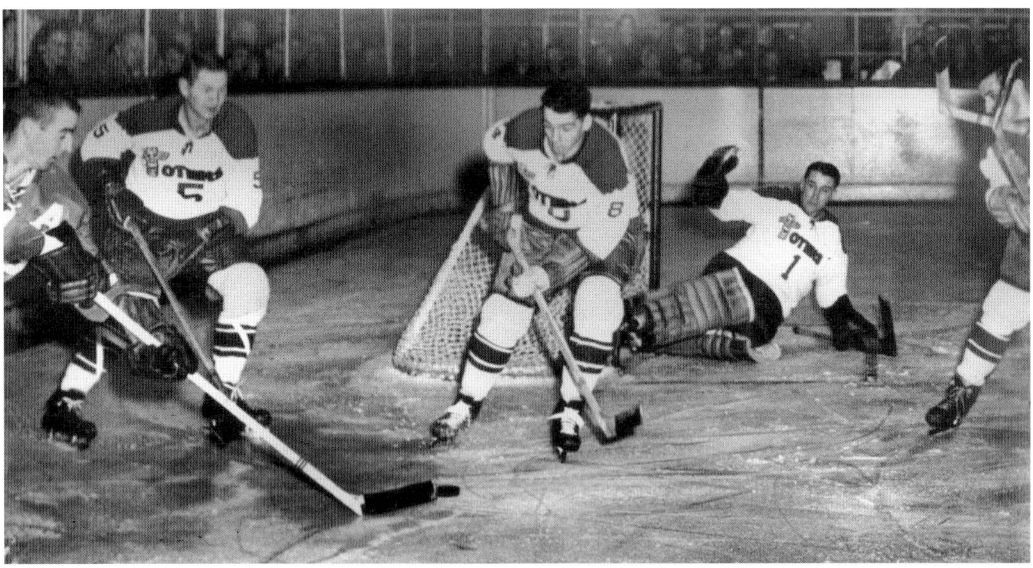

Bev Bentley (No. 1) protects the near post as Bill Davidson (No. 5) and Tom McVie (No. 8) close in on the opposing puck handler. Bentley was exactly what the Totems needed to position themselves as an elite team, and his 1.64 goals against average, two shutouts, and 11-1 record in the 1958–1959 playoffs rank among the best by a Seattle goaltender in the professional era.

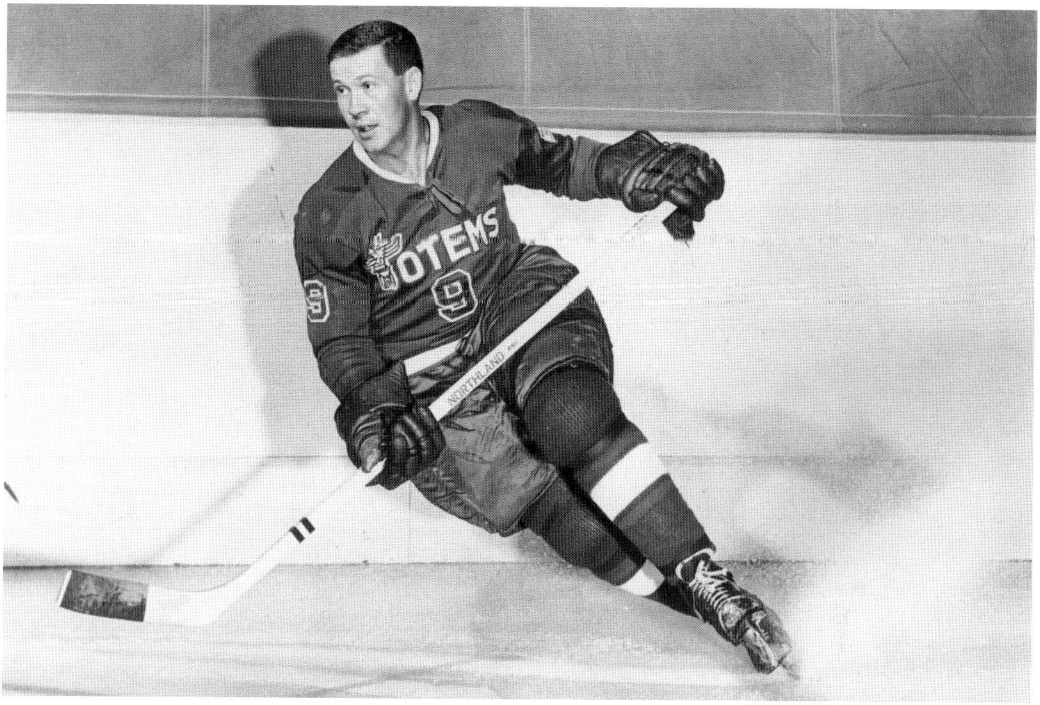

Early in the 1958–1959 season, the Totems sent Alex Kuzma to Vancouver in exchange for Jim Powers. Powers quickly paid dividends, scoring 26 goals in only 56 games for Seattle. Unfortunately, a late-season leg injury kept him out of the playoffs. Powers returned to Vancouver to start the 1959–1960 season, but Allen reacquired him in another trade.

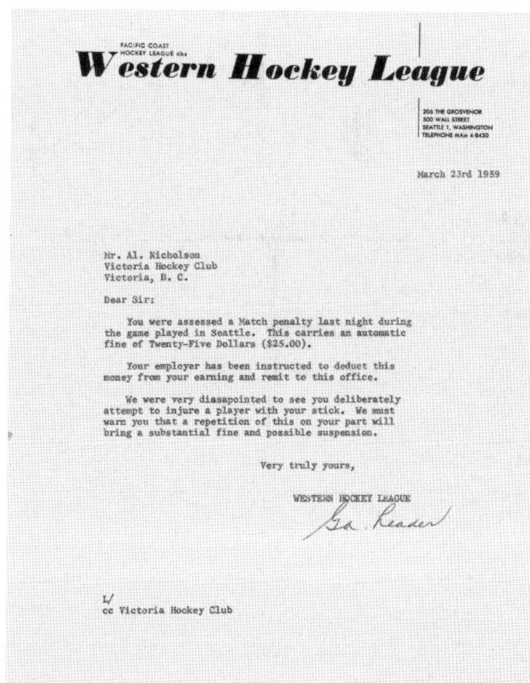

PACIFIC COAST HOCKEY LEAGUE dba
Western Hockey League

206 THE GROSVENOR
500 WALL STREET
SEATTLE 1, WASHINGTON
TELEPHONE MAin 4-8430

March 23rd 1959

Mr. Al. Nicholson
Victoria Hockey Club
Victoria, B. C.

Dear Sir:

You were assessed a Match penalty last night during the game played in Seattle. This carries an automatic fine of Twenty-Five Dollars ($25.00).

Your employer has been instructed to deduct this money from your earning and remit to this office.

We were very diasapointed to see you deliberately attempt to injure a player with your stick. We must warn you that a repetition of this on your part will bring a substantial fine and possible suspension.

Very truly yours,

WESTERN HOCKEY LEAGUE

L/
cc Victoria Hockey Club

The final game of the 1958–1959 regular season was also the craziest, with Seattle and Victoria combining for 93 penalty minutes. Not only were there four fights happening simultaneously at one point in the second period, but Cougar Al Nicholson attacked Frank Arnett with two different sticks. That performance earned Nicholson this written rebuke from WHL president Al Leader and a $25 fine.

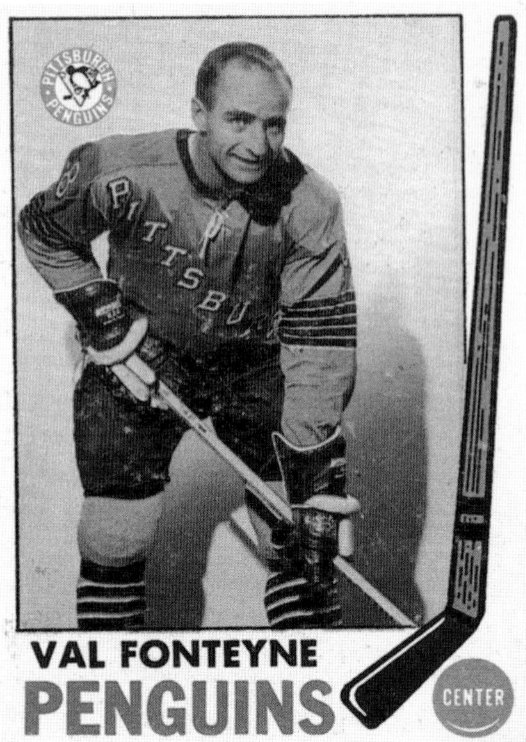

The success of the 1958–1959 Totems benefitted Val Fonteyne, who was called up to the Detroit Red Wings the following year, the start of a 13-season NHL career. Unfortunately, he found goals harder to come by there, scoring 75 times in 820 NHL games. (Topps hockey cards used courtesy of the Topps Company, Inc. For more information about The Topps Company, please see our website at www.topps.com.)

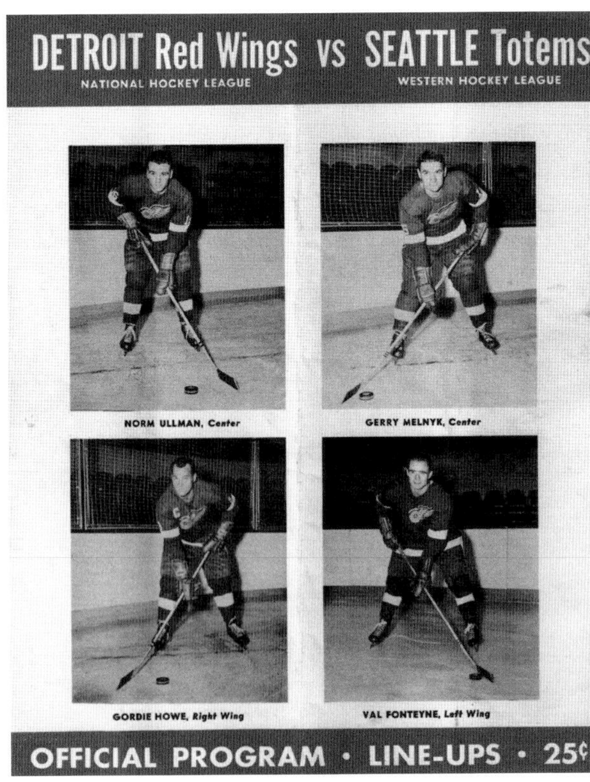

Val Fonteyne returned to Seattle at the start of the 1959–1960 season, but in a Detroit Red Wings uniform, as the NHL club defeated the Totems 5-4 in a preseason matchup. The Wings also had their eyes on Seattle's star center Guyle Fielder, but their offers to purchase his contract were rebuffed by the Totems.

4

Guyle Fielder

A fan would have been forgiven for arriving at the October 31, 1951, matchup between the Seattle Ironmen and New Westminster Royals and not realizing that they were about to witness an important moment in Seattle hockey history. And frankly, even after the game was over, there would have been no reason to think anything notable happened other than an early season tie against the league-leading Royals. But playing for the Royals that night was a 20-year-old center who would go on to win the PCHL Rookie of the Year that season. A young man who, while kept off the scoreboard that night, would go on to become the most prolific scorer in Seattle hockey history. It was the first night on Seattle ice for Guyle Fielder.

Fielder's journey to Seattle was an unusual one. Prior to arriving in the city for the Bombers' 1953–1954 campaign, he had already played two years of junior hockey, won Rookie of the Year honors in both the PCHL (1952) and American Hockey League (1953), and made two all-too-brief appearances in the NHL, including three games with Chicago in 1950–1951 and four with Detroit in 1953. Seattle seemed like a temporary way station, even more so when the Bombers left the WHL prior to the 1954–1955 season. But the league's commissioner, Al Leader (who also happened to be Fielder's uncle), ensured that he returned to Seattle in 1955 with the newly re-formed Seattle Americans, and the rest is history.

Fielder's impact on Seattle hockey is hard to overstate. He was part of three championship teams, led his team in scoring in 13 of his 15 Seattle seasons, and earned six WHL Most Valuable Player awards. He led the league in scoring nine times, and in assists 13 times. He was truly Mr. Seattle Hockey and earned the nickname "Golden Guyle" with his flashy play, incredible skating, and scoring touch.

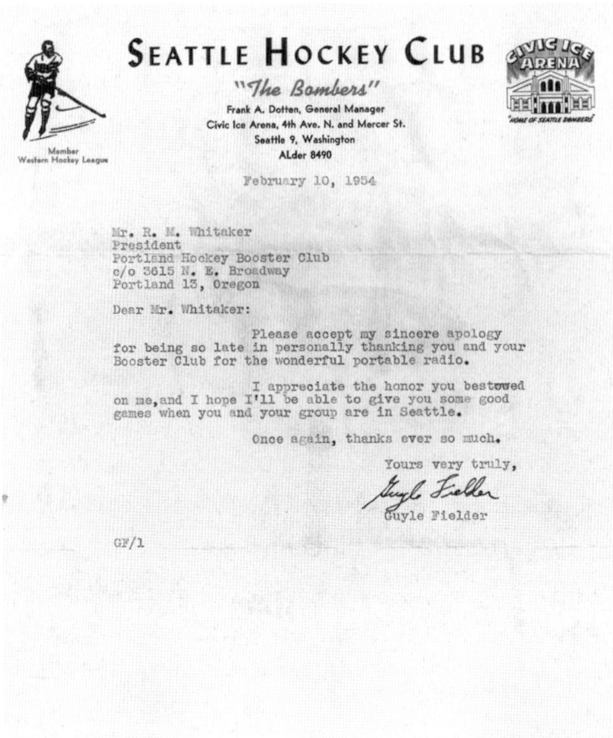

SEATTLE HOCKEY CLUB

"The Bombers"

Frank A. Dotten, General Manager
Civic Ice Arena, 4th Ave. N. and Mercer St.
Seattle 9, Washington
ALder 8490

Member
Western Hockey League

CIVIC ICE ARENA
"HOME OF SEATTLE BOMBERS"

February 10, 1954

Mr. R. M. Whitaker
President
Portland Hockey Booster Club
c/o 3615 N. E. Broadway
Portland 13, Oregon

Dear Mr. Whitaker:

Please accept my sincere apology for being so late in personally thanking you and your Booster Club for the wonderful portable radio.

I appreciate the honor you bestowed on me, and I hope I'll be able to give you some good games when you and your group are in Seattle.

Once again, thanks ever so much.

Yours very truly,

Guyle Fielder
Guyle Fielder

GF/l

It did not take long for Fielder to make a splash with the fans in the Western Hockey League. In this letter dated February 10, 1954, he thanks the Portland Hockey Booster Club for presenting him with a gift—quite an honor for a 23-year-old to be recognized by the hockey fans of another city. (Courtesy of Dave Eskenazi.)

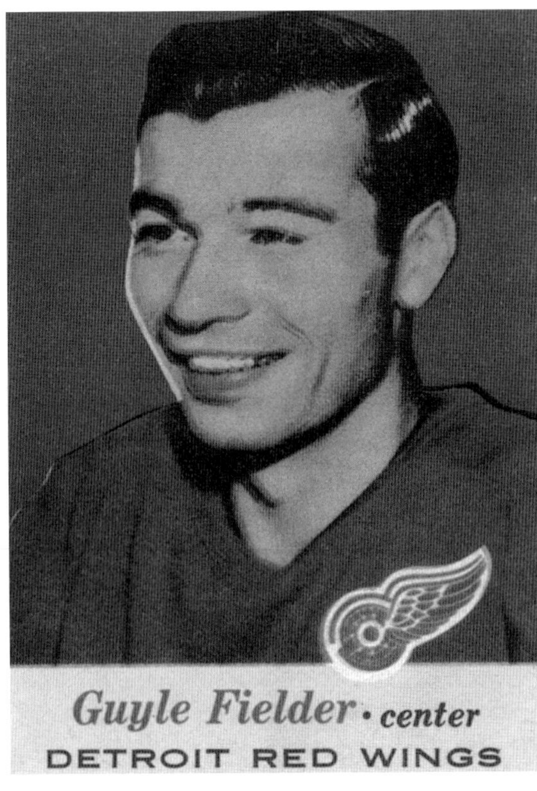

Guyle Fielder only appeared in 15 NHL games, so it is very fortunate that he made it onto a hockey card. He is shown here in 1957–1958 with the Detroit Red Wings. He played six games in Detroit to start the season before returning to Seattle. (Topps hockey cards used courtesy of The Topps Company, Inc. For more information about The Topps Company, please see our website at www.topps.com.)

While primarily known for his scoring ability, Fielder also had a reputation for being a classy player. He generally kept himself out of the penalty box and earned the Fred J. Hume Cup as the WHL's most gentlemanly player three times (1966, 1967, and 1969). (Courtesy of Dave Eskenazi.)

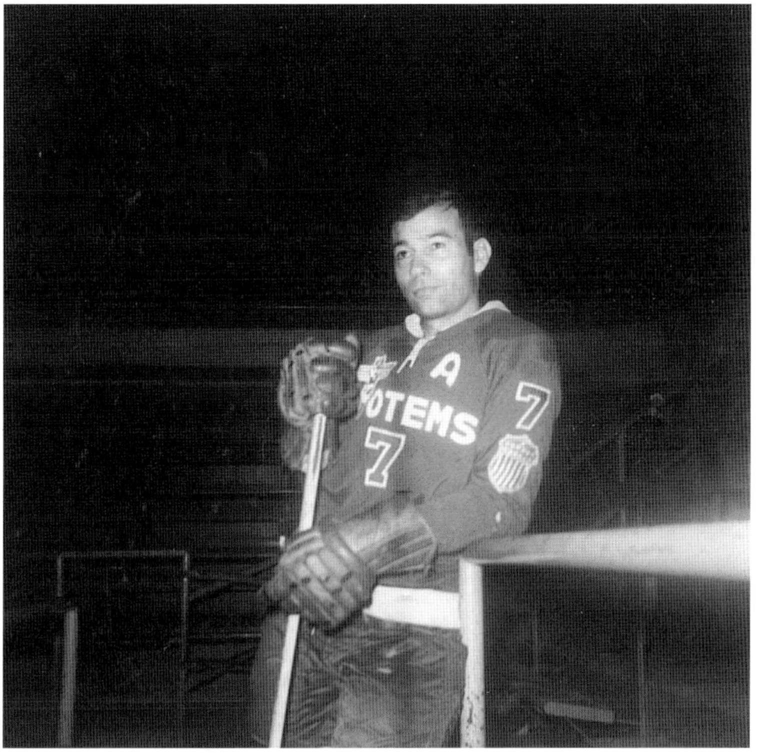

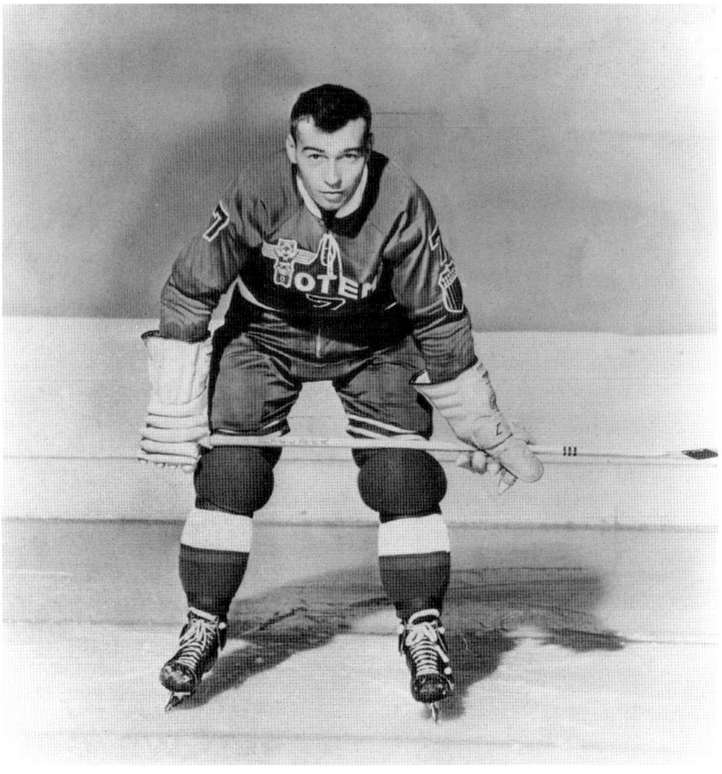

Small of stature at five feet nine inches tall and 160 pounds, Fielder relied on speed, agility, and tremendous hand-eye coordination to keep him productive and out of harms way. Many forwards, like Bob Barlow in 1962–1963, had the most productive goal-scoring seasons of their careers when moved to Fielder's line. Barlow lit the lamp for the Totems 47 times that season, the best total ever for a Totems player. (Courtesy of Dave Eskenazi.)

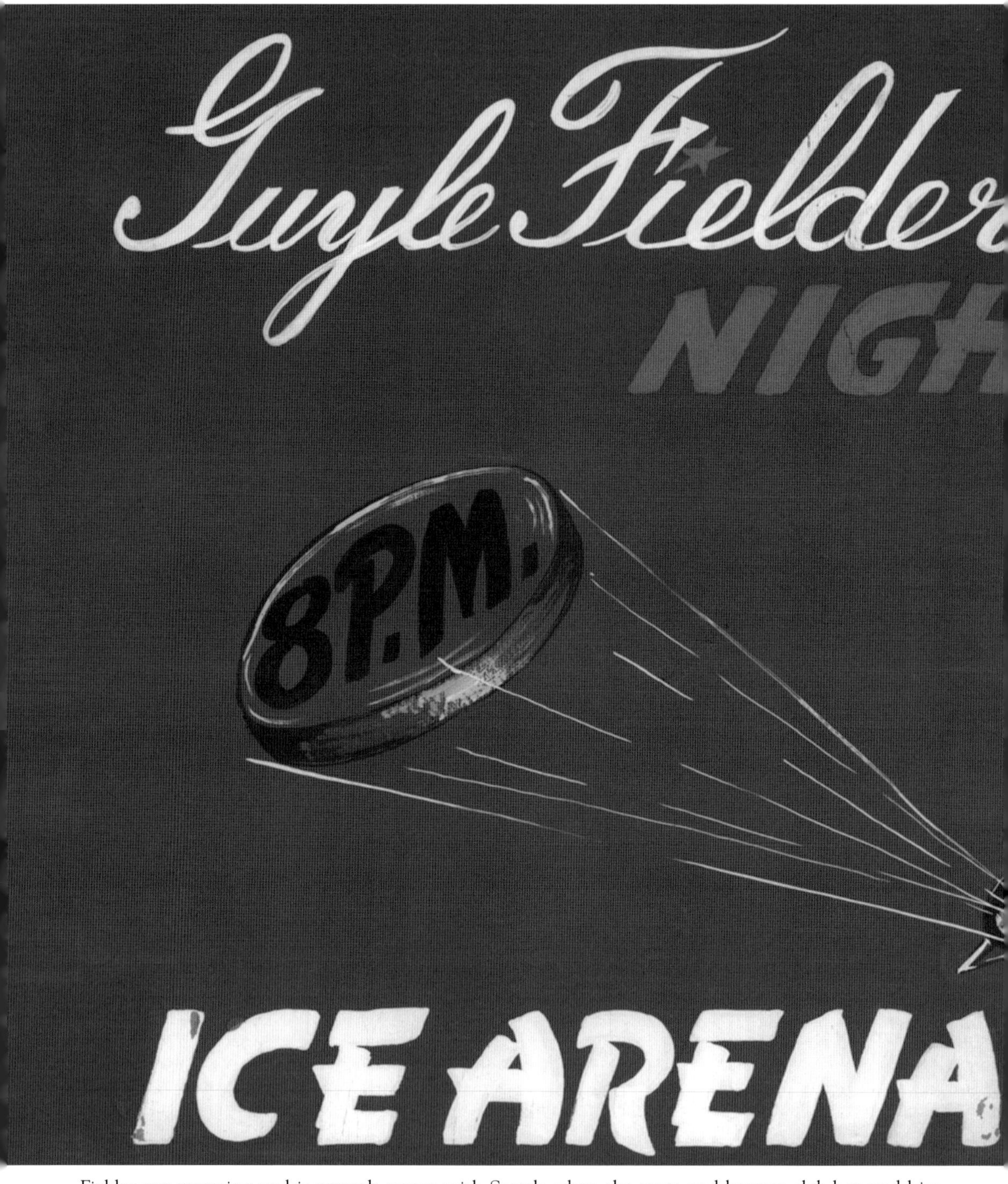

Fielder was wrapping up his seventh season with Seattle when the team and booster club honored him with Guyle Fielder Night on April 2, 1961. He was presented with an array of gifts from the league, team, booster club, and even opponents and their fan clubs. Congratulatory telegrams arrived from the four corners of the hockey world recognizing the man who was the league's all-time leading scorer. Ironically,

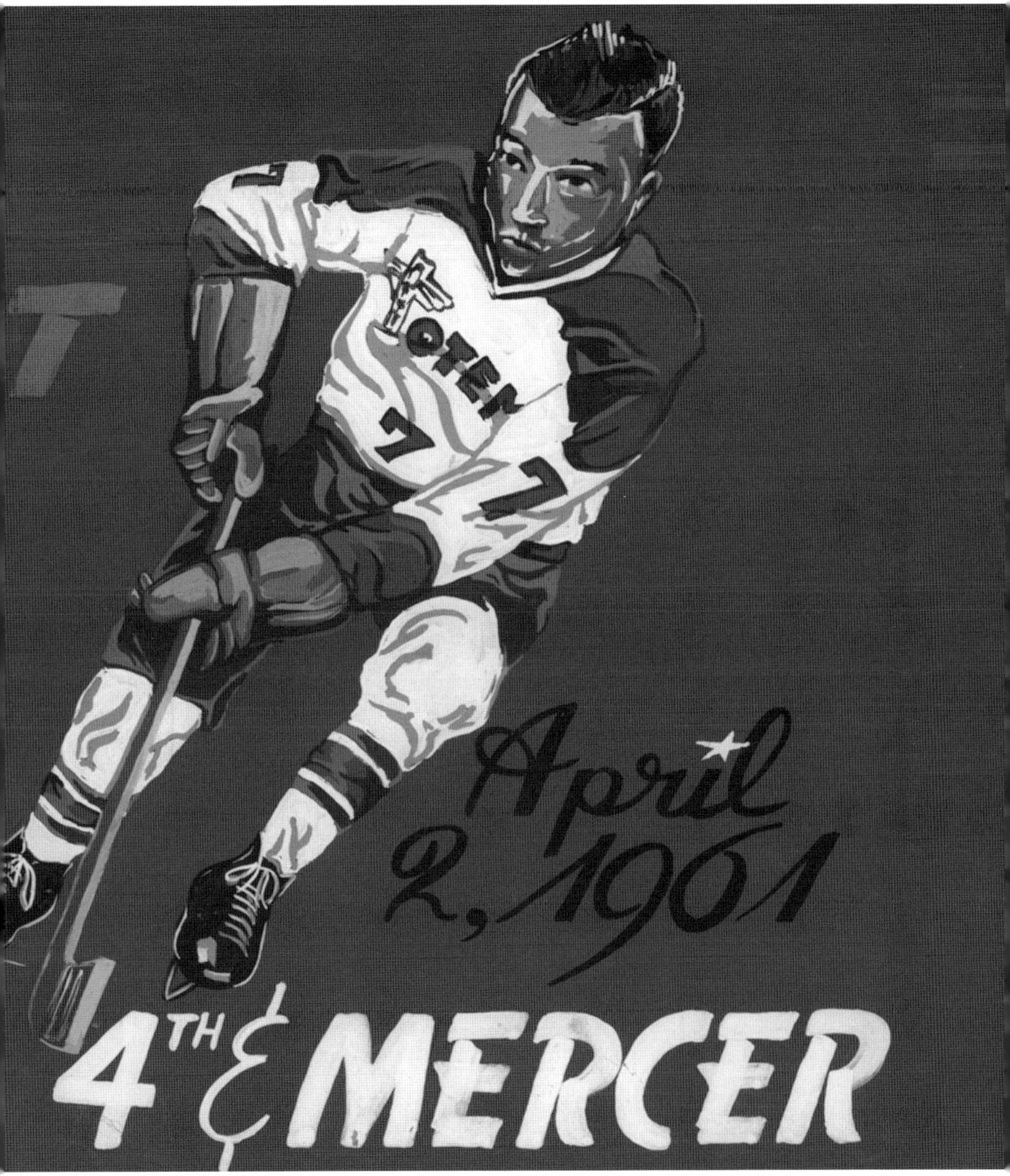

he went into that last game of the regular season in third place in team scoring with 92 points, trailing both Rudy Filion (95) and Bill MacFarland (94). Despite Fielder scoring a goal and two assists in the 8-5 win, Filion got an assist of his own to finish as the team's top scorer, a rare honor and one of only two occasions in Fielder's Seattle career that he did not lead his team in scoring.

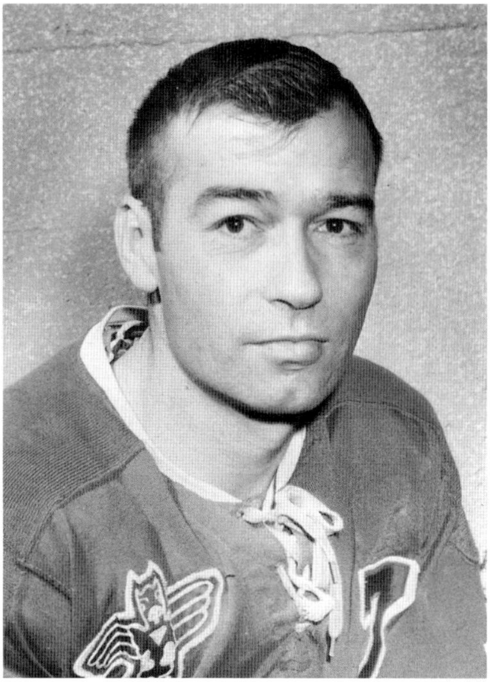

Guyle Fielder holds a number of Seattle career records. He appeared in 1,127 games in a Seattle uniform (including playoffs), earning 347 goals, 1,169 assists, and 1,516 total points. With no professional hockey team in the city as of 2014, and junior-league players having limited career spans, Fielder's position in the top spot in these areas appears secure for decades to come. (Courtesy of Dave Eskenazi.)

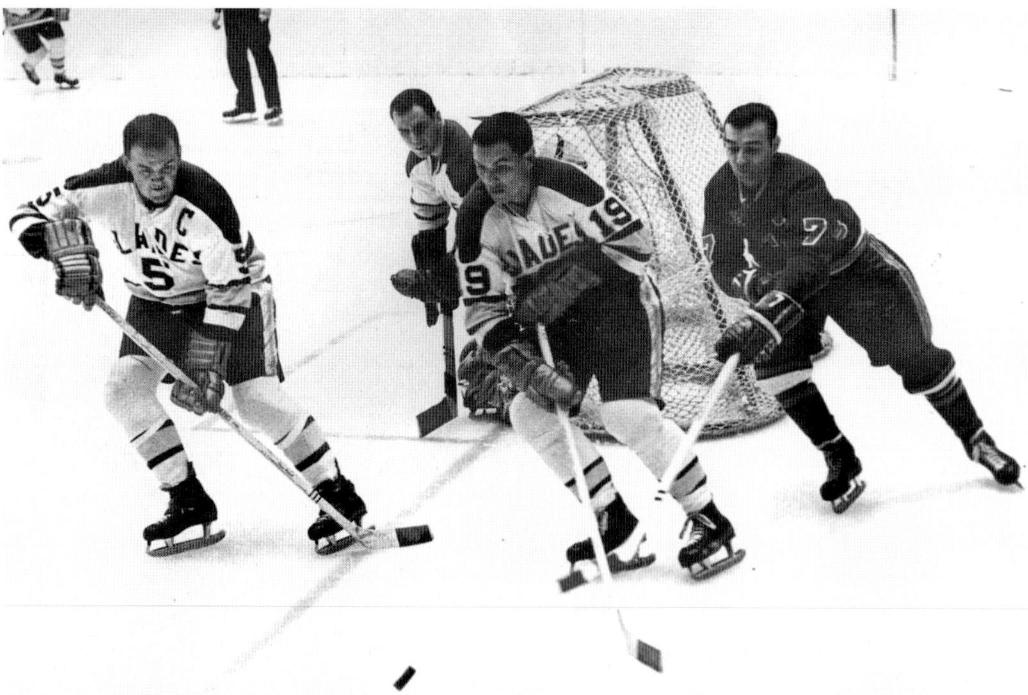

As a significant scoring threat throughout his career, Fielder always drew a crowd when he was in the offensive zone. In this 1964–1965 matchup with the Los Angeles Blades, he is pictured circling around the back of the net chasing the loose puck as defensemen Jack Evans (No. 5) and Harley Hodgson (No. 19) attempt to clear and goaltender Jack McCartan looks on with concern.

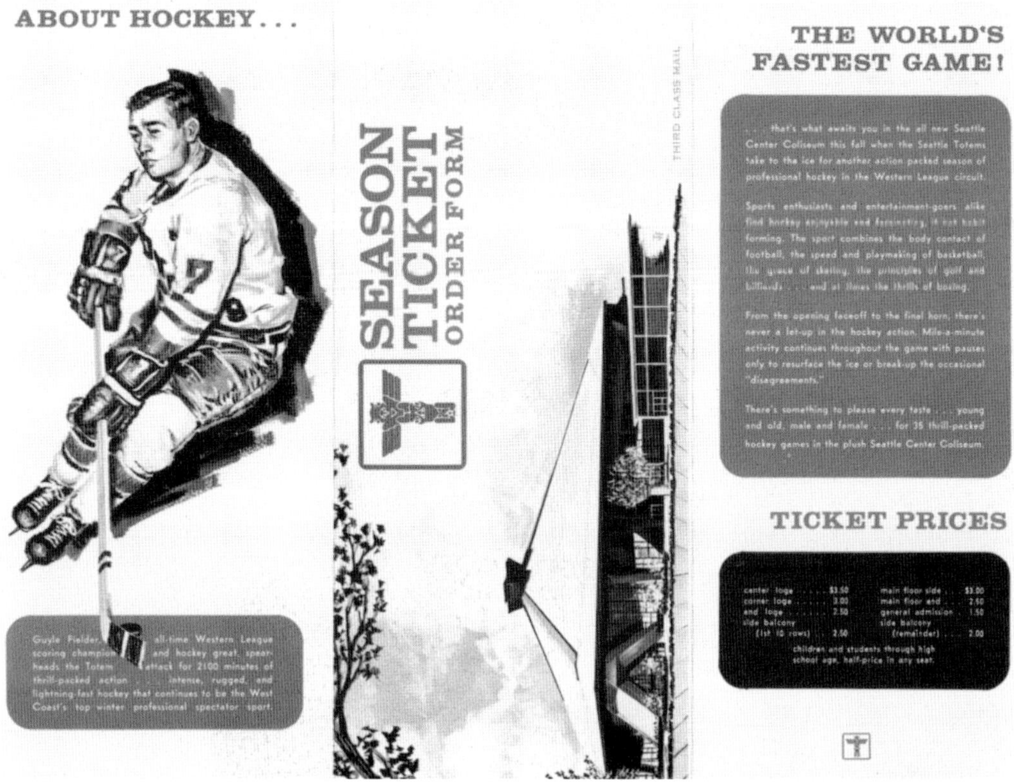

The Totems front office fully recognized how valuable Guyle Fielder was to the team, both on and off the ice. He frequently appeared at events and for photo opportunities, and was an important part of the club's marketing efforts. Here, he appears on a ticket brochure from the mid-1960s alongside the team's brand new facility, the 12,000-plus-seat Coliseum. (Courtesy of Dave Eskenazi.)

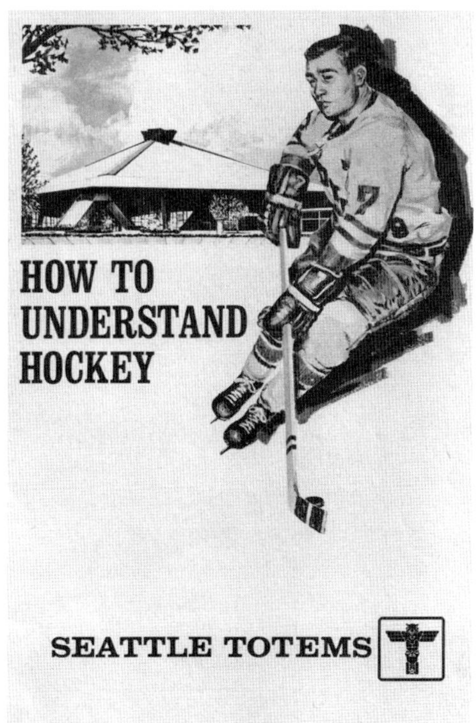

Who better to grace the cover of the Seattle Totems "How to Understand Hockey" guide than the team's best player, Guyle Fielder? The guide included all the important information that a new hockey fan would need to understand the game, including basic rules, referee signals, and explanations of offside and icing.

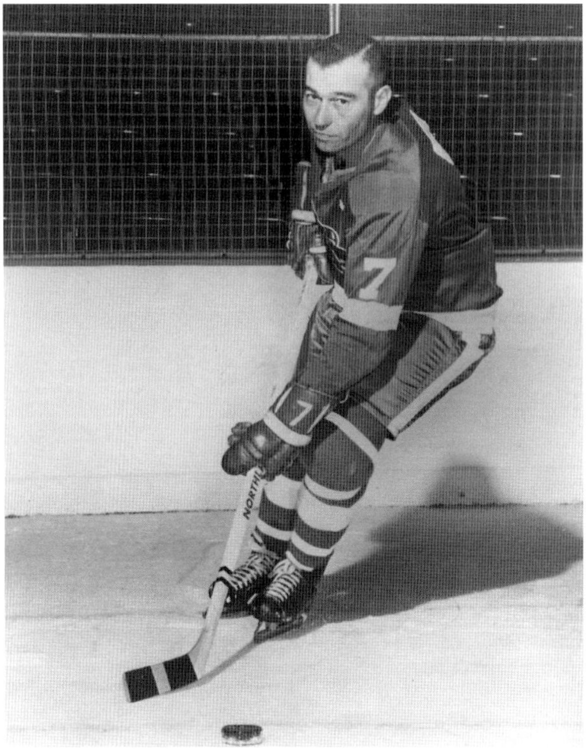

Guyle Fielder played his last season with the Totems in 1968–1969, but even as a 38-year-old he led the team in assists (74) and points (94). He still had a lot more hockey left in him, playing four more productive seasons in the WHL with Salt Lake City and Portland before retiring at the close of the 1972–1973 campaign. (Courtesy of Dave Eskenazi.)

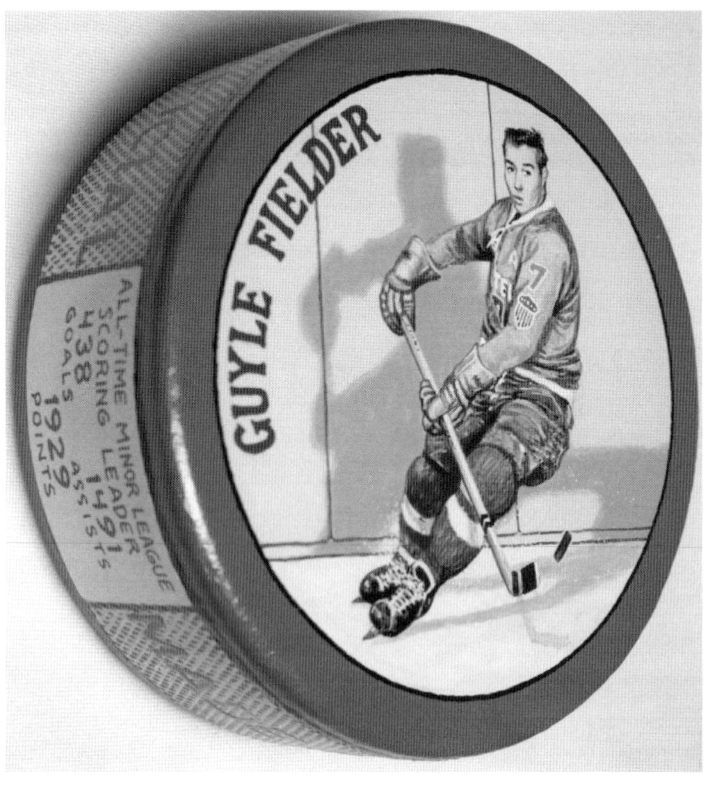

Renowned comic book and sports artist Monty Sheldon painted this one-of-a-kind hockey puck for the author in 2000 to commemorate the hockey career of Guyle Fielder. Fielder's reign as the all-time minor-league scoring champion (1,929 total points) is likely to remain intact for quite some time. (Original art by Monty Sheldon.)

5

The Fabulous 1960s

If one decade can be said to represent the golden age of Seattle hockey, it would probably be the 1960s. To be fair, the 1910s were pretty good, too, with the Metropolitans hosting two Stanley Cup Finals and winning the vaunted trophy in 1917. But the Mets only existed for half that decade, and just five years later they were gone for good. They had an amazing nine-season run, and certainly built the foundation for hockey in Seattle, but they lacked a certain bit of continuity.

The 1960s, however, saw the continued growth in popularity of the Totems, a team that evolved from the Ironmen of the 1940s and closed out the 1950s with their first professional championship. The team existed throughout the decade, posting seven winning records in nine seasons from 1960 to 1969, making four WHL Finals appearances and winning the league title twice. They had the best player in the league, and arguably in all of minor-league hockey, in Guyle Fielder, and moved into the brand-new 12,000-plus–seat Coliseum. They had a booster club with hundreds of active members who were not afraid to travel to away games. Everything seemed to go their way.

The cracks started to show only as the decade came to a close. The NHL muscled into the Los Angeles and San Francisco/Oakland markets in 1967–1968, depriving the WHL of its two largest cities. Guyle Fielder retired at the end of the 1968–1969 season (though he came out of retirement the following season to join Salt Lake City), ending an incredible run of success in Seattle. And though no one knew it at the time, 1968–1969 was the Totems' last winning season, as the 1970s ushered in a decline on the ice and at the gate that culminated in the disastrous 12-win 1971–1972 season. When the fall came, it came fast, and it came hard.

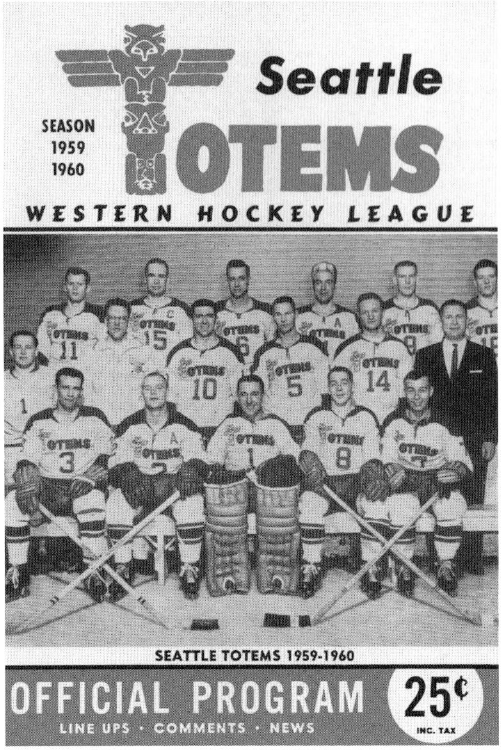

The 1959–1960 Totems were arguably a deeper club than the one that won the championship the prior season. The three top scorers in the WHL were all on the Totems: Guyle Fielder (31 goals, 64 assists, 95 points), Bill MacFarland (35-51-86), and Rudy Filion (36-49-85). However, their offensive prowess disappeared in the playoffs, and the club managed only four goals in a four-game first-round sweep by Victoria.

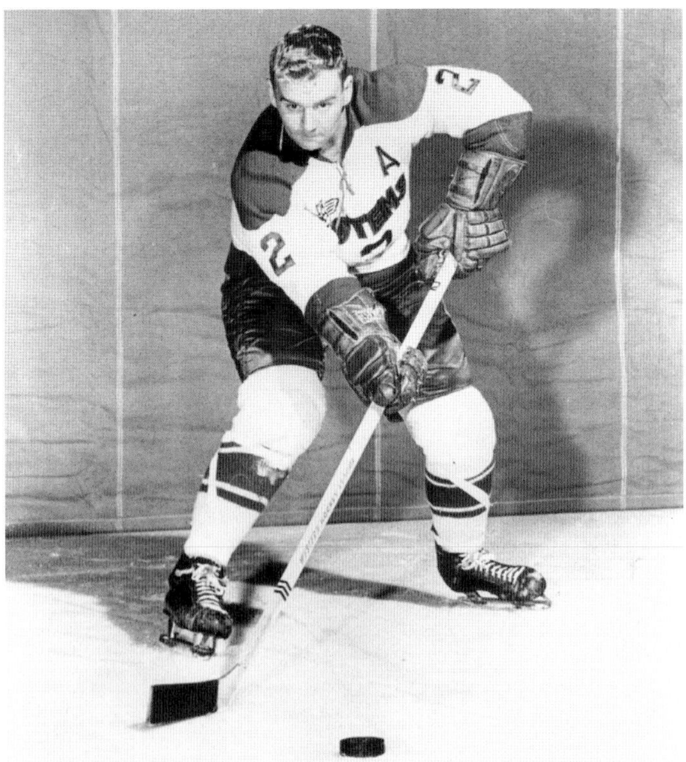

Totems defenseman Les Hunt was no stranger to the more physical side of the game, earning over 100 minutes in the penalty box in 1959–1960. He also ended the season of Vancouver Canuck Eddie Dorohoy with an open-ice hit on December 13 that left Dorohoy with his right leg broken in two places, one of the worst injuries ever on Seattle ice.

The Totems rebounded from their disappointing postseason the previous year to go 37-28-5 in 1960–1961, though this was only good enough for fourth place in the eight-team WHL. Despite having to play their first three playoff games on the road, the Totems swept regular-season champs Calgary to earn a trip to the WHL Finals, where they fell to Portland in six games.

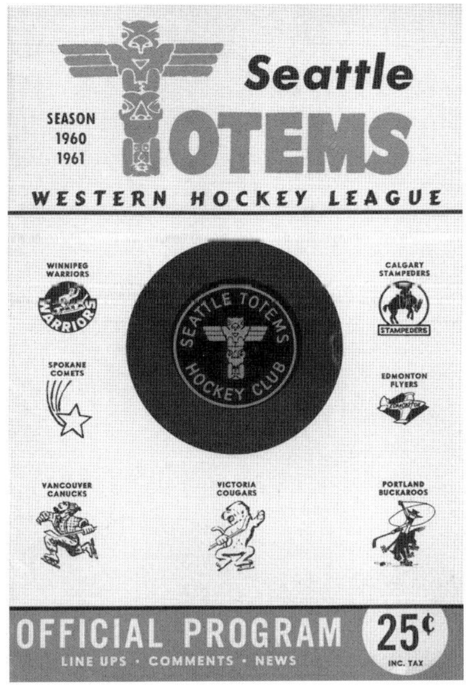

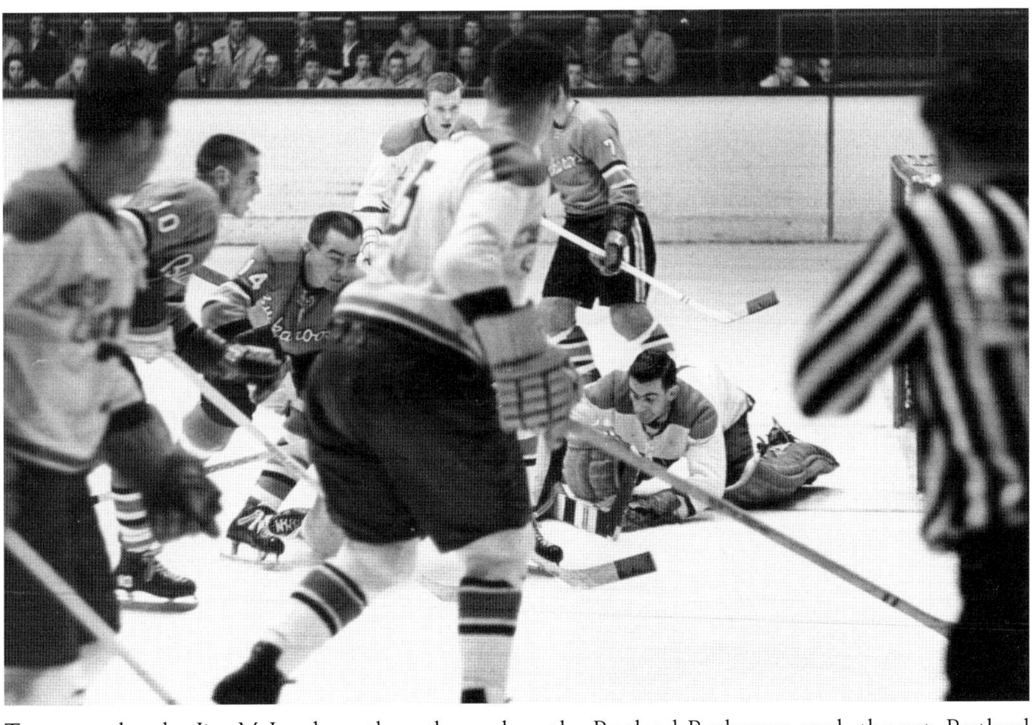

Totems goaltender Jim McLeod smothers the puck as the Portland Buckaroos crash the net. Portland joined the WHL in 1960–1961 and won the league championship in their first year, guaranteeing the start to what would quickly become one of the most intense rivalries in the WHL. The Totems and Buckaroos met twice in the league finals, each coming away with a championship against their nemesis.

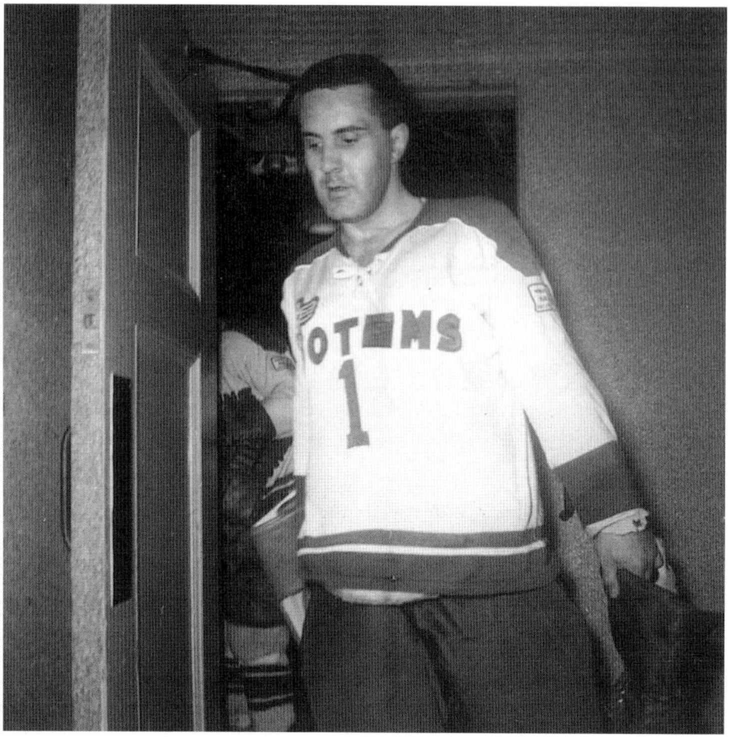

Al Millar joined the Totems in 1961 and came up just short of playing in every minute of all 87 Totems games (including playoffs) in 1962–1963. He was pulled in the middle of the second period during a game in Calgary, only to suffer the indignity of being replaced by a local junior leaguer named Lorne Thornycroft who just happened to be attending the game that night. (Courtesy of Dave Eskenazi.)

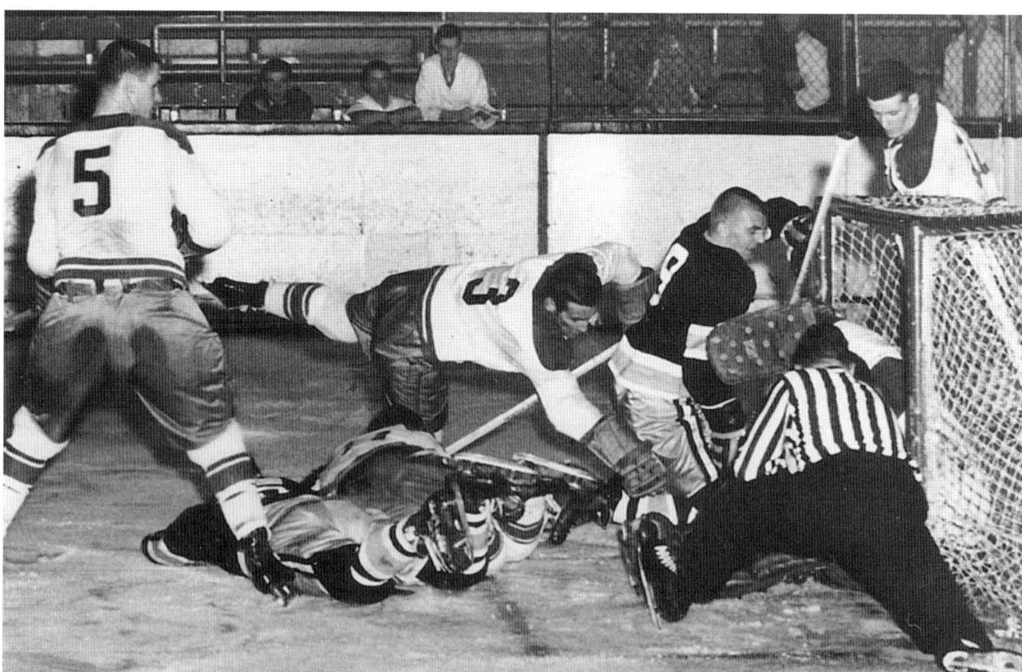

Al Millar desperately tries to keep the puck out of the net while Don Ward (No. 5) looks on and Gordie Sinclair (No. 3) dives in to cover it up. Bob Barlow is the Totem lying flat on the ice (No. 11), while Gerry Leonard (No. 16) looks in from behind the net. (Photograph by Bob Carver, courtesy of Dave Eskenazi.)

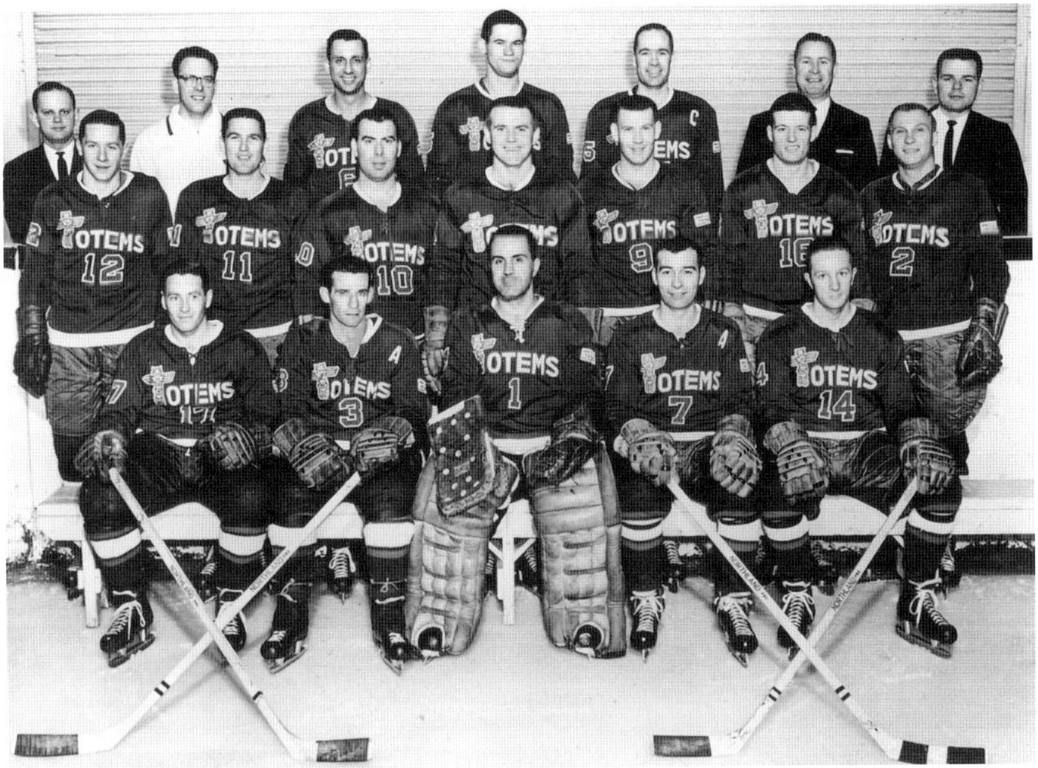

The 1962–1963 Seattle Totems are, from left to right, (first row) Wayne Hall, Gordie Sinclair, Al Millar, Guyle Fielder, and Don Chiupka; (second row) Barney Krake, Bob Barlow, Bob Sabourin, Jim Hay, Jim Powers, Gerry Leonard, and Lou Kazowski; (third row) Gerald Lonn, Dick Bielous, Rudy Filion, Don Ward, Bill MacFarland, Keith Allen, and George Konik.

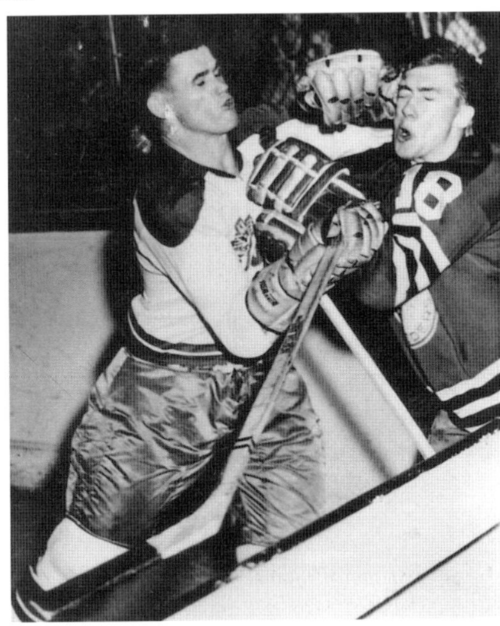

Defenseman Don Ward (in white) joined the Totems in 1961–1962 and became a mainstay on the blue line for the next 11 seasons. Here, he shows Calgary Stampeders center Cliff Bristow exactly why the Totems acquired him. Ward was known for his physical play and punishing hits. (Photograph by Bob Carver, courtesy of Dave Eskenazi.)

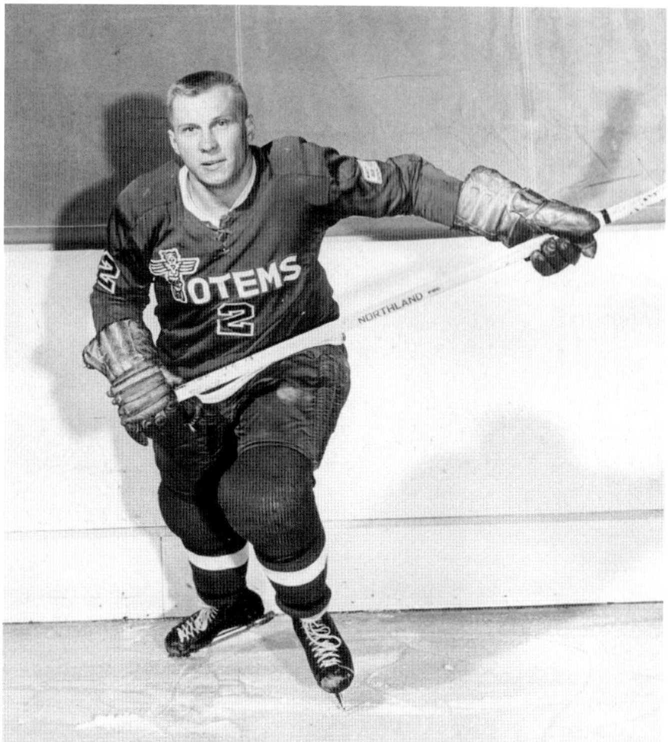

The 1962–1963 season saw the Totems make it all the way to the WHL Finals, but it was not without some bumps in the road. Lou Kazowski (shown) missed two months after separating his shoulder in a fight and on his first day back at practice collided with teammate George Konik, separating Konik's shoulder and reinjuring his own.

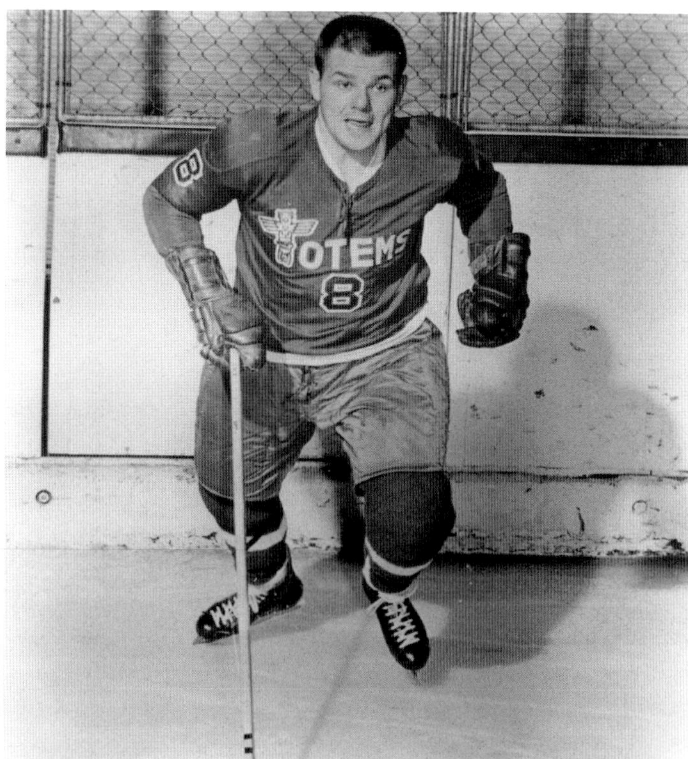

The Totems acquired George Konik off waivers from Portland in November 1962 to toughen up their front line. Unfortunately, he only appeared in 42 games that season as a result of a collision with teammate Lou Kazowski. Ironically, the shoulder injuries to Konik and Kazowski gave more ice time to Barney Krake, who had himself suffered a severe shoulder injury the prior season and was getting back into form.

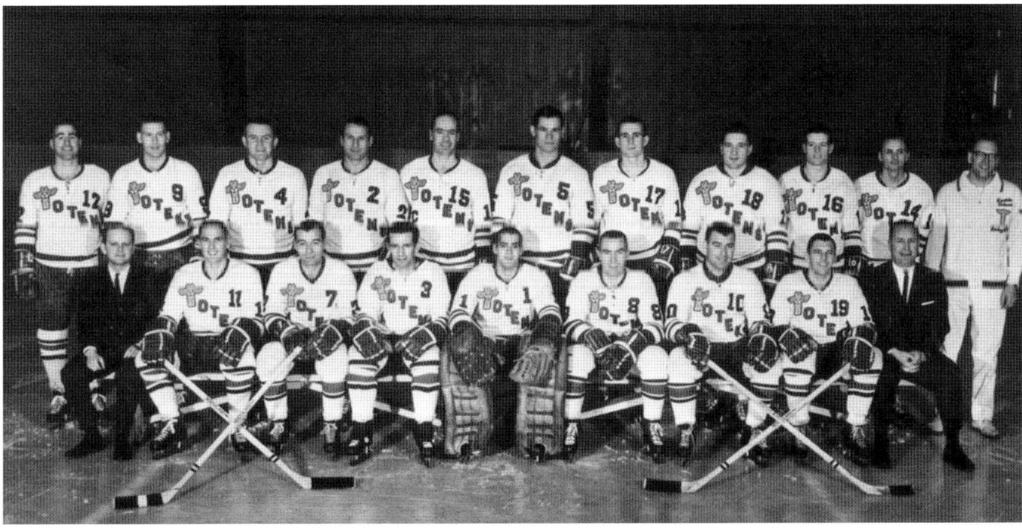

The 1963–1964 Totems posted the franchise's first losing record since 1955–1956, going 29-35-6 and missing the playoffs. From left to right are (first row) Gerald Lonn, Bob Barlow, Guyle Fielder, Gordie Sinclair, Claude Dufour, Bev Bell, Bob Sabourin, Jean-Marie Cossette, and Keith Allen; (second row) Del Topoll, Jim Powers, Jim Hay, Larry Zeidel, Bill MacFarland, Don Ward, Larry Hale, Tom Burgess, Gerry Leonard, Bill Carter, and Dick Bielous.

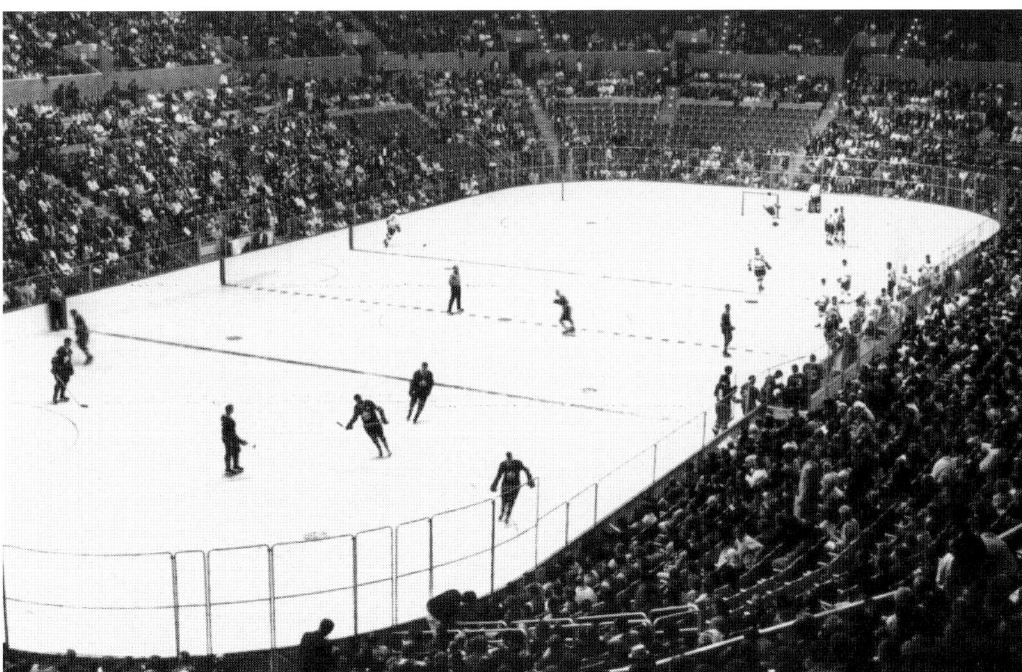

The Totems christened their new home, the 12,700-seat Seattle Coliseum, with an exhibition game against the NHL's Toronto Maple Leafs on September 30, 1964. A crowd of 8,601 turned out for the evening's festivities, almost double the largest crowd that could fit into the Civic Arena. Toronto won easily 7-1. (Courtesy of the *Seattle Post-Intelligencer* Collection, Museum of History and Industry.)

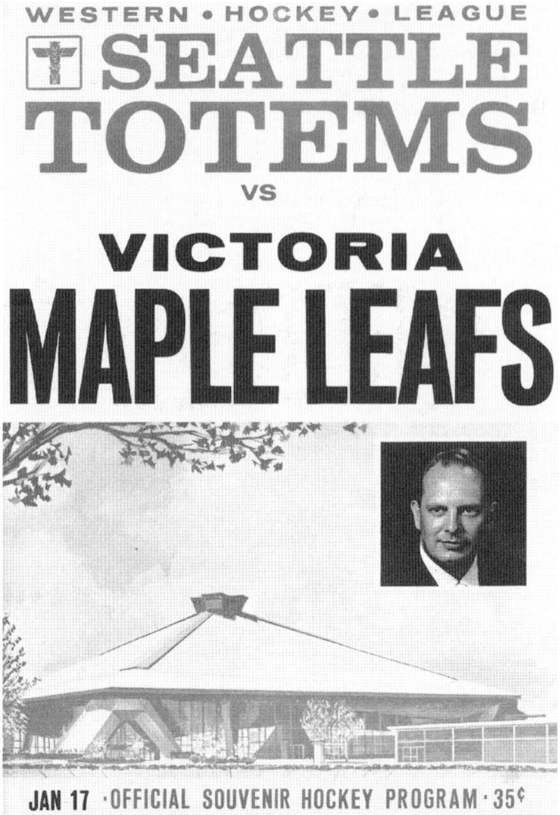

On January 17, 1965, the Totems hosted the Victoria Maple Leafs, and the home fans were treated to one of the worst incidents ever seen on home ice when Seattle defenseman Larry Zeidel repeatedly tried to spit on referee Willie Papp. Zeidel earned a five-game suspension for the display and did not return to the Totems the following season.

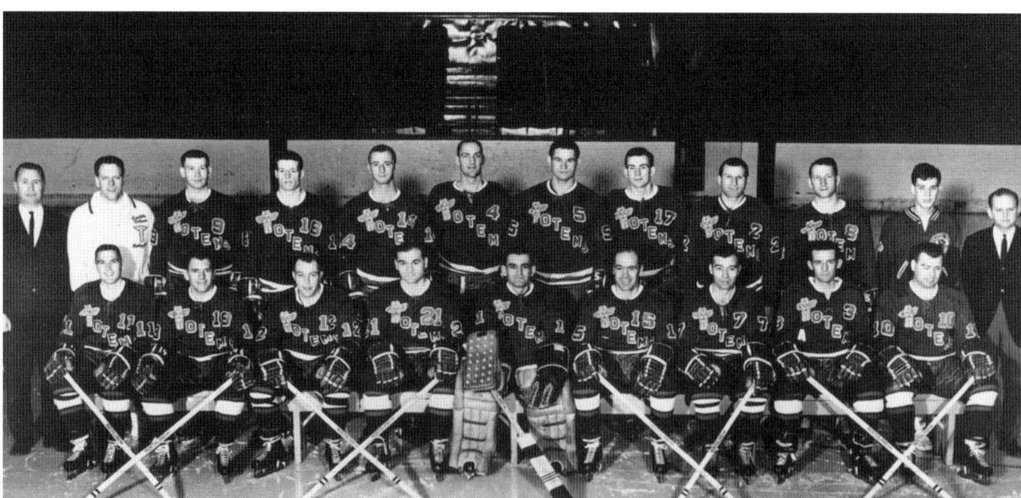

The 1964–1965 Totems got back over .500 (36-30-4) but lost in the first round of the playoffs. From left to right are (first row) Bob Barlow, Jean-Marie Cossette, Gerry Brisson, Ray Kinasewich, Jim McLeod, Bill MacFarland, Guyle Fielder, Gordie Sinclair, and Bob Sabourin; (second row) Keith Allen, Dick Bielous, Jim Powers, Gerry Leonard, Chuck Holmes, Maurice Mantha, Don Ward, Larry Hale, Larry Zeidel, Bill Dineen, Danny O'Brien, and Gerald Lonn.

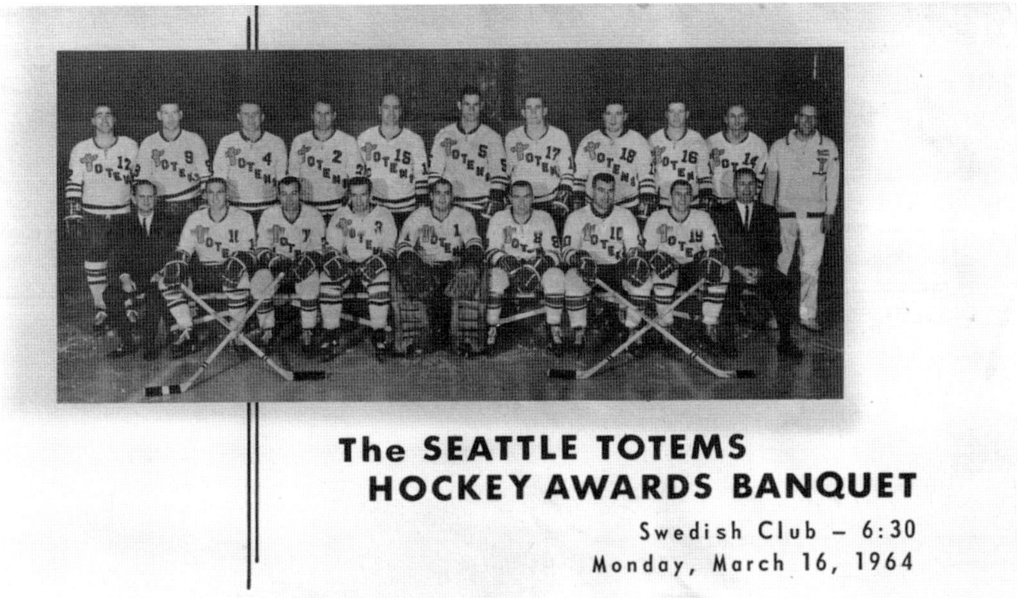

The Seattle Totems Booster Club was a large organization that at its peak numbered roughly 400 members. The annual awards banquet was a big event on the hockey calendar, with Totems players and staff attending to take part in the festivities, spending time with their fans and receiving awards and gifts.

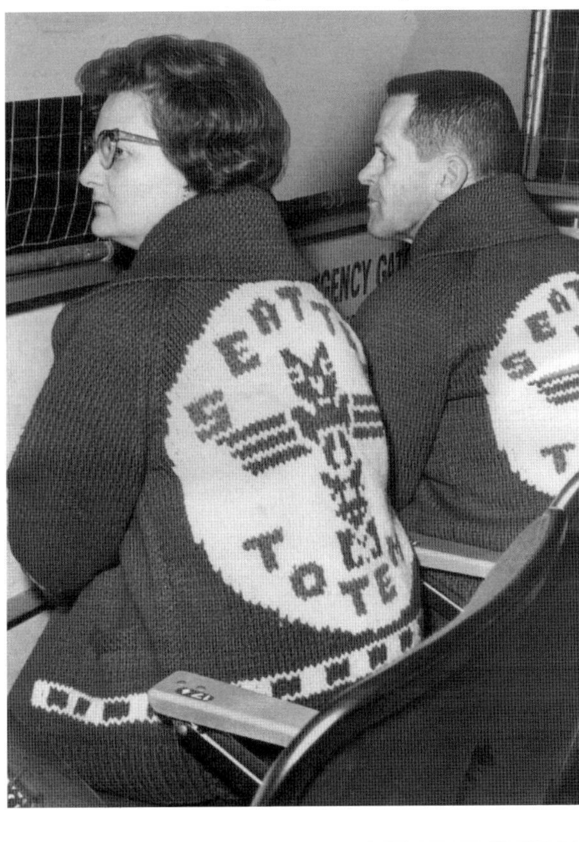

Perhaps nothing showed a fan's passion more than sporting a custom, handmade Seattle Totems sweater at the games. Here Mr. and Mrs. Leonard Capps show their Totems pride while seated in the front row, a dangerous position in those days, with only a wire fence separating fans from the players. (Courtesy of the *Seattle Post-Intelligencer* Collection, Museum of History and Industry.)

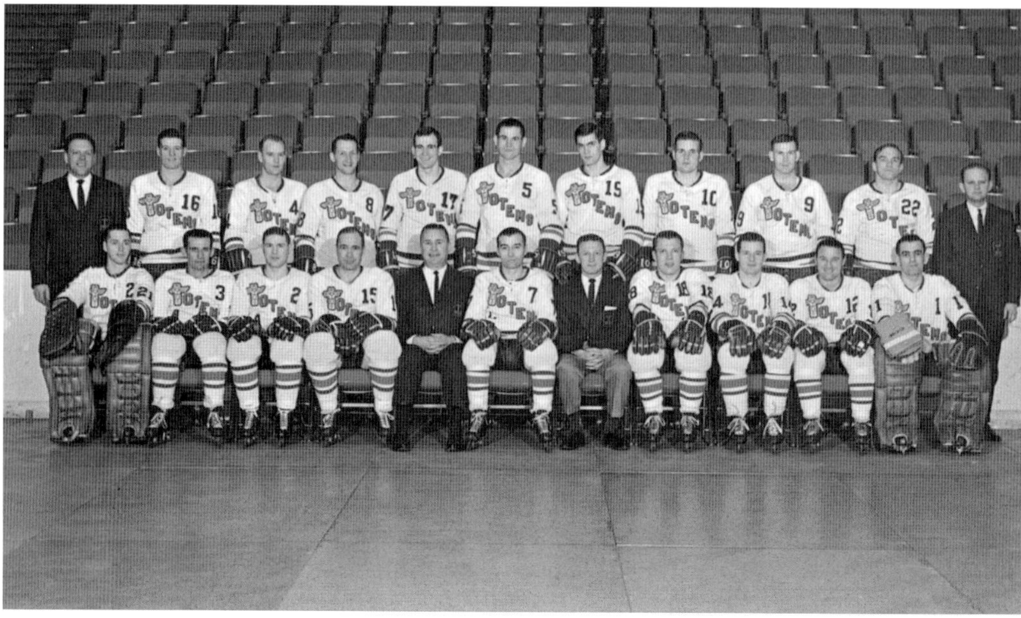

The 1965–1966 Seattle Totems are, from left to right, (first row) Ernie Wakely, Gordie Sinclair, Adam Keller, Bill MacFarland, Keith Allen, Guyle Fielder, Bobby Kromm, Ken Campbell, Don Chiz, Len Haley, and Jim McLeod; (second row) Dick Bielous, Gerry Leonard, Les Hunt, Bill Dineen, Larry Hale, Don Ward, Larry Lund, Earl Heiskala, Jim Powers, Bob Taylor, and Gerald Lonn.

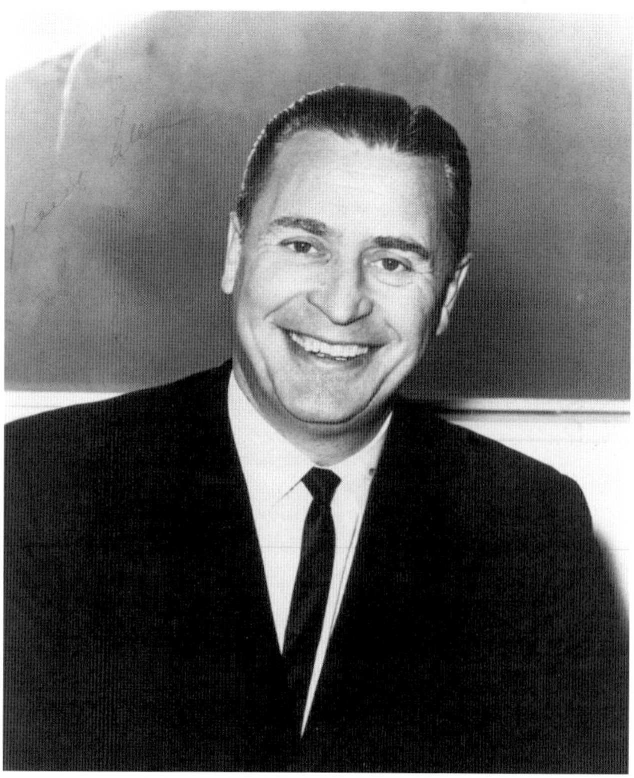

Keith Allen hung up his whistle and moved from behind the bench to the front office as the Totems general manager prior to the start of the 1965–1966 season. During his nine seasons as head coach, he amassed a 319-270-41 record with Seattle, taking the team to the WHL Finals three times and earning one championship. His replacement, Bobby Kromm, only lasted one season as head coach.

The Totems suffered their second losing season in three years in 1965–1966, going 32-37-3 under new head coach Bobby Kromm. Kromm's intensity and vocal nature, which included criticizing players in the press, did not go over well with his veteran team, which likely contributed to their lackluster performance and his departure at the end of the season.

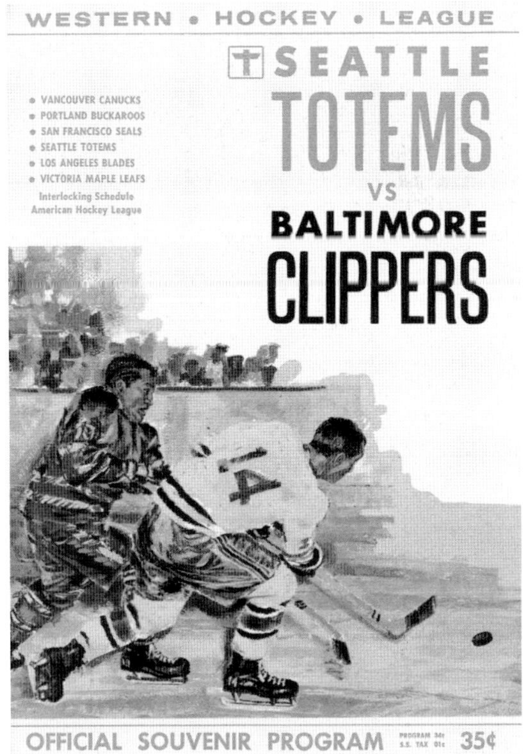

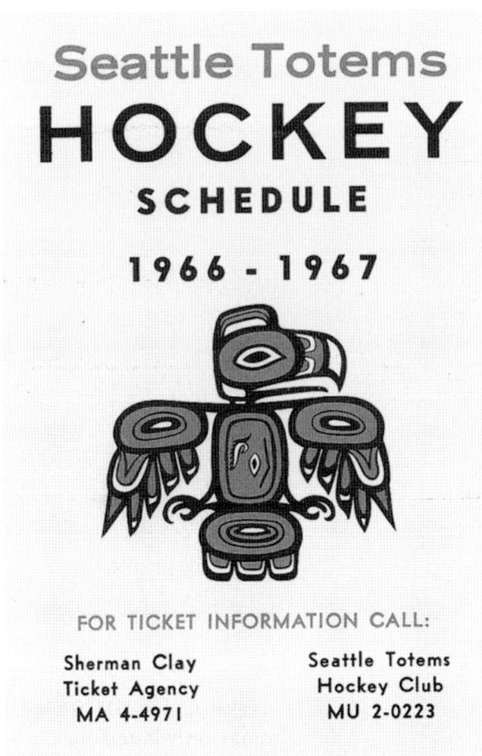

After the failure of the Bobby Kromm experiment the previous season, Keith Allen made sure he put a man behind the Totems bench who was guaranteed to have the respect of the team, none other than their teammate for the last decade Bill MacFarland. Along with the new coach came a new logo, the green Native American thunderbird motif that is so familiar to Seattle hockey fans.

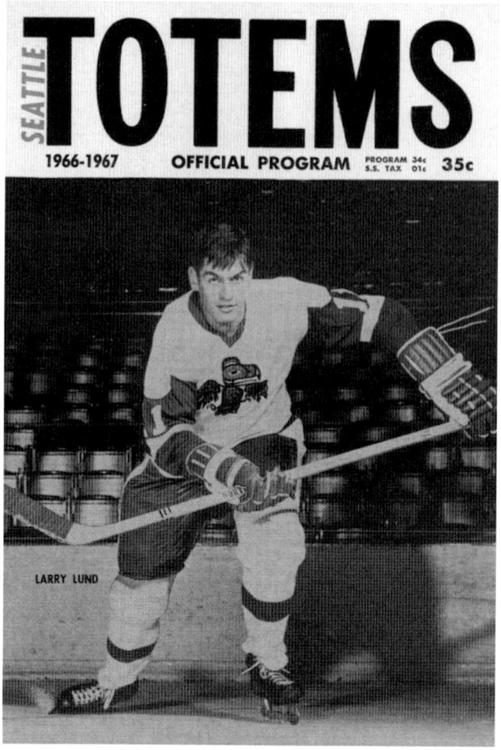

With new green jerseys and five defensemen who each weighed over 200 pounds, the 1966–1967 Totems earned themselves the nickname the "Jolly Green Giants." They allowed the fewest goals in the league and though not an offensive powerhouse, scored enough to finish the regular season in second place with a 39-26-7 record.

Totems forward Howie Hughes (No. 15) maneuvers around diving Canuck goaltender Don Simmons in game three of the 1967 WHL Finals. The Totems went 8-2 in the playoffs, sweeping Vancouver in the finals to earn their first WHL championship since 1959. (Courtesy of the *Seattle Post-Intelligencer* Collection, Museum of History and Industry.)

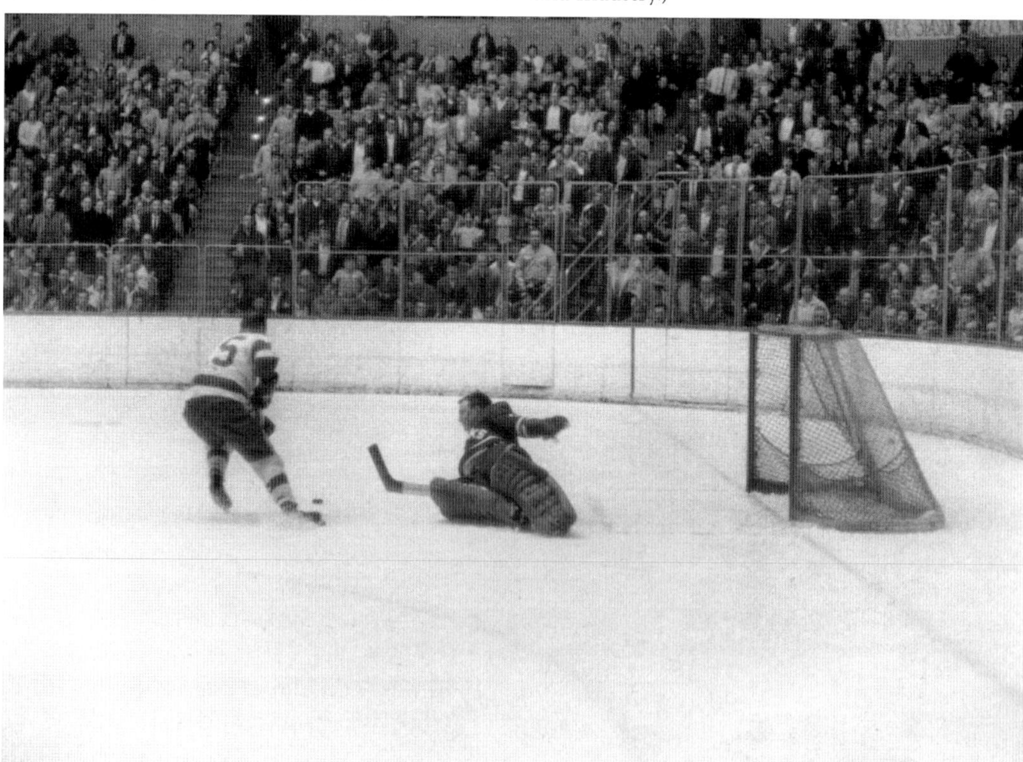

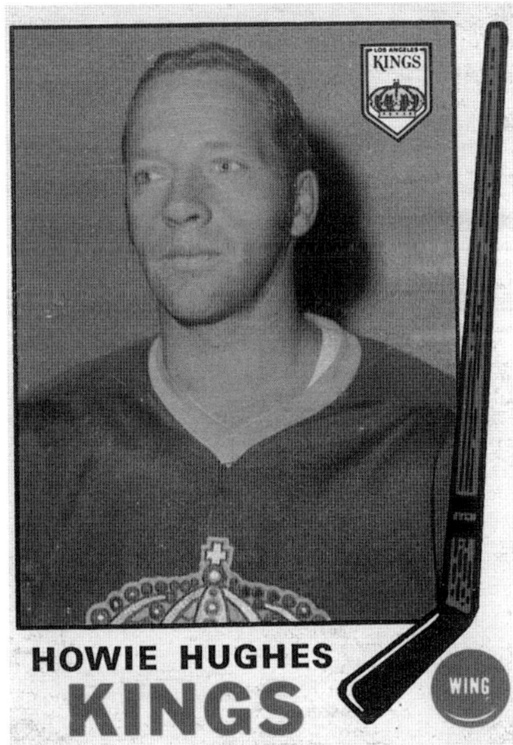

A successful 26-goal and 71-point campaign with Seattle in 1966–1967 earned Howie Hughes a promotion to the Los Angeles Kings of the NHL the following season as a 28-year-old rookie. He played three seasons in the NHL before returning to the WHL. (Topps hockey cards used courtesy of the Topps Company, Inc. For more information about The Topps Company, please see our website at www.topps.com.)

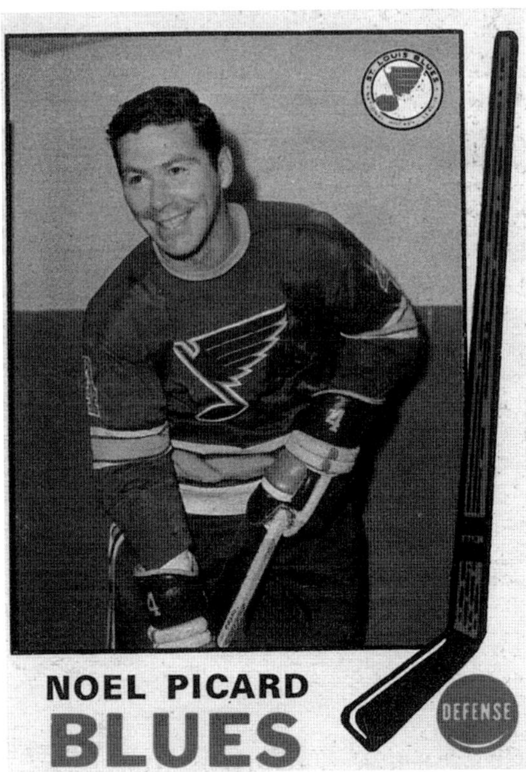

One of the Jolly Green Giants, Noel Picard also earned a shot at the NHL following the 1966–1967 championship run, spending the next six seasons with St. Louis and Atlanta, where he continued to be a physical presence on the blue line. (Topps hockey cards used courtesy of the Topps Company, Inc. For more information about The Topps Company, please see our website at www.topps.com.)

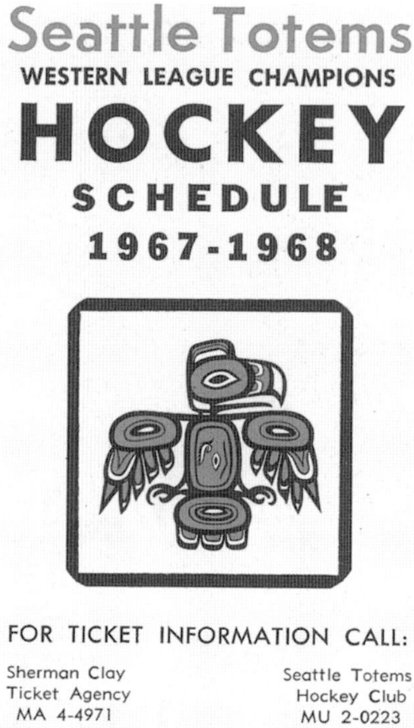

During the summer of 1967 Jack Kent Cooke, owner of the new Los Angeles Kings NHL expansion franchise, attempted to buy a controlling interest in the Totems so he could use the club as a farm team. When word of Cooke's plan leaked, a group of Totems owners bought out the last wavering shareholder to ensure the team remained in local hands.

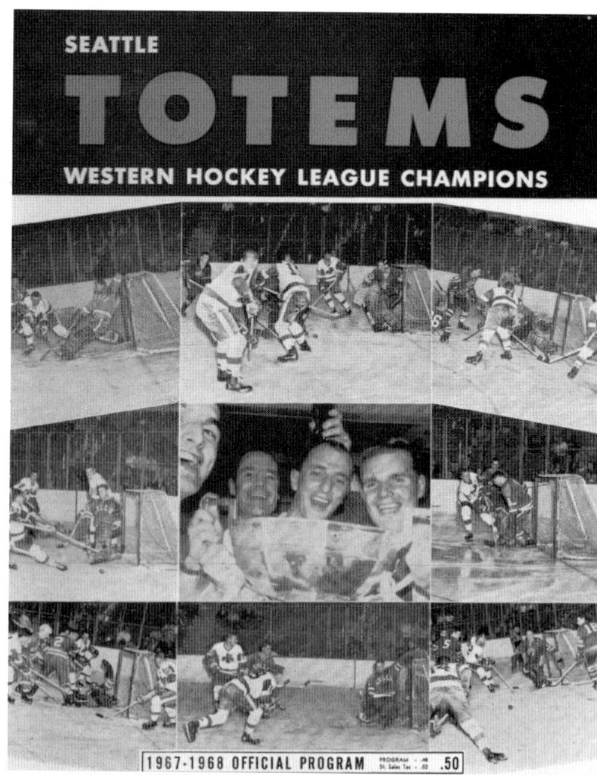

The 1967–1968 Totems came out of the gate strong, opening the campaign with a 10-game unbeaten streak that included eight wins. They eventually came back to earth and slid comfortably into second place in the now five-team WHL, finishing with a 35-30-7 record, despite having the lowest-scoring offense in the league.

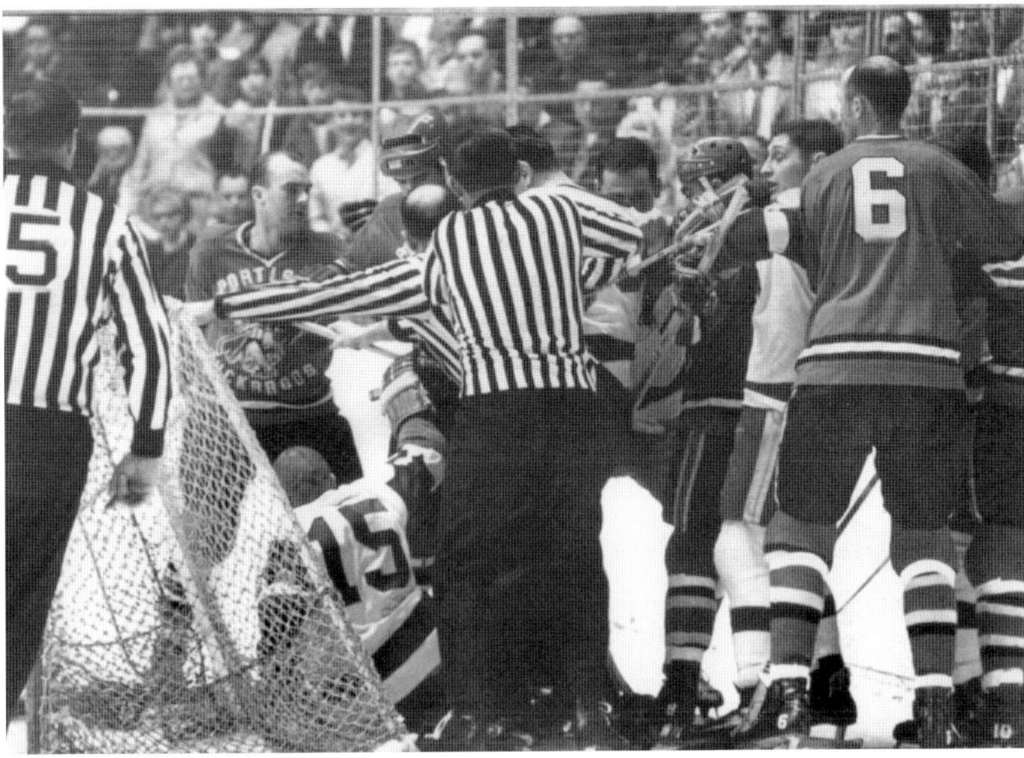

The rivalry with the Portland Buckaroos reached its boiling point in 1967–1968. The teams engaged in a series of brutal, brawl-filled encounters in the last month of the season that generated multiple ejections and culminated with a Seattle fan throwing a can of coffee (yes, a can of coffee) at Buckaroo Connie Madigan. (Courtesy of the *Seattle Post-Intelligencer* Collection, Museum of History and Industry.)

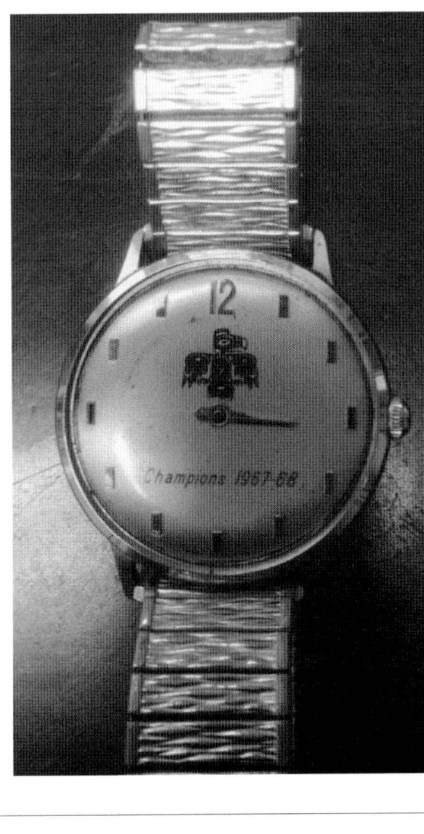

The Totems defeated the Portland Buckaroos in the finals to win the 1968 WHL championship, their second in two years and unfortunately their last. In the second game, they rallied from a 6-2 third-period deficit to beat the Buckaroos in overtime. Members of the organization received various items, such as this watch, to commemorate the championship. (Courtesy of Dave Eskenazi.)

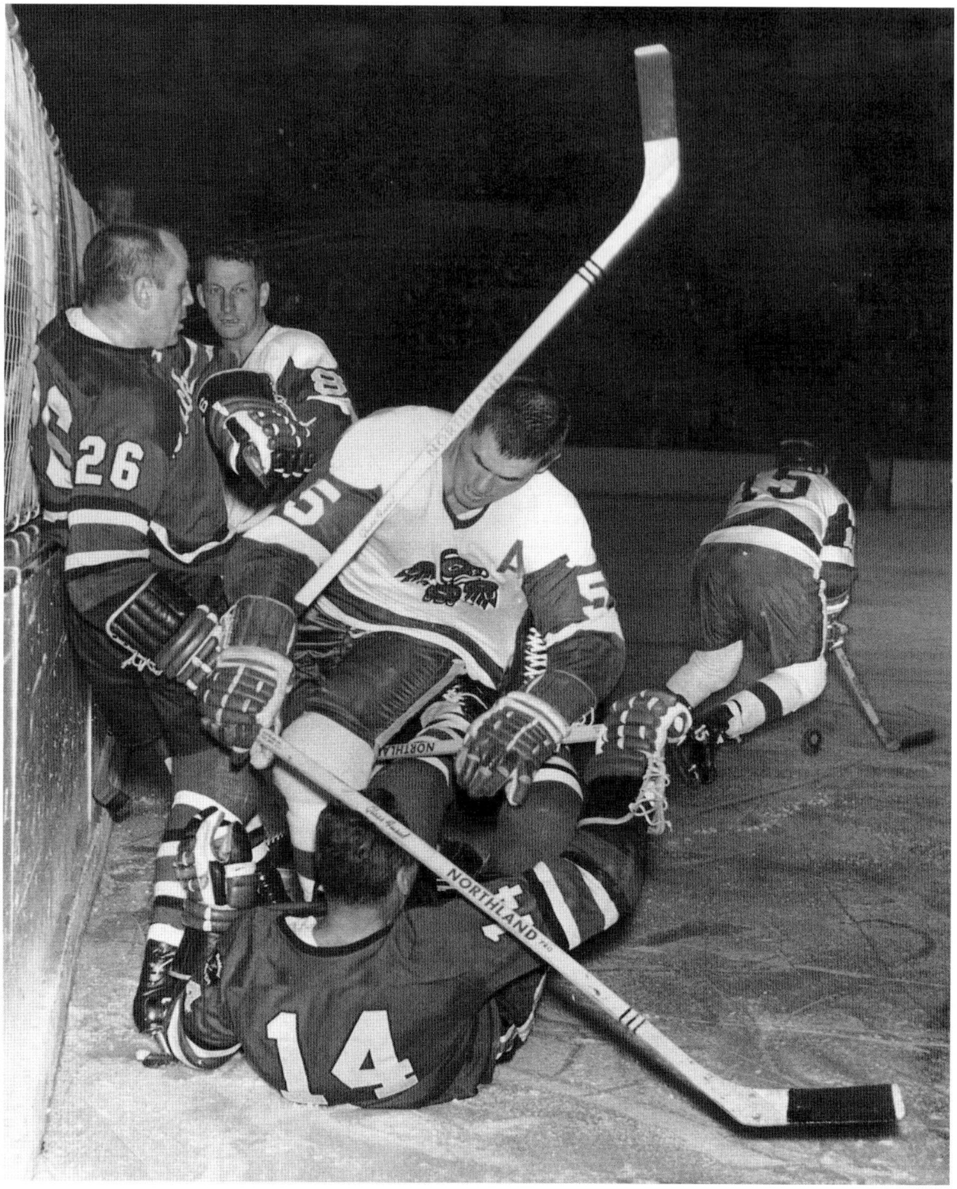

In arguably the most iconic action photograph of the Totems era, defenseman Don Ward (No. 5) demolishes Portland Buckaroo Andy Hebenton (No. 14), while Bill Dineen (No. 8) and Connie Madigan (No. 26) tangle on the boards. Art Stratton (No. 15) of the Totems takes the loose puck from the scene. An artistic rendering of this hit, created by Stu Moldrem, graced the cover of Seattle game programs in 1969–1970. Portland was arguably the better team over the course of the 14-season rivalry, earning eight first-place finishes and three WHL titles while the Totems failed to top the standings during that period. Regardless of their respective records, however, when the two teams met, it was sure to be a battle. Perhaps the most infamous of these was on March 31, 1967, when a 20-minute bench-clearing brawl erupted right before the end of the game, which resulted in Connie Madigan being escorted from the ice by police and $1,200 in fines levied by the league. (Photograph by Bob Carver.)

Winning back-to-back championships is marketing gold, and the Totems made sure to play up the team's recent successes in their advertising, such as this season ticket brochure for the 1968–1969 season. Unfortunately, the Totems had won their last championship and were about to embark on a period of decline, posting their last-ever winning record in 1968–1969. (Courtesy of Dave Eskenazi.)

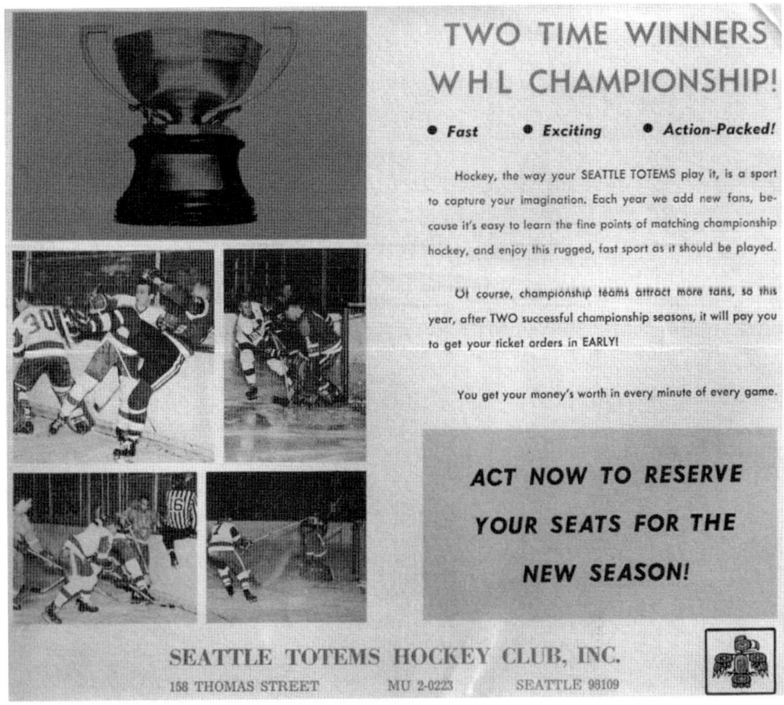

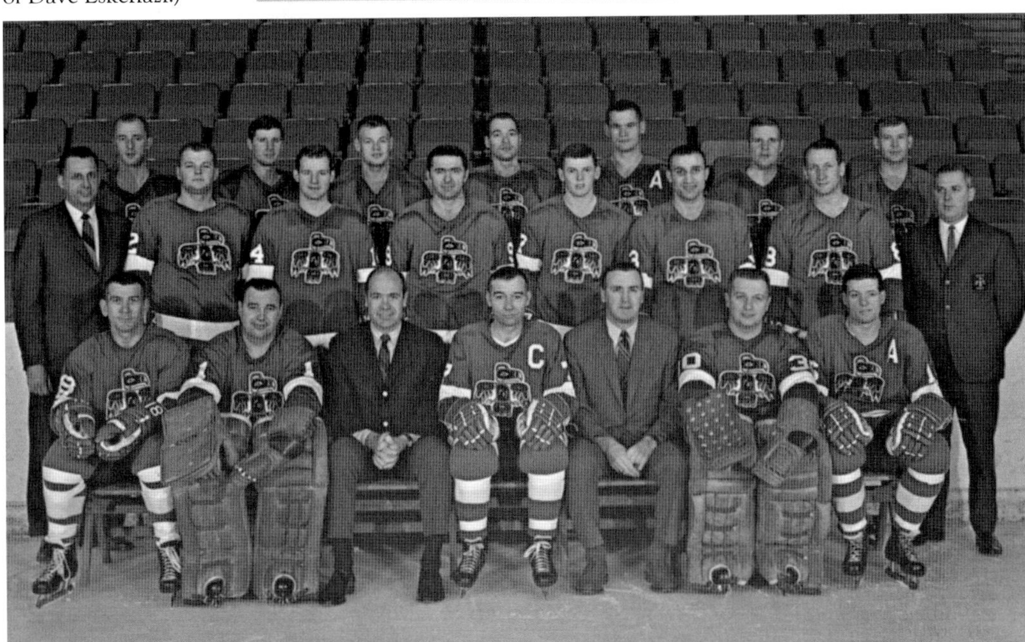

The fourth-place 1968–1969 Seattle Totems are, from left to right, (first row) Bob Courcy, Don Head, Bill MacFarland, Guyle Fielder, Murray Costello, Jim Armstrong, and Gerry Leonard; (second row) Rudy Filion, Ken Rodgers, Don Chiz, Marc Boileau, Jack Michie, John Hanna, Bill Dineen, and Pat Dunn; (third row) Chuck Holmes, Gary Kilpatrick, Ray Larose, Art Stratton, Don Ward, Earl Heiskala, and Jim Powers.

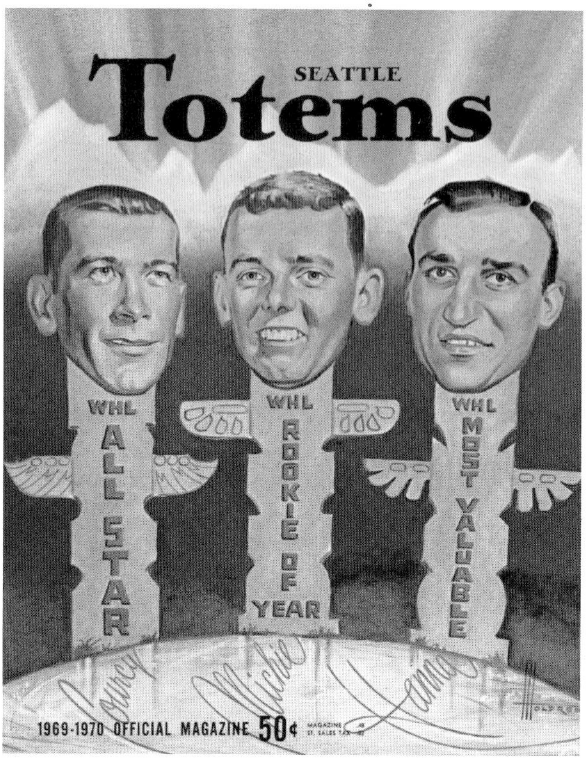

While the 1968–1969 season was a disappointment, there was reason for hope in 1969–1970. The Totems were returning with the 1968–1969 Rookie of the Year in Jack Michie, a first-team all-star in Bob Courcy, and the league's top defenseman and MVP John Hanna. What they did not have, however, was Guyle Fielder, who left Seattle for Salt Lake City.

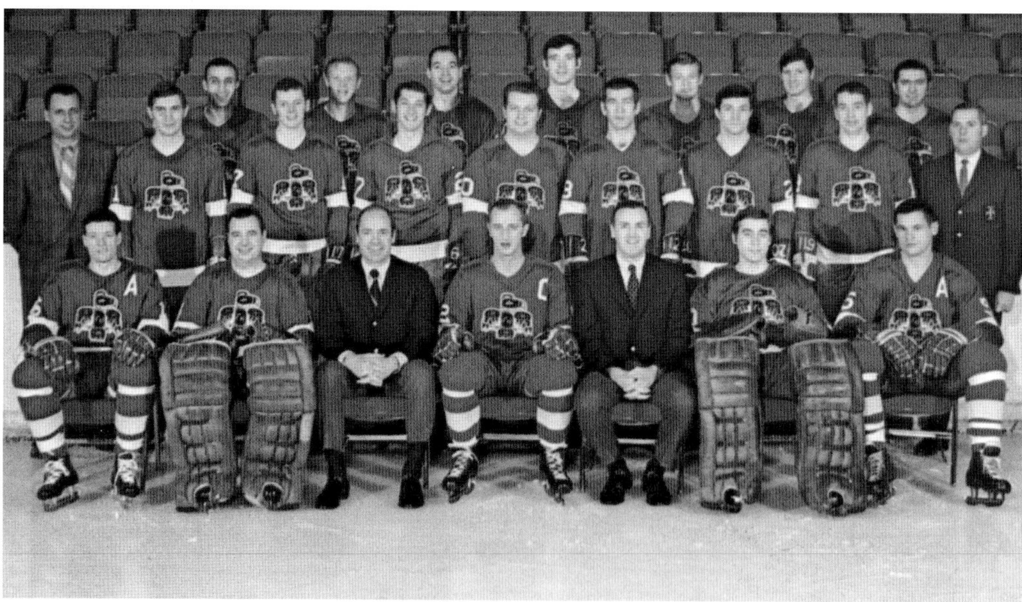

The 1969–1970 Seattle Totems are, from left to right, (first row) Gerry Leonard, Don Head, Bill MacFarland, Chuck Holmes, Murray Costello, Chris Worthy, and Don Ward; (second row) Rudy Filion, Bobby Schmautz, Jack Michie, Dwight Carruthers, Jim Armstrong, Bob Courcy, Jack Dale, Tom McVie, and Pat Dunn; (third row) John Hanna, Ron Ingram, Art Stratton, Gerry Meehan, Ray Larose, Gary Kilpatrick, and Marc Boileau.

6

Bill MacFarland

The Seattle Totems went into the 1968 WHL playoffs trying to repeat as league champions. However, their first-round opponents, the Phoenix Roadrunners, were none too impressed by the Totems style of play. According to Roadrunners coach Alf Pike, "What I mean is Seattle is dirty. We're aggressive." Pike should have known better than to serve up a softball like that to Totems coach Bill MacFarland, who when he was not busy with hockey worked as an attorney. When asked for a comment about Pike's accusation, MacFarland replied, "The Roadrunners play a pretty good game of hockey. But the referee plays a dirty trick on them when he drops the puck." The Totems went on to sweep the Roadrunners on the way to their second consecutive WHL title.

In many ways, Bill "Packy" MacFarland was not a typical professional hockey player. He earned his undergraduate degree from the University of Michigan, where he also played hockey and led the Wolverines to back-to-back NCAA championships in 1955 and 1956. From there he went to the WHL for 11 seasons as a player (10 in Seattle), followed by four more as Totems head coach. Along the way, he also went to law school and was admitted to the Washington State Bar Association in 1964. Even with his coaching days behind him, he still remained involved in the sport, serving as president of the WHL from 1972 to 1974 and holding the same position with the upstart World Hockey Association from 1975 to 1977. He made another splash in the local scene in 1990 as part of a group that sought to bring an NHL expansion franchise to Seattle, an effort unfortunately doomed to failure due to the unexpected last-minute withdrawal of the group's application.

Bill MacFarland passed away in 2011 at the age of 79. His passion for the game and importance to Seattle hockey cannot be overstated and is worthy of recognition and celebration.

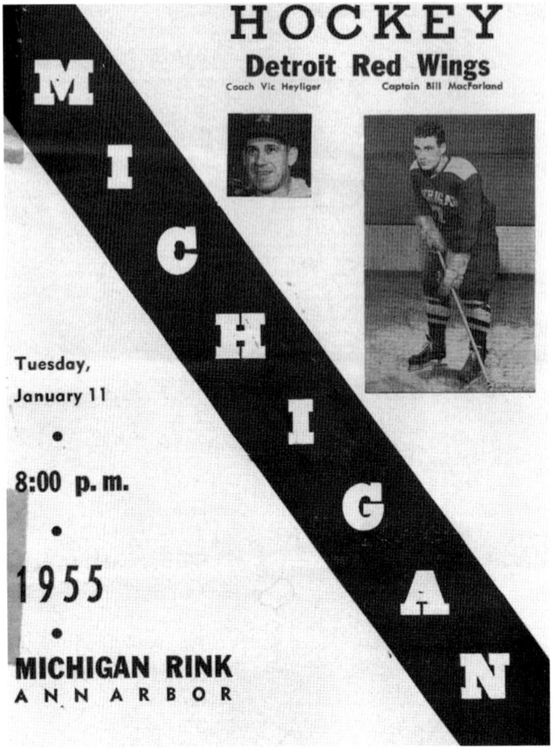

Team captain Bill MacFarland is prominently featured on the cover of this 1955 program for an exhibition game between the University of Michigan and the Detroit Red Wings. In addition to winning back-to-back NCAA championships with the Wolverines, MacFarland was also named to the 1955 NCAA Frozen Four All-Tournament Team. He continued his academic career while in Seattle, attending law school at the University of Washington.

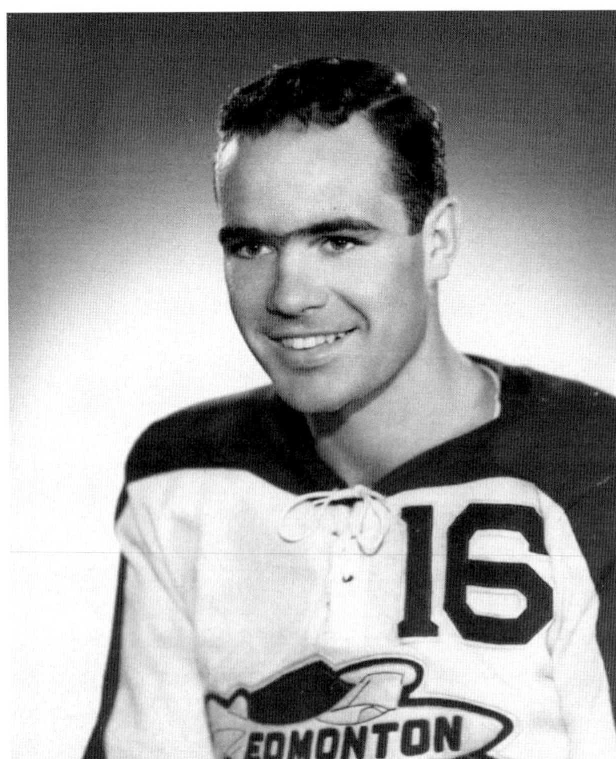

Bill MacFarland arrived in the WHL as a 24-year-old rookie in 1956–1957, scoring 16 goals and 49 points with the Edmonton Flyers. His stay in Edmonton only lasted one season, and he was transferred to the Americans in 1957–1958, the start of a successful 10-year playing career in Seattle (excluding the one game he played in 1967 while head coach, a ploy to make himself playoff-eligible in an emergency).

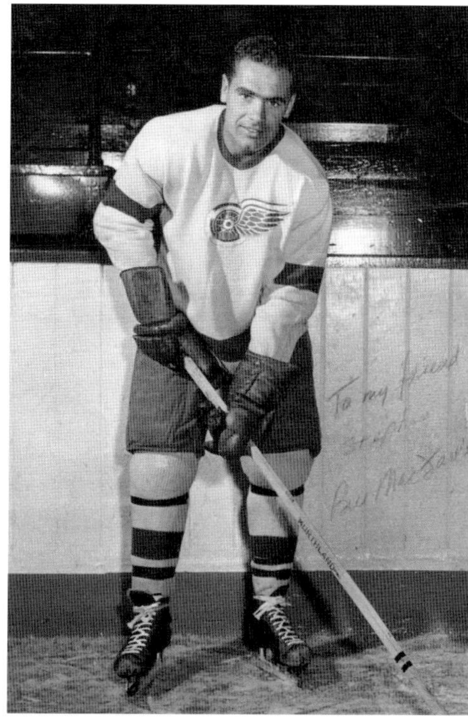

Like many minor-league hockey players, an NHL team held MacFarland's rights. In his case, that team was the Detroit Red Wings, the same club he played against while in college at the University of Michigan. However, MacFarland never saw the ice in an NHL game, spending his entire decade-long professional career in the WHL.

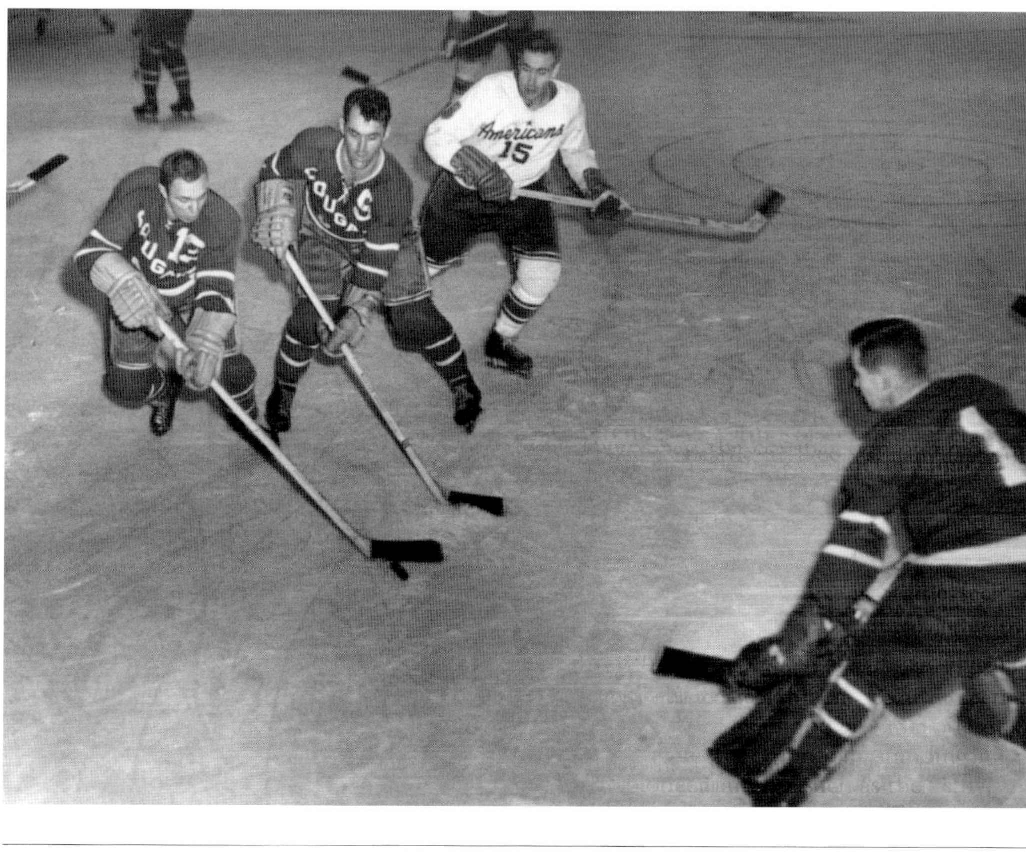

MacFarland (No. 15) quickly established himself as an offensive threat upon arriving in Seattle, notching the first of his seven 30-plus–goal seasons. He also showed a willingness to get physical and protect his smaller line mates by earning 57 penalty minutes in 1957–1958, the second most among Americans forwards.

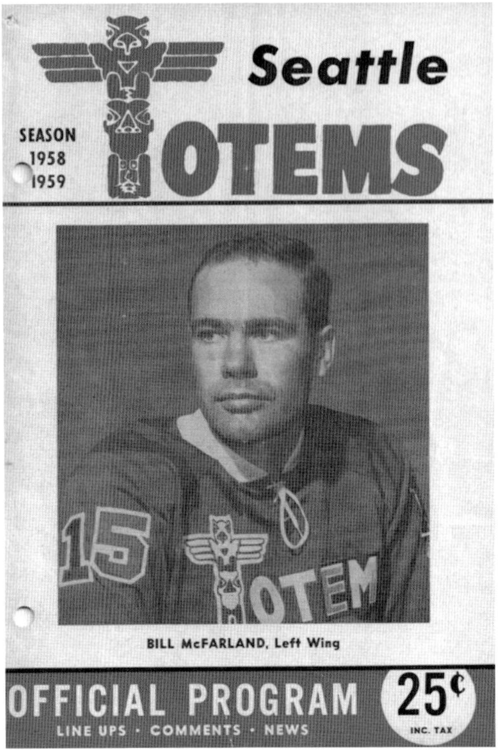

MacFarland truly came into his own as a player in 1958–1959, earning a five-point night in the home opener and never looking back, despite being slowed somewhat by an early-season knee injury. His 35 goals led the team, and he added six more in the postseason as the Totems rolled on to an 11-1 playoff record and won their first WHL championship.

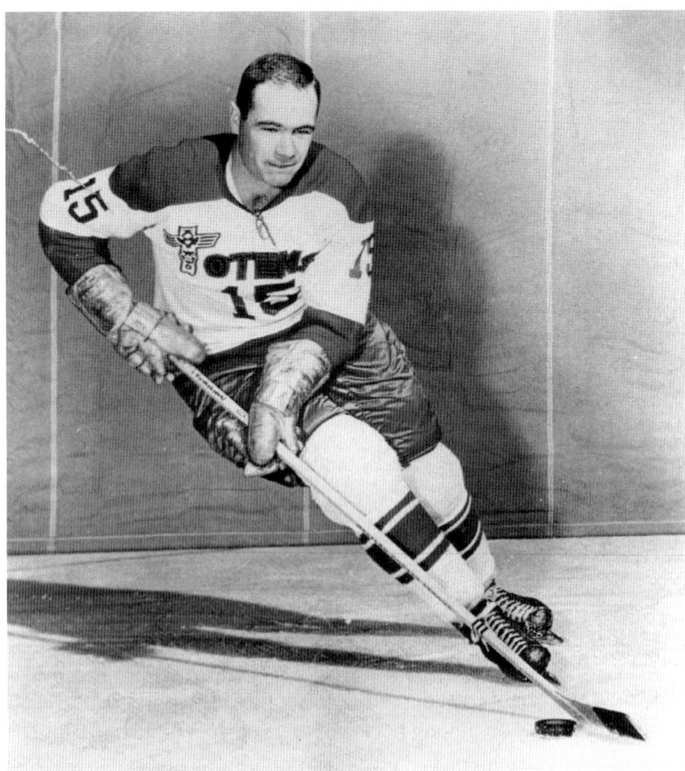

Bill MacFarland ranks in the top five all-time among Seattle players in every offensive category, with 299 regular season goals (third), 344 assists (fourth), and 643 total points (third) over the course of 626 games. He led the Americans/Totems in goals five times in 10 seasons and was the WHL MVP in 1962. He ranks second all-time among Seattle professionals in playoff goals (25), assists (43), and points (68).

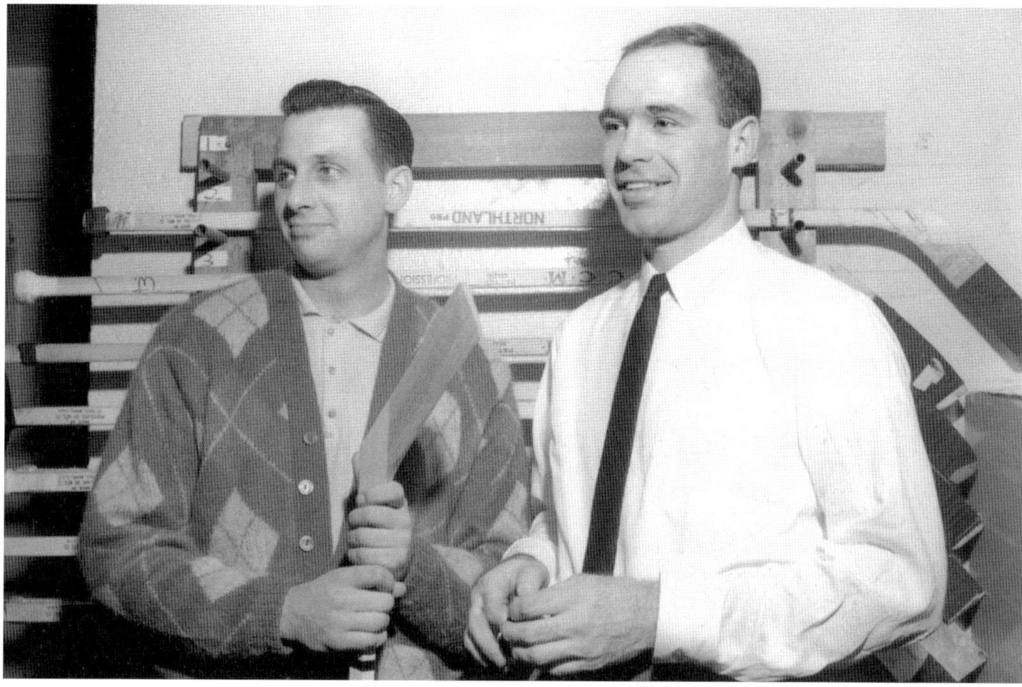

The careers of Rudy Filion (left) and Bill MacFarland (right) were intertwined throughout the 1960s and into the 1970s. They were line mates on the ice, and both moved on to front-office roles with the Totems after their playing careers ended. (Courtesy of the *Seattle Post-Intelligencer* Collection, Museum of History and Industry.)

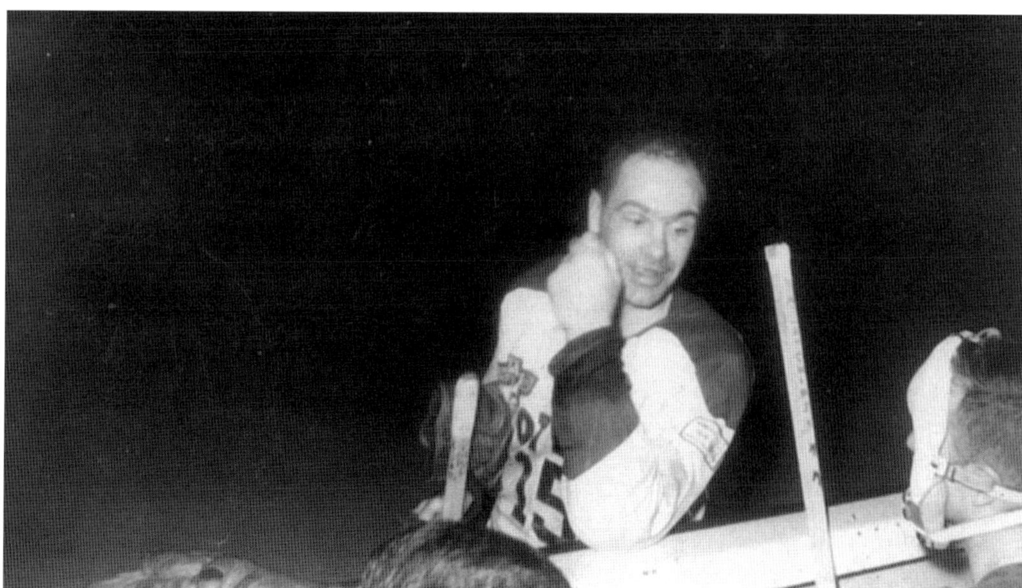

MacFarland was always quick to flash a smile, one that on the ice revealed a notable lack of front teeth, a common condition among hockey players of the era. Despite his friendly nature, however, he was also a fierce competitor who racked up 340 penalty minutes in Seattle. (Courtesy of Dave Eskenazi.)

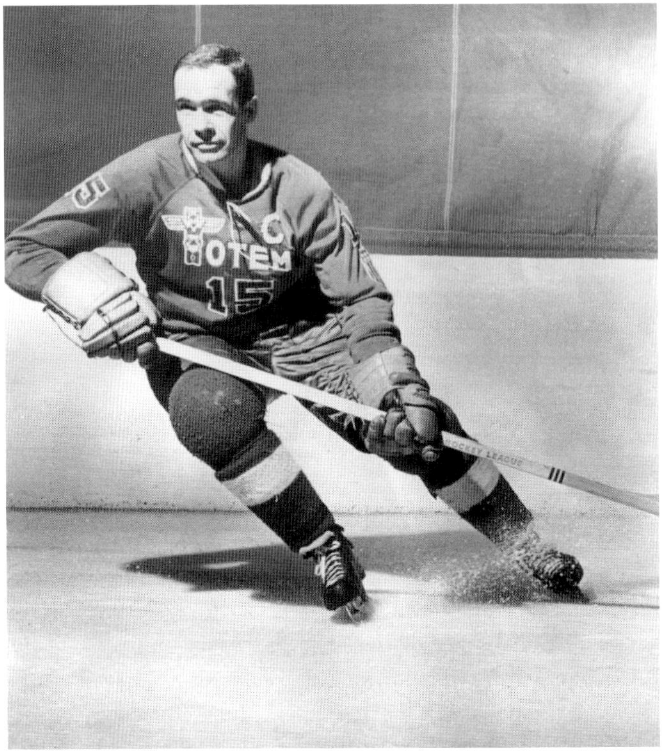

Bill MacFarland's influence extended beyond the ice, even during his playing days. He represented the WHL players in their negotiations with the owners, helped establish a player pension fund, and was also part of the group that published the *Western Hockey World* newspaper during the mid-1960s, the WHL version of *The Hockey News*. (Courtesy of Dave Eskenazi.)

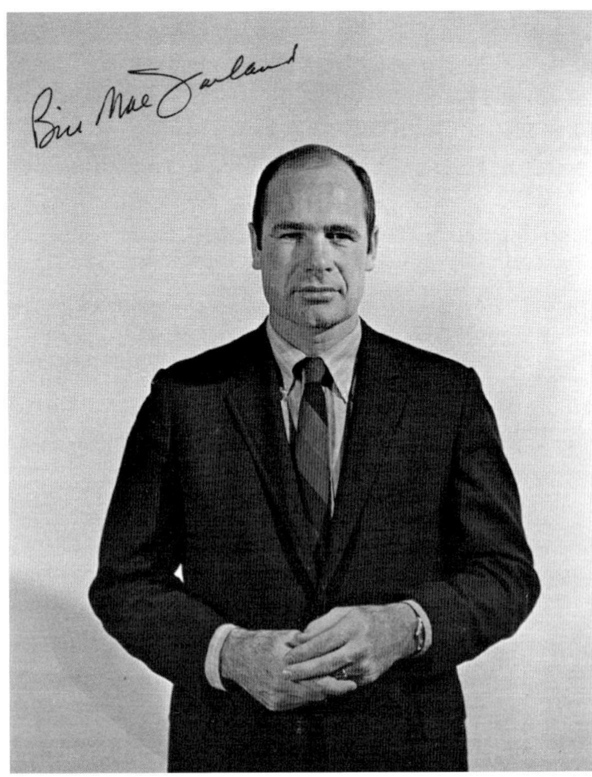

MacFarland remained involved with hockey after his playing days. He served as Totems coach and general manager, president of the WHL, and was a franchise owner and league president in the World Hockey Association. He was also part of a group that tried to bring an NHL expansion franchise to Seattle in the early 1990s.

7

The Tough 1970s

Sometimes it is staggering how fast things change. The Totems finished in fourth place in 1968–1969 with a lackluster 33-30-11 record, but there were a lot of reasons to be hopeful about the future. That team boasted the WHL Rookie of the Year Jack Michie as well as John Hanna, who captured honors as both the league's top defenseman and the MVP award. Things looked to be moving in the right direction.

But, in fact, they were not. They were moving in the entirely wrong direction. Just three seasons later, the Totems and their fans endured a tortuous 12-win 1971–1972 campaign that was capped off by a staggering 18-game losing streak. It was truly rock bottom. There were, however, some positives. The Totems played two exhibition games against the powerhouse Russian national teams, the second of which resulted in a 8-4 Seattle win that sent shockwaves through the hockey world. It was definitely something to cheer about, and hockey fans who were at one or both of those games still remember them fondly today.

The WHL folded in 1974, forcing the Totems to join the Central Hockey League for what turned out to be their last season in 1974–1975. But on the surface, Seattle's hockey future appeared bright, as the Totems ownership group was awarded an NHL expansion franchise in 1974. The NHL was finally coming to Seattle. Unfortunately, the decline that was the 1970s continued on this front as well, with the promised expansion team failing to materialize and relations between the ownership group and the NHL deteriorating into an antitrust lawsuit that took a decade to resolve. In the end, professional hockey left Seattle in 1975, and while there has been some discussion in recent years of a new arena and an NHL team, the city's hockey fans are still waiting for the professional game to return to the home of America's first Stanley Cup–winning team.

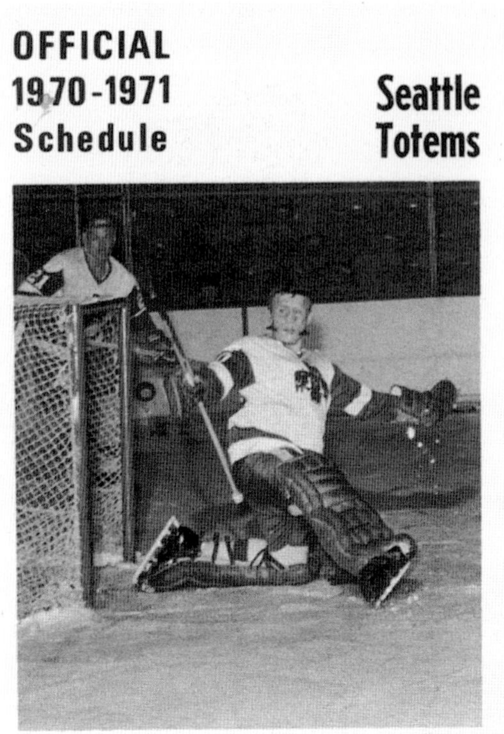

The Totems continued their slide to the bottom in 1970–1971, dropping a position in the standings to finish the season in fifth place with their second consecutive losing record (27-36-9). They missed the playoffs for the first time since 1965–1966 and never again made it to the postseason.

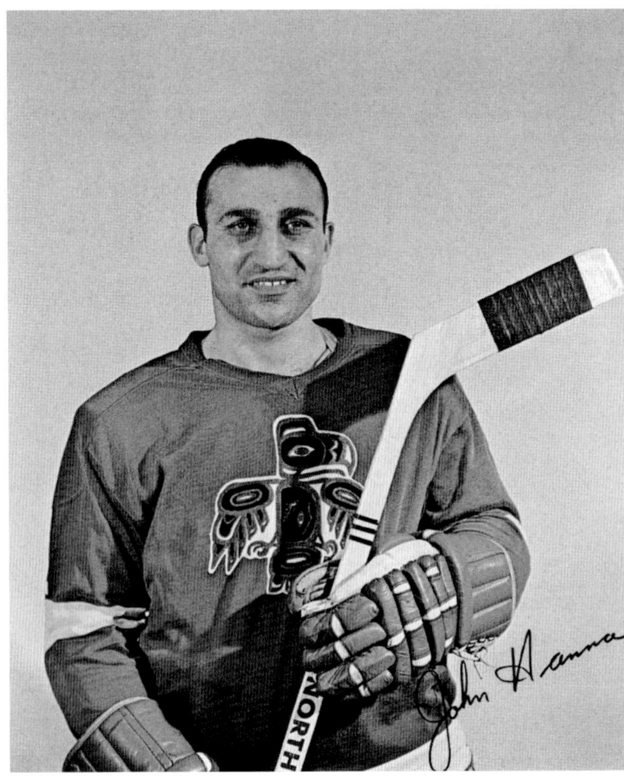

NHL veteran blue liner John Hanna was one of the few bright spots on the Totems during the 1970–1971 season. He won his second Hal Laycoe Cup as the league's top defenseman and became the only defenseman ever to lead the Totems in scoring, his 60 points (20 goals, 40 assists) tying him with Bob Jones.

The Totems rebounded after the disastrous 1971–1972 season, more than doubling their win total and posting a respectable 26-32-14 record in 1972–1973. Unfortunately, that was only good enough for a fifth-place finish, as they fell one point shy of the Denver Spurs for the fourth playoff spot. It was the closest the franchise came to the playoffs during the 1970s.

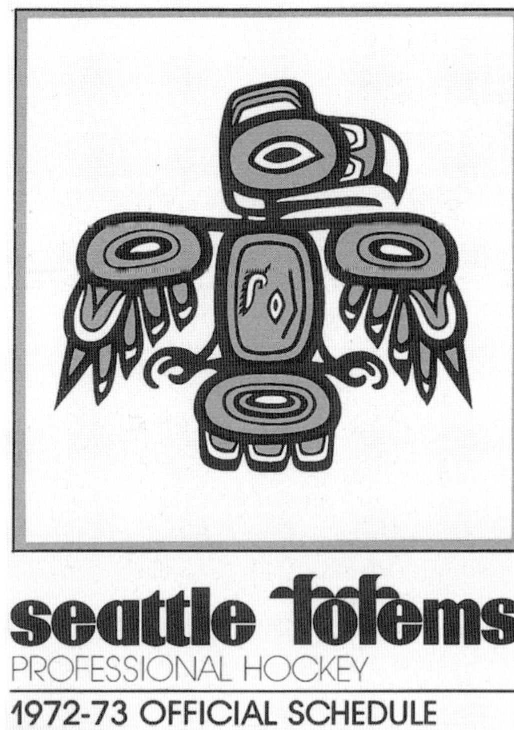

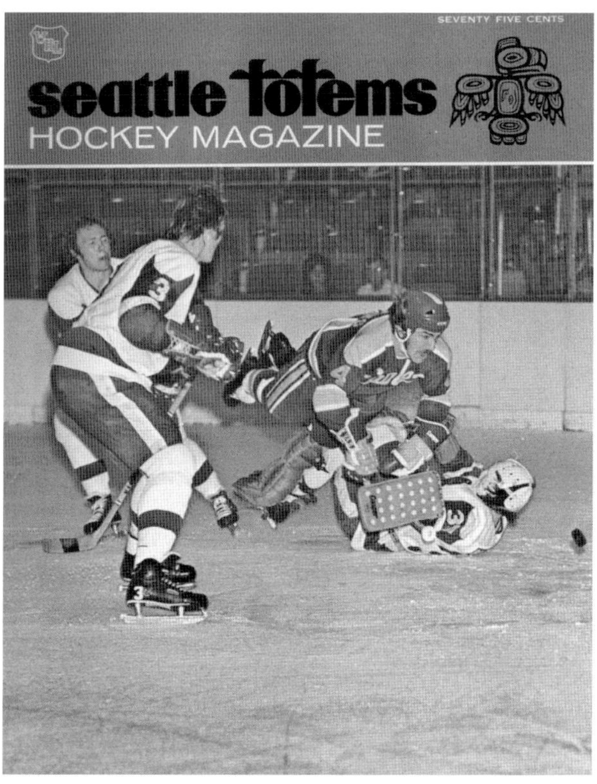

To understand how close the Totems came to breaking their postseason dry spell in 1972–1973, one only needs to look at how they played on home ice, where they suffered a 14-game winless streak (0-9-5) from mid-December to March. Just one win or two more ties during that period would have moved them into fourth place and the playoffs. (Photograph by Jerry Berg.)

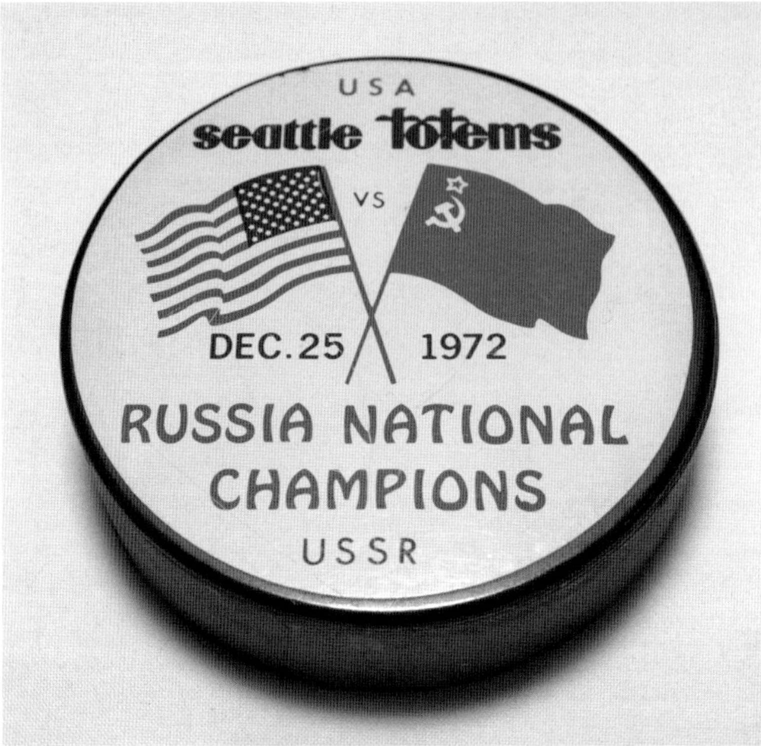

WHL president Bill MacFarland scored a coup by arranging for the Russian national team to play a series of four exhibition games against WHL opponents in 1972–1973. The Russian team that visited Seattle in 1972 was one of the greatest in history, featuring 17 players who were part of the team that almost defeated Canada's best professionals in the infamous eight-game Summit Series just four months prior.

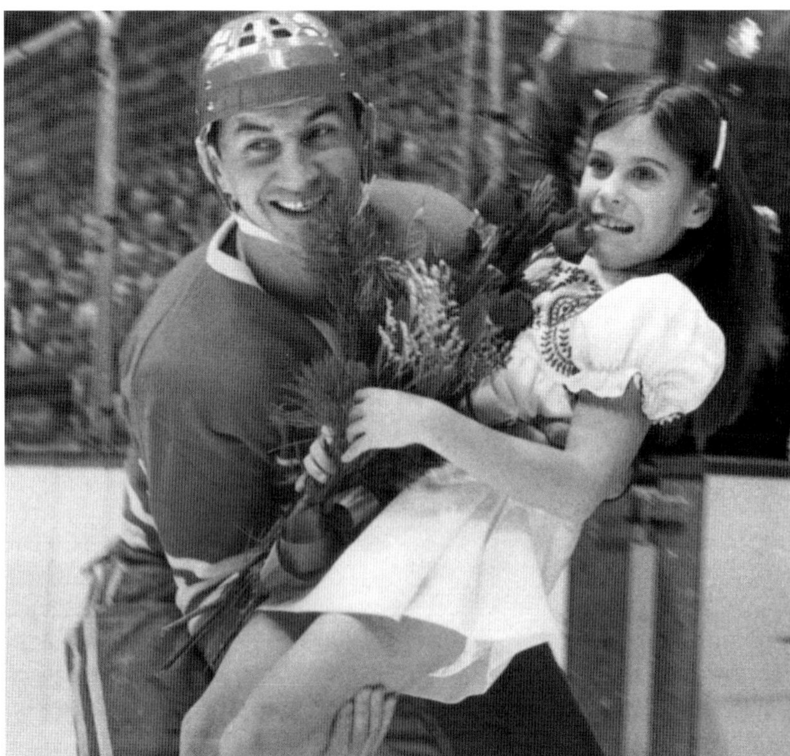

Russian captain Viktor Kuzkin won over the fans when he scooped up Annette Daggett, daughter of Totems play-by-play announcer Joe Daggett, and skated her over to the Russian bench so she could give her flowers to the team's coach. (Courtesy of the *Seattle Post-Intelligencer* Collection, Museum of History and Industry.)

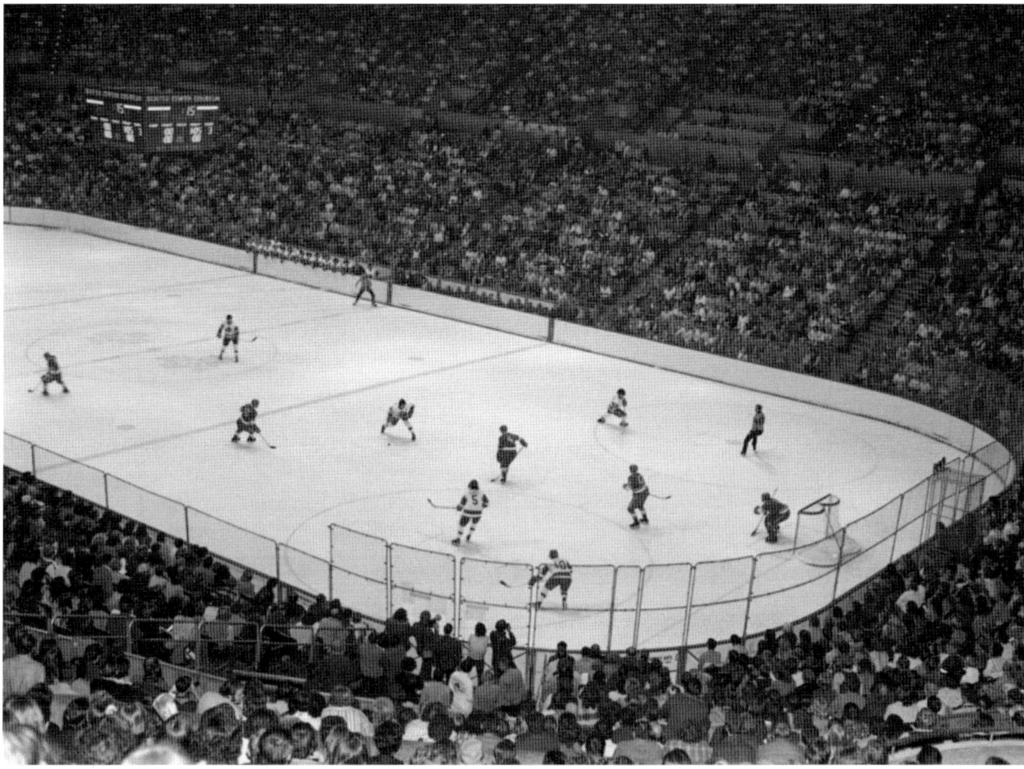

The Totems quickly fell behind 3-0 within the first 10 minutes of action but came back with goals by Paul Raymer and Danny Seguin to close out the first period. The 3-2 period rallied the fans, and while the Totems tied the score 4-4 in the second, the Russians scored five unanswered goals to win 9-4. (Photograph by Jerry Berg.)

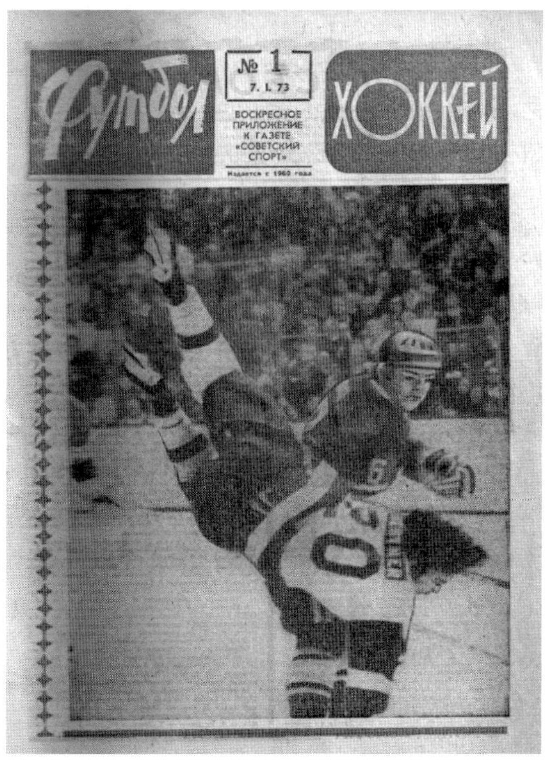

The news of the Russian victory over the Totems even made it into Russian-language publications, like this one dated January 7, 1973. Shown on the cover is Russian defenseman Aleksandr Gusev (No. 6) checking Totems forward Dave Westner (No. 20). Despite being overwhelming favorites, it was still important to the Russians that they show their superiority on the ice.

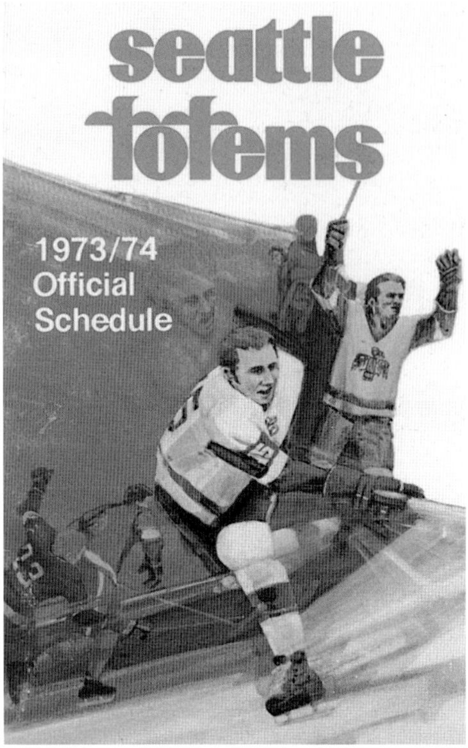

The Western Hockey League's last season was in 1973–1974. The offseason announcement that Denver and Seattle had been awarded NHL franchises, combined with the departure of Phoenix to the World Hockey Association, left the WHL a shell of its former self. The Totems finished out of the playoffs for the fourth consecutive season with a 32-42-4 record.

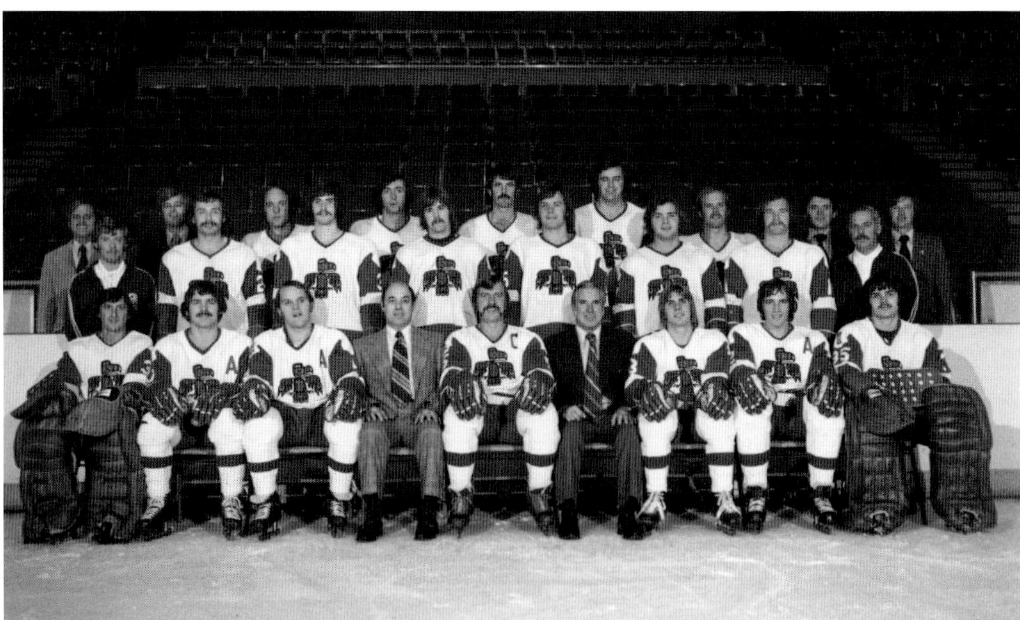

Seattle hockey teams played in 21 of the Western Hockey League's 22 seasons, missing only the 1954–1955 campaign when the franchise was in financial straits. They were the only original Pacific Coast Hockey League club to transition into the WHL and survive until the league's ultimate demise in the summer of 1974. (Photograph by Jerry Berg.)

The Russians returned for a rematch with the Totems in 1974, this time bringing along the Czechoslovakian army team (Dukla Jihlava). The teams had already competed in the world cup, the Russians having swept the tournament to once again be crowned amateur world champions. Seattle was the last stop on the tour for the Russians, who had already defeated Phoenix (3-1), Portland (8-3), and San Diego (11-3).

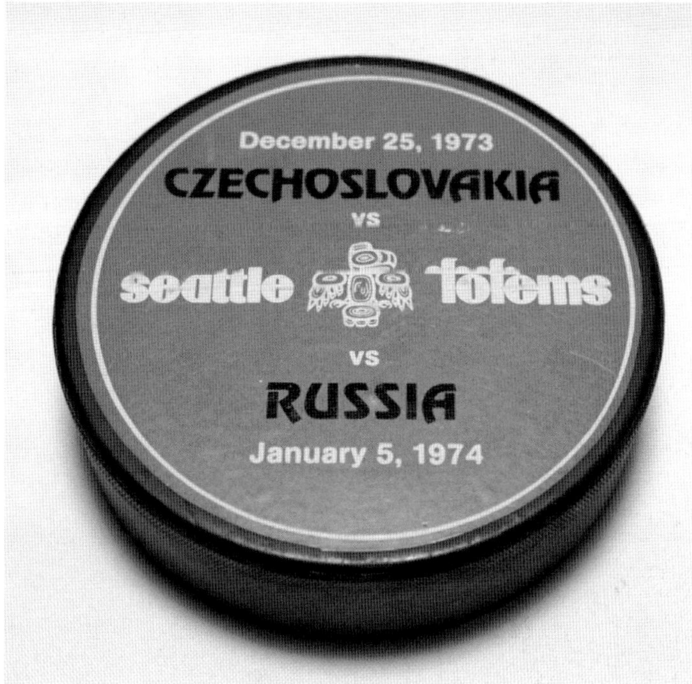

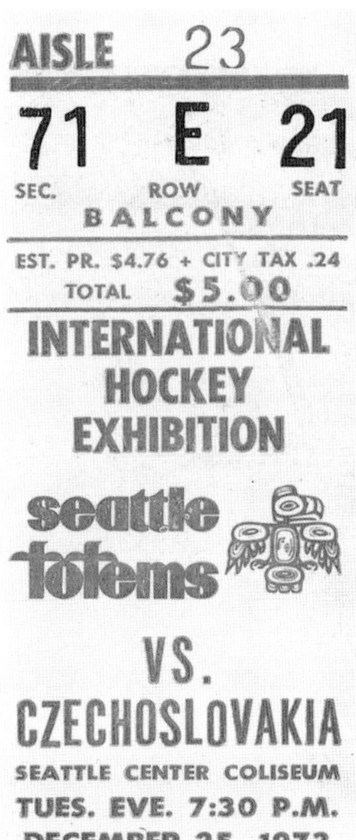

Exactly one year after they first faced the Russians, the Totems hosted Czechoslovakia at the Coliseum. The Czechs were not as dominant as the Russians, having played in a pair of 2-2 ties prior to arriving in Seattle. The crowd was somewhat disappointing, with only 6,041 on hand; the game against the Russians 11 nights later was the bigger draw.

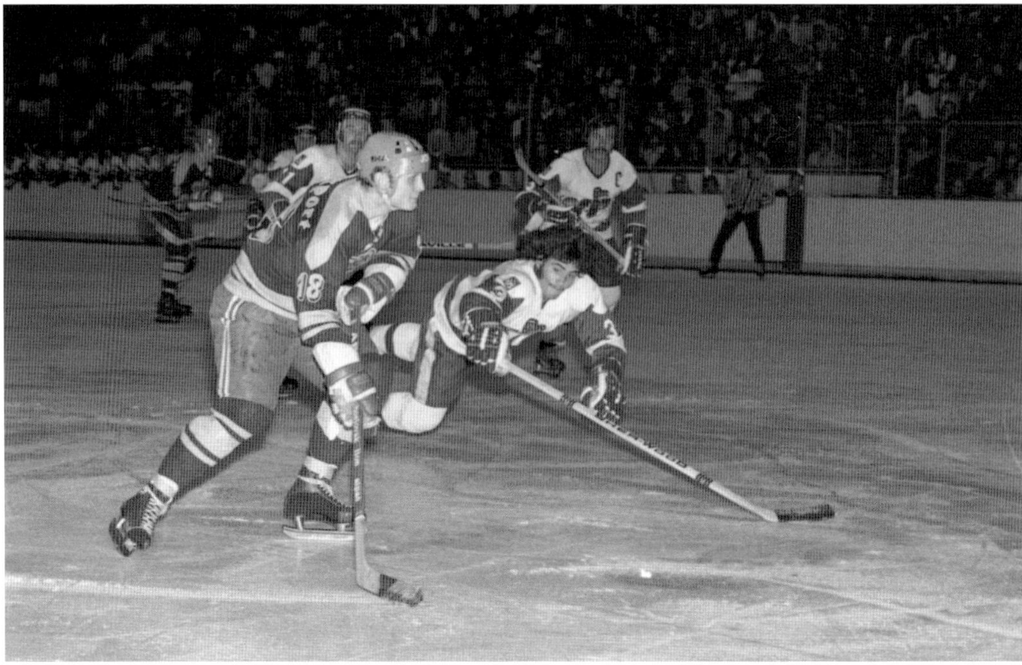

Defenseman Pete Folco (No. 3) attempts to disrupt Czech left winger Milos Kupc (No. 18). The Czechs jumped out to a 3-0 first-period lead, but Totems coach Phil Maloney told his club to get physical, which turned the tide. The frustrated Czechs threatened to not come out for the third period but relented when told they would forfeit their game check. The Totems won 6-4. (Photograph by Jerry Berg.)

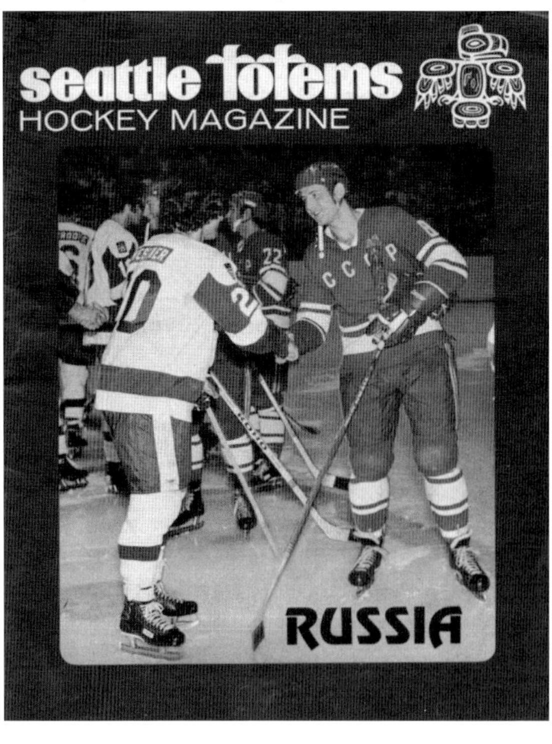

The Russian team that arrived in Seattle in January 1974 was virtually the same squad the Totems faced a year earlier. While the Totems no longer had high-scoring forward Rob Walton, the 1973–1974 squad had a much more balanced attack, though no one gave them much of a chance against the world champions. (Photograph by Jerry Berg.)

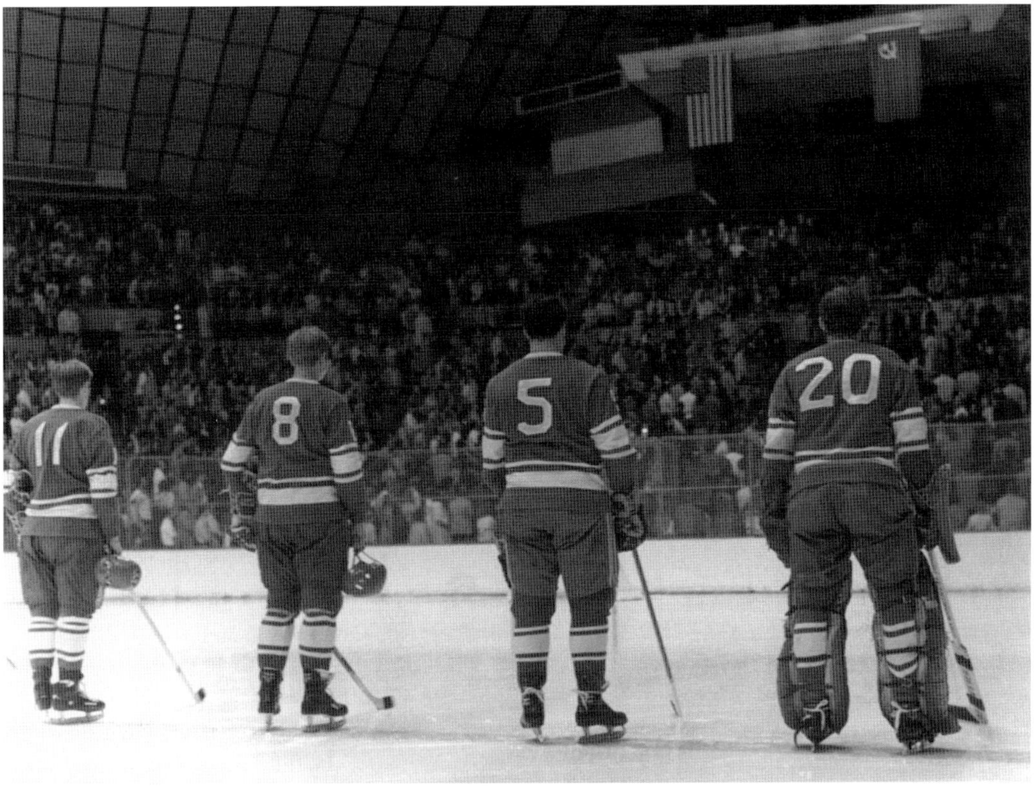

In the net for the Russians in 1974 was future Hockey Hall of Famer Vladislav Tretiak (No. 20). Tretiak was also with the team when they visited Seattle in 1972, but he did not play in that game. This time around, the Totems got the chance to face one of the world's greatest goaltenders. (Photograph by Jerry Berg.)

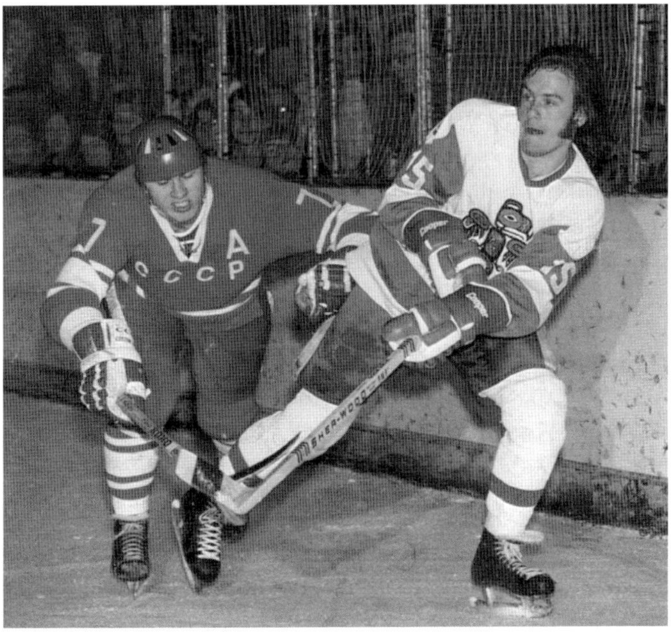

Totem Dave Wisener (No. 15) fights off a check along the boards by Russian defenseman Gennady Tsygankov (No. 7) to get a pass off to a teammate. Wisener was having a decent offensive season, but the high point may have been the four assists he earned that night against the Russians. (Photograph by Jerry Berg.)

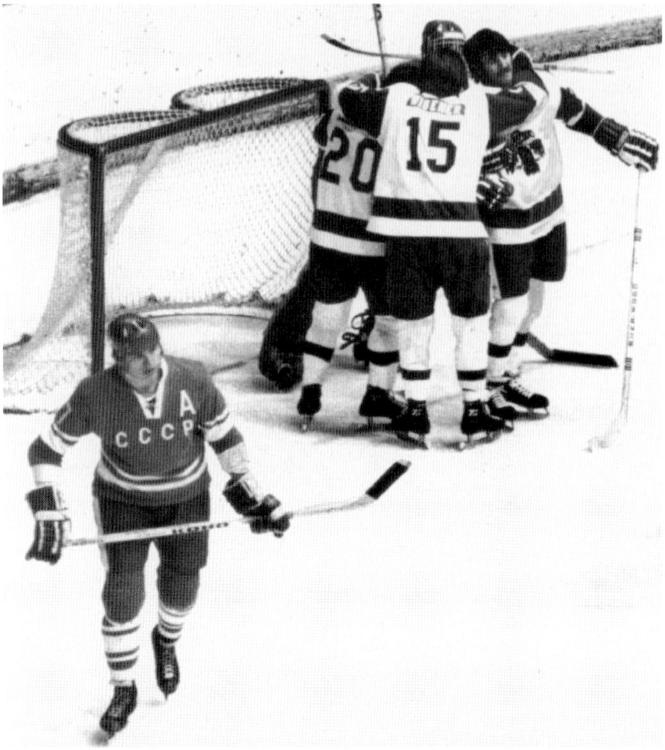

Totems Dave Westner (No. 20), Dave Wisener (No .15), and Don Westbrooke (right) celebrate a goal in front of the Russian net. Their line was dominant, with Westbrooke earning a hat trick and Westner picking up a pair as Seattle upset the Russians 8-4 in front of 12,710 euphoric fans. (Courtesy of the *Seattle Post-Intelligencer* Collection, Museum of History and Industry.)

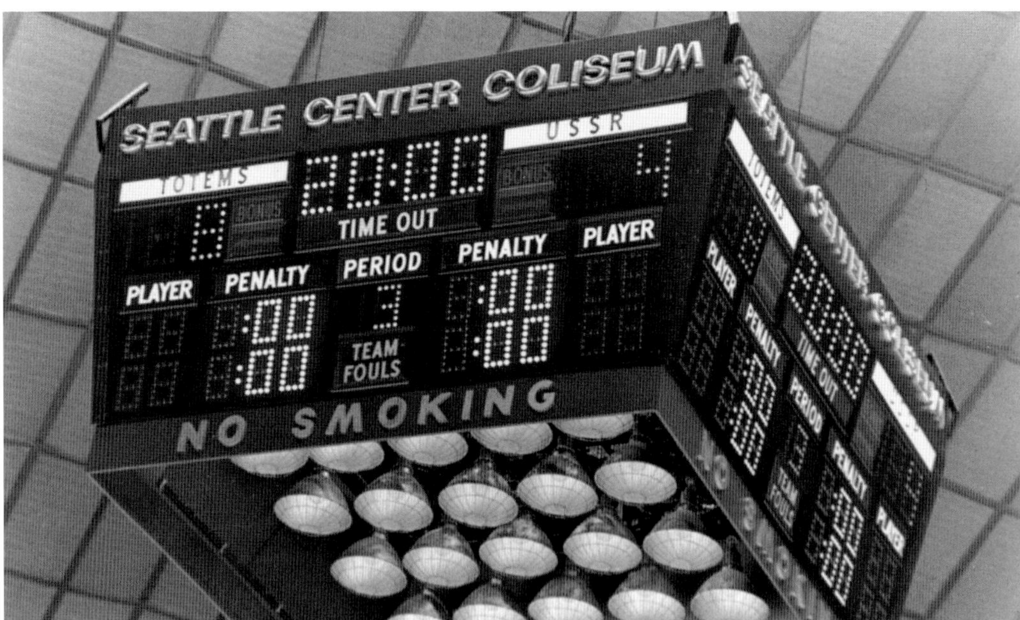

When the final whistle blew, the Totems had stunned the Russians 8-4. The Russians did not suit up their top line for the start of the game, but once it became clear the Totems were for real, the players quietly made their way to the locker room and put on their uniforms. It was too little, too late on a night that saw everything go Seattle's way. (Photograph by Jerry Berg.)

On June 12, 1974, the NHL announced that Seattle and Denver had been awarded expansion franchises for 1976–1977. This led to the immediate demise of the WHL and forced both clubs to join the Central Hockey League while they prepared. Denver made the transition, but Seattle was left out in the cold and found itself mired in a decade-long lawsuit against the NHL.

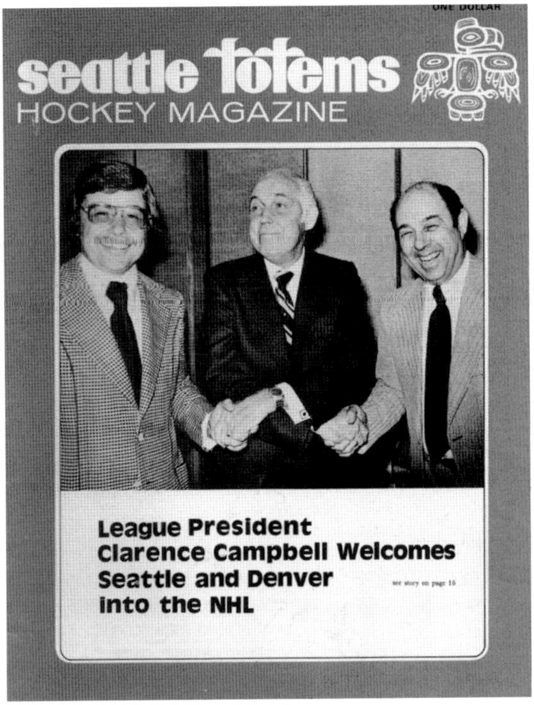

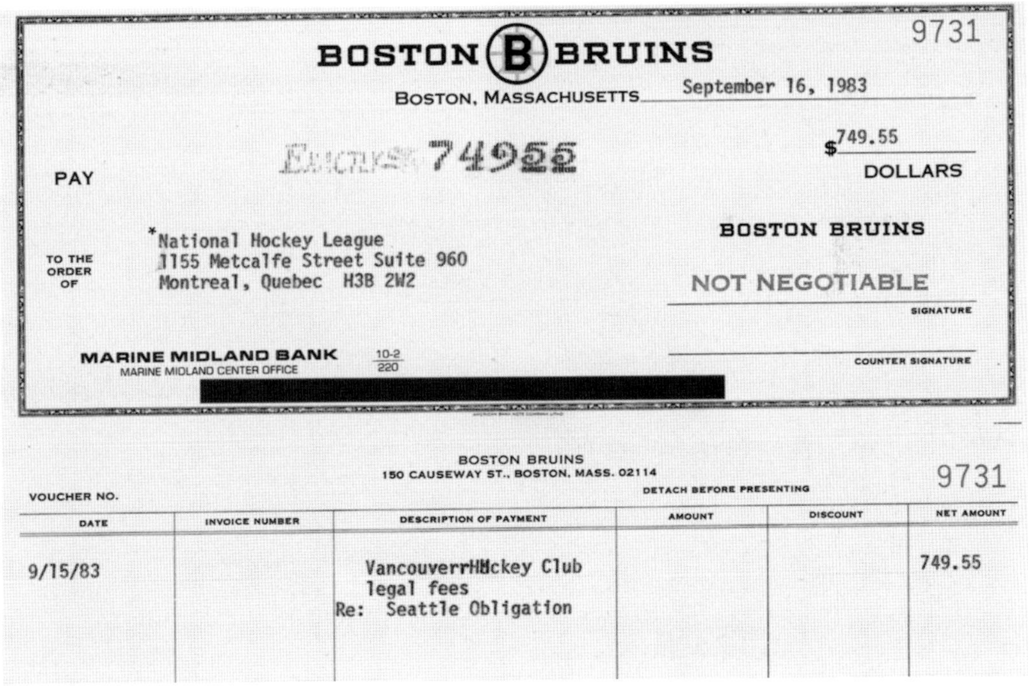

BOSTON BRUINS — 9731

BOSTON, MASSACHUSETTS September 16, 1983

PAY 74955 $749.55 DOLLARS

TO THE ORDER OF *National Hockey League
1155 Metcalfe Street Suite 960
Montreal, Quebec H3B 2W2

BOSTON BRUINS

NOT NEGOTIABLE

SIGNATURE

COUNTER SIGNATURE

MARINE MIDLAND BANK
MARINE MIDLAND CENTER OFFICE
10-2
220

BOSTON BRUINS
150 CAUSEWAY ST., BOSTON, MASS. 02114

VOUCHER NO. 9731

DETACH BEFORE PRESENTING

DATE	INVOICE NUMBER	DESCRIPTION OF PAYMENT	AMOUNT	DISCOUNT	NET AMOUNT
9/15/83		VancouverrHHckey Club legal fees Re: Seattle Obligation			749.55

The Seattle Totems sued the NHL and the Vancouver Canucks for antitrust violations in the wake of losing their expansion franchise. The litigation continued until 1987, marking the end of the road for Seattle's NHL dreams. NHL teams, like the Boston Bruins, were required to financially contribute to the defense of the league and the Canucks.

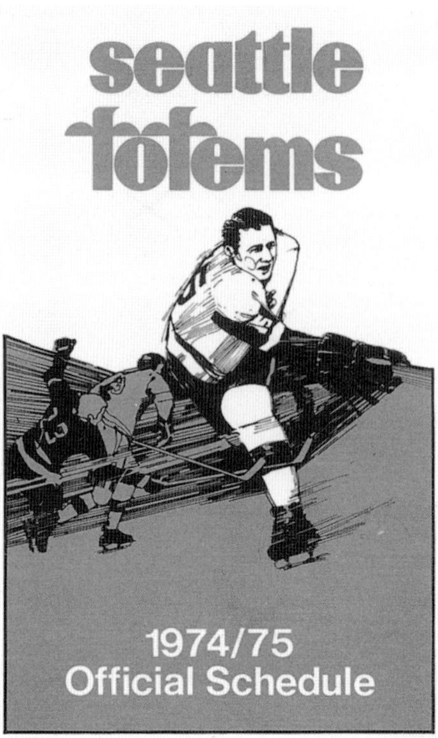

Twice, the Totems found themselves within three points of third place and a playoff spot in the CHL's north division in 1974–1975, but an eight-game winless streak doomed them to a last-place finish in the division. Attendance dropped to 2,500 fans per game, making the Coliseum seem more like a mausoleum, and with the NHL expansion bid in jeopardy, the team folded during the off-season.

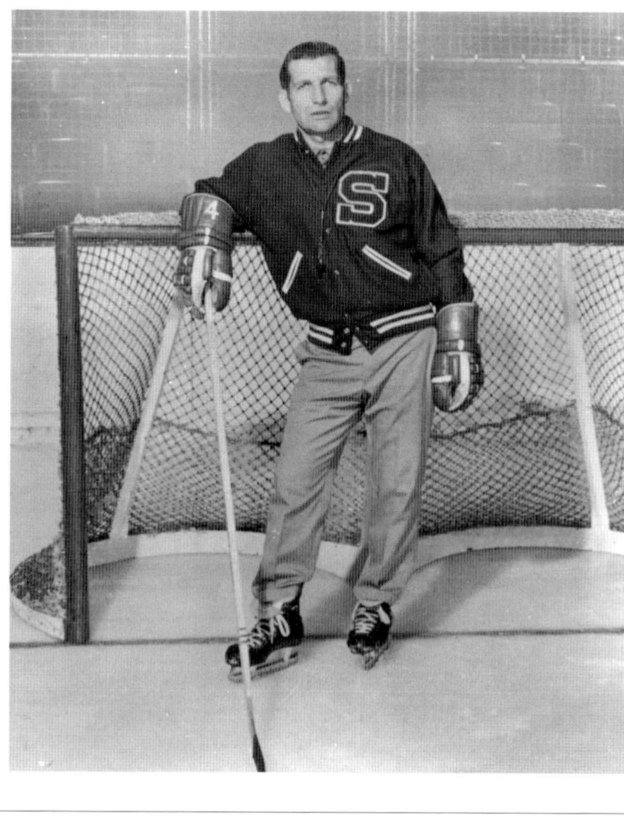

Larry Popein was the head coach of the Totems during 1970–1971, the start of a coaching carousel that saw five men behind the bench over the franchise's last five seasons. When he began complaining about his players in the press and fining them for poor play, he likely sealed his own fate and was gone following that season. (Courtesy of Dave Eskenazi.)

Former Totem player Chuck Holmes replaced Popein as head coach for the disastrous 1971–1972 season. While known as a player's coach, Holmes had little to work with, and the Totems crashed into the WHL cellar, setting a number of dubious league records along the way, including least wins (12), least goals (175), and most home losses (24). It was Holmes's only season as Totems coach.

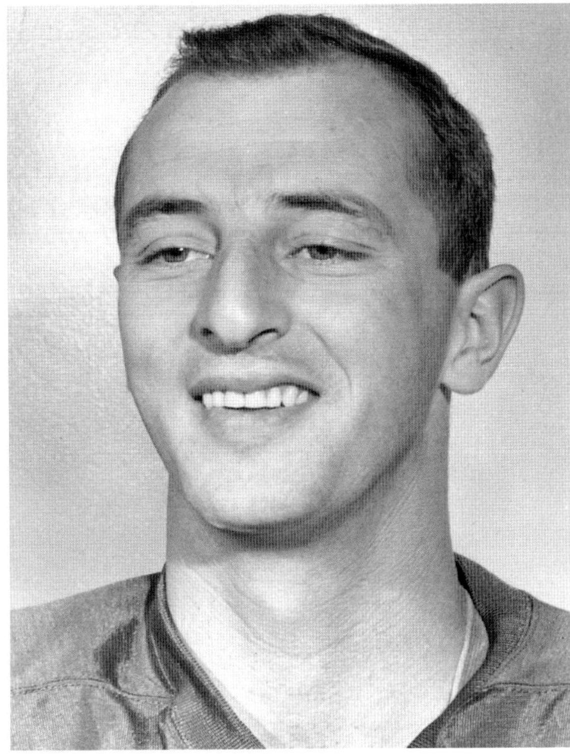

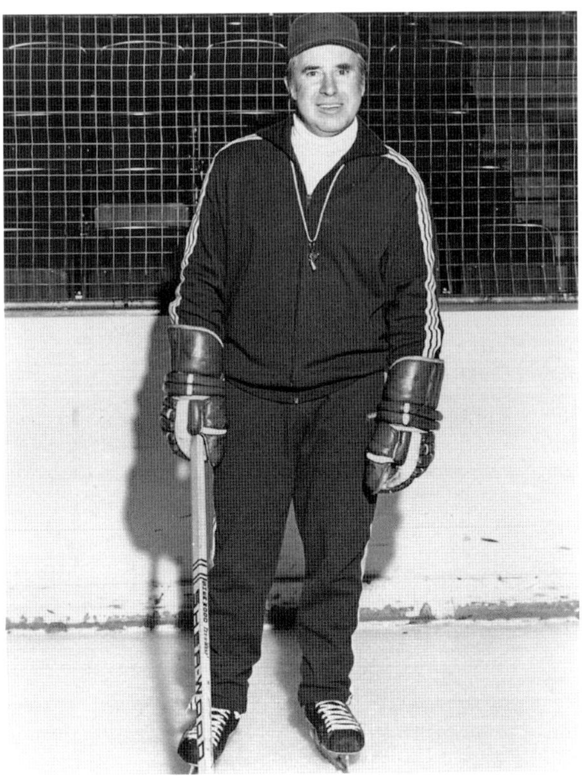

Phil Maloney survived longer as Totems coach than anyone else in the 1970s, lasting just over a season and a half. In fact, it was his success at revitalizing the team that led to his departure, as the Vancouver Canucks called him up to take over the NHL team in January 1974. His replacement in Seattle for the remainder of the season was none other than Rudy Filion.

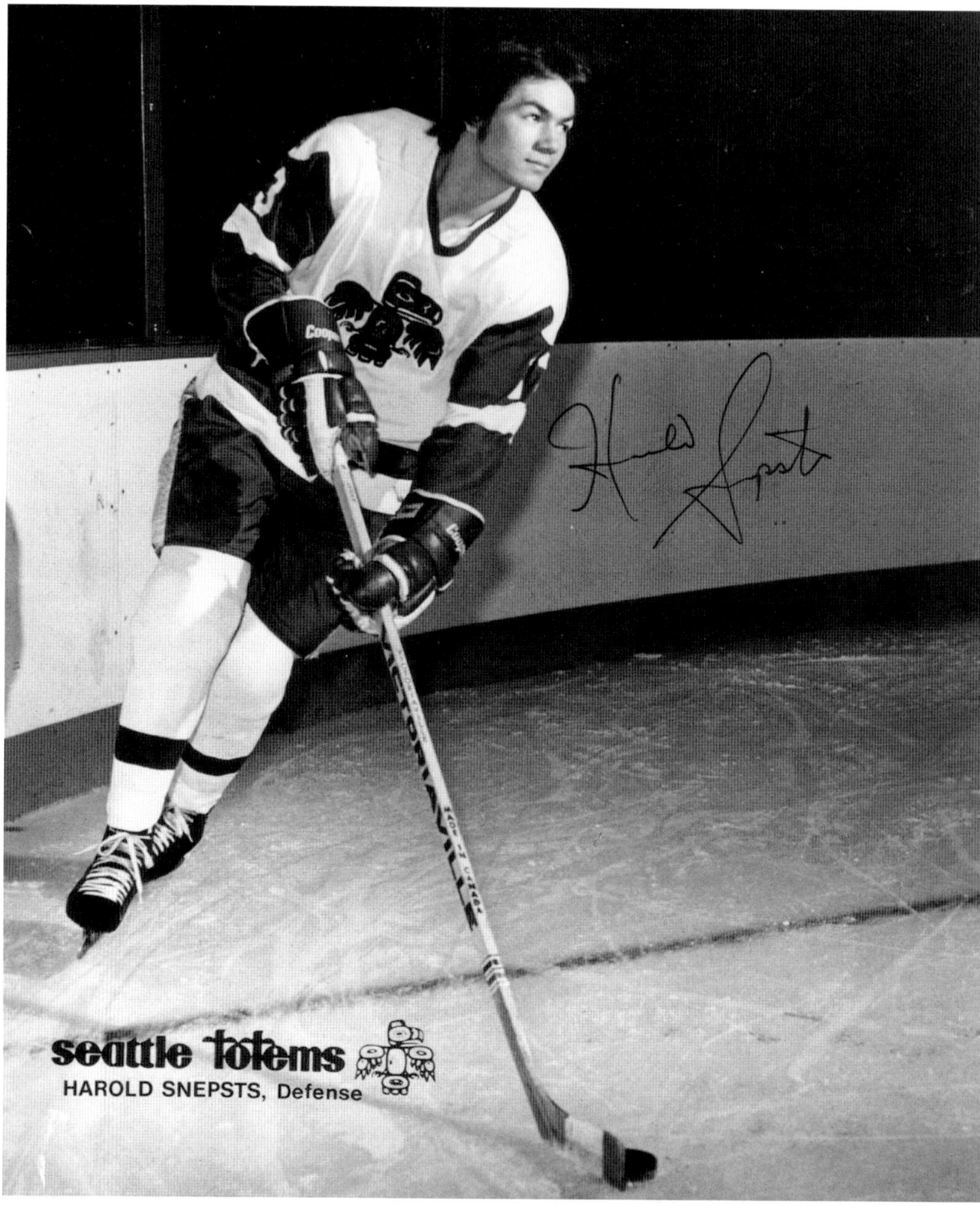

Harold Snepsts holds the distinction as being the last former Totem player to appear in an NHL game. Snepsts joined the Totems as a 20-year-old defenseman in 1974–1975, picking up a goal and six assists in 19 games while wearing the green and white. He was promoted to the Vancouver Canucks and finished out the season with 27 games in the NHL. At that time, the Canucks had an ownership stake in the Totems, and the club operated as a farm team for Vancouver. Snepsts was a mainstay with the Canucks, playing 10 seasons with them before embarking on a period that saw him play for four different teams (including Vancouver again) over the course of his last seven professional seasons. He hung up his skates after playing 54 games with the St. Louis Blues in 1990–1991, the last of the Totems. (Courtesy of Dave Eskenazi.)

8

The Players

Roughly 210 skaters and 25 goaltenders suited up and appeared in at least one game for the Seattle Totems between 1958 and 1975. Some were veritable fixtures with the club. Men like Gerry Leonard (842 games), Guyle Fielder (767), and Don Ward (691) were with the team for so long that it is hard to imagine them in a uniform from another city, even though all three did play elsewhere. For others like brothers Bill (11 games) and Roger Christian (5), or mid-game emergency substitute goaltender Lorne Thornycroft who was literally plucked out of the crowd one night to fill in for an injured goalie, it is hard to even think of them as having been Totems at all. Regardless, they are all part of the story of Seattle Totems hockey, men who put on the uniform and gave it their best regardless of how many games they played. They are worthy of respect and are part of the hockey family.

Through the story of Seattle Totems hockey, many of these players appeared in the narrative. Some were mentioned due to a specific incident, others their impact on a given season, and a fortunate few earned the right to their own standalone chapters. But that still leaves most of them unmentioned up to this point. So with that in mind, the remainder of the story is dedicated to the individuals who were part of the Seattle Totems, whether as long-standing impact players or guys who passed through for the proverbial "cup of coffee." The scorers. The grinders. The tough guys. Cheers to them. Thanks for playing a part in the success of the Totems and hockey in Seattle.

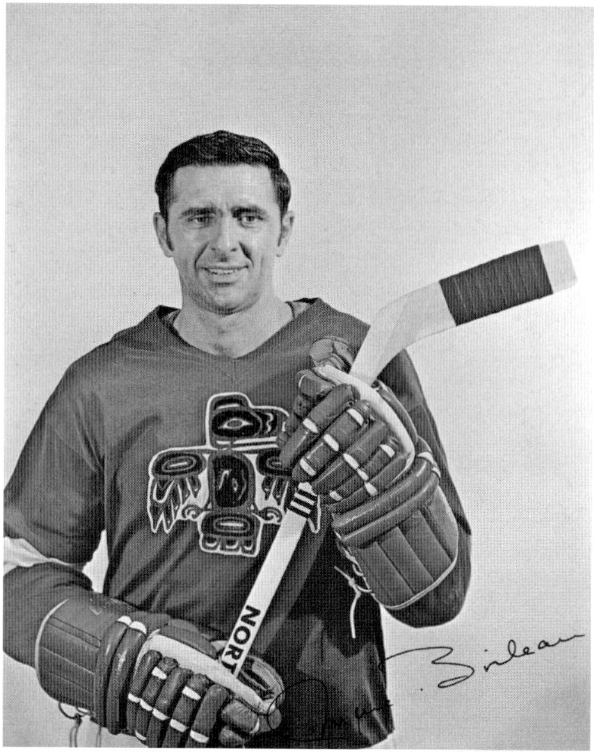

Marc "The Shark" Boileau had two runs with the Totems, from 1958 to 1961, then again from 1967 to 1970. He won championships with the club in 1959 and 1968, and his 42 goals in 1960–1961 led the team. Boileau played one season in the NHL, appearing with Detroit in 1961–1962, though the heavy-handed way the Red Wings handled his transfer permanently soured the working arrangement between Detroit and Seattle.

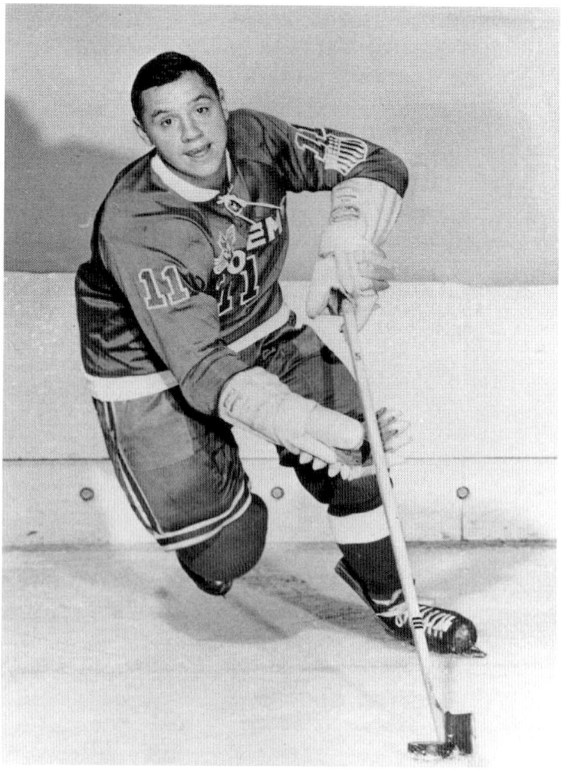

Cummy Burton opened the 1958–1959 WHL season with Seattle and made his presence felt, scoring 41 points and racking up 60 penalty minutes over the course of 50 games. He also appeared in another 14 games with the Detroit Red Wings, which caused him to miss out on the Totems WHL championship in his only season in Seattle. (Courtesy of Dave Eskenazi.)

Don "Chips" Chiupka played six full seasons in Seattle from 1957 to 1963, but unfortunately a shoulder injury kept him out of much of the Totems 1959 playoff run, and other injuries kept him off the ice for parts of 1960 and 1962. He still remained productive, however, notching 20 or more goals in four of his six Seattle seasons.

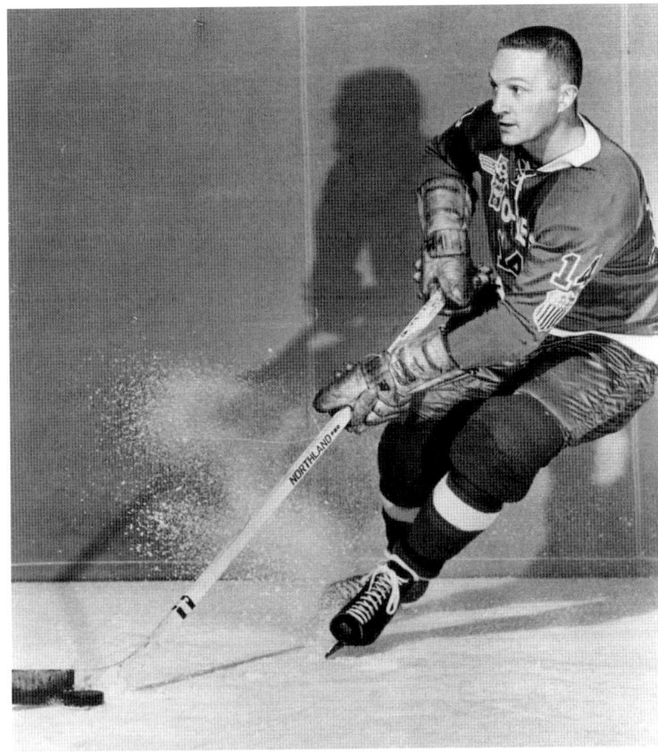

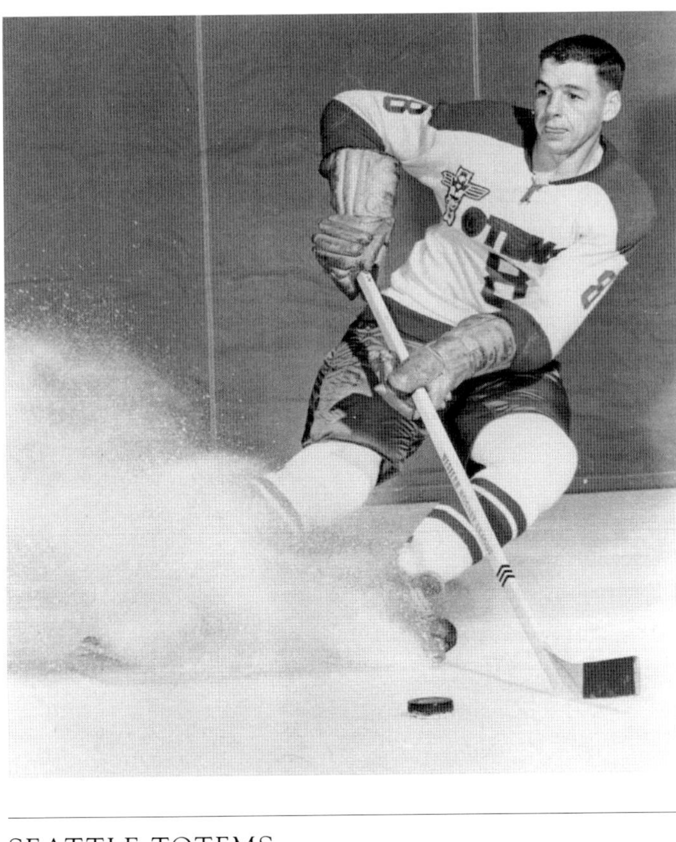

As was true of many players, Tom McVie's career took him through Seattle on multiple occasions. He first played with the Americans as a 22-year-old, appearing in 193 games between 1957 and 1961 and scoring an impressive 86 goals. He came back to Seattle for three more seasons from 1969 to 1972, and though he had slowed, he was still good for another 30 tallies.

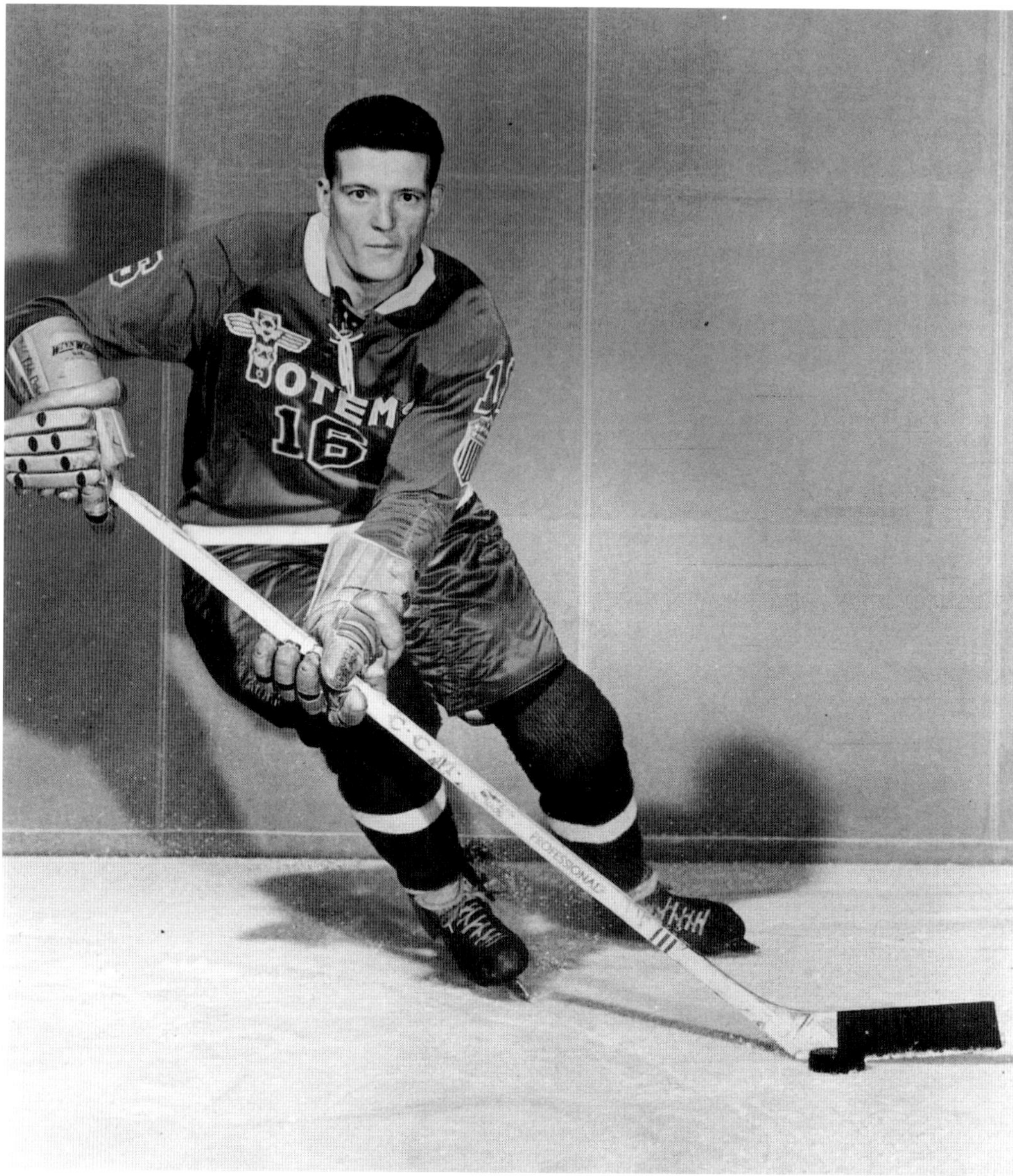

Gerry "Grump" Leonard was one of the most versatile players to lace up skates for the Totems. He was, in many ways, the perfect role player. While flashy skaters like Guyle Fielder and goal scorers like Bill MacFarland plied their trades, Leonard did whatever was necessary—playing on the checking line, stepping up to the scoring line, killing penalties, dropping the gloves, and at times even wearing the captain's C. Leonard is one of three players to appear on all three Totems championship teams (though MacFarland could be included if one considers his coaching), skating in 12 seasons between 1958 and 1970. His 924 games (including playoffs) place him third all-time among Seattle skaters, and he ranks in the top 10 all time in every offensive category and in penalty minutes. His best offensive season came in 1961–1962, when he finished second on the Totems in goals (25) and fourth in points (61).

"Jumbo" Jim Powers knew how to score goals and score them by the bushel. He was so good that the Totems kept bringing him back, making deals to acquire him four different times and putting him in a Totems uniform in nine different seasons between 1958 and 1970. He played on all three Totems championship teams, though an injury kept him out of the 1959 postseason.

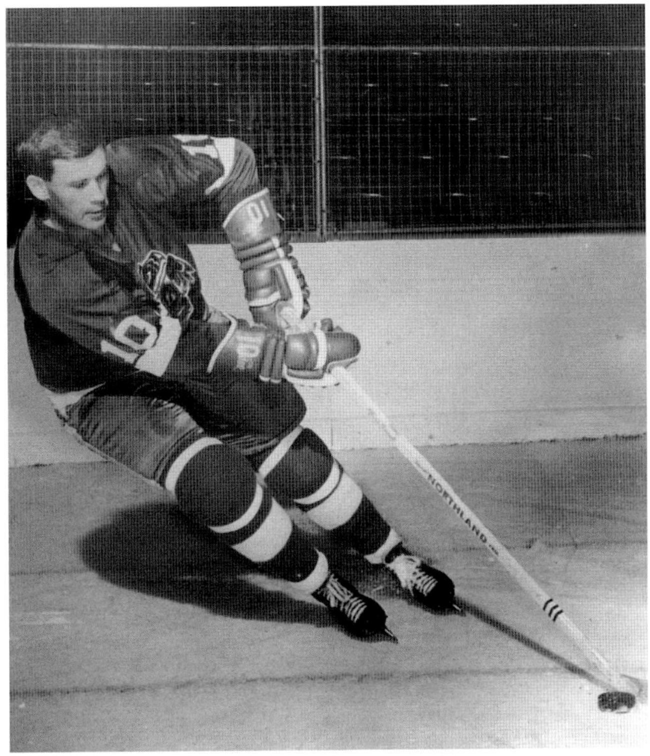

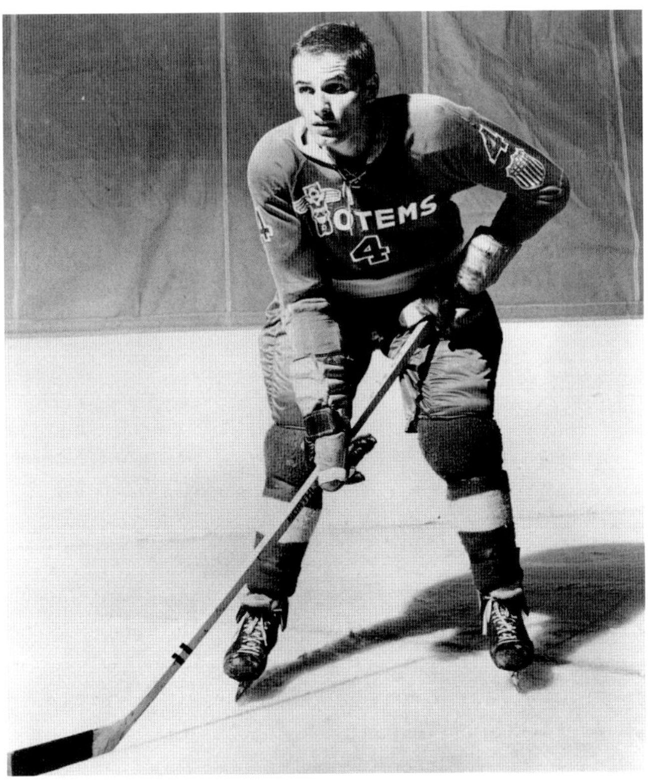

Gordon "Tans" Tansley only played one year in Seattle, but he made the most of it, finishing second on the team in penalty minutes (108) in 1960–1961, his only professional season. A broken right forearm in late 1960 seemed to derail his season, but Tansley toughed it out and only missed nine games.

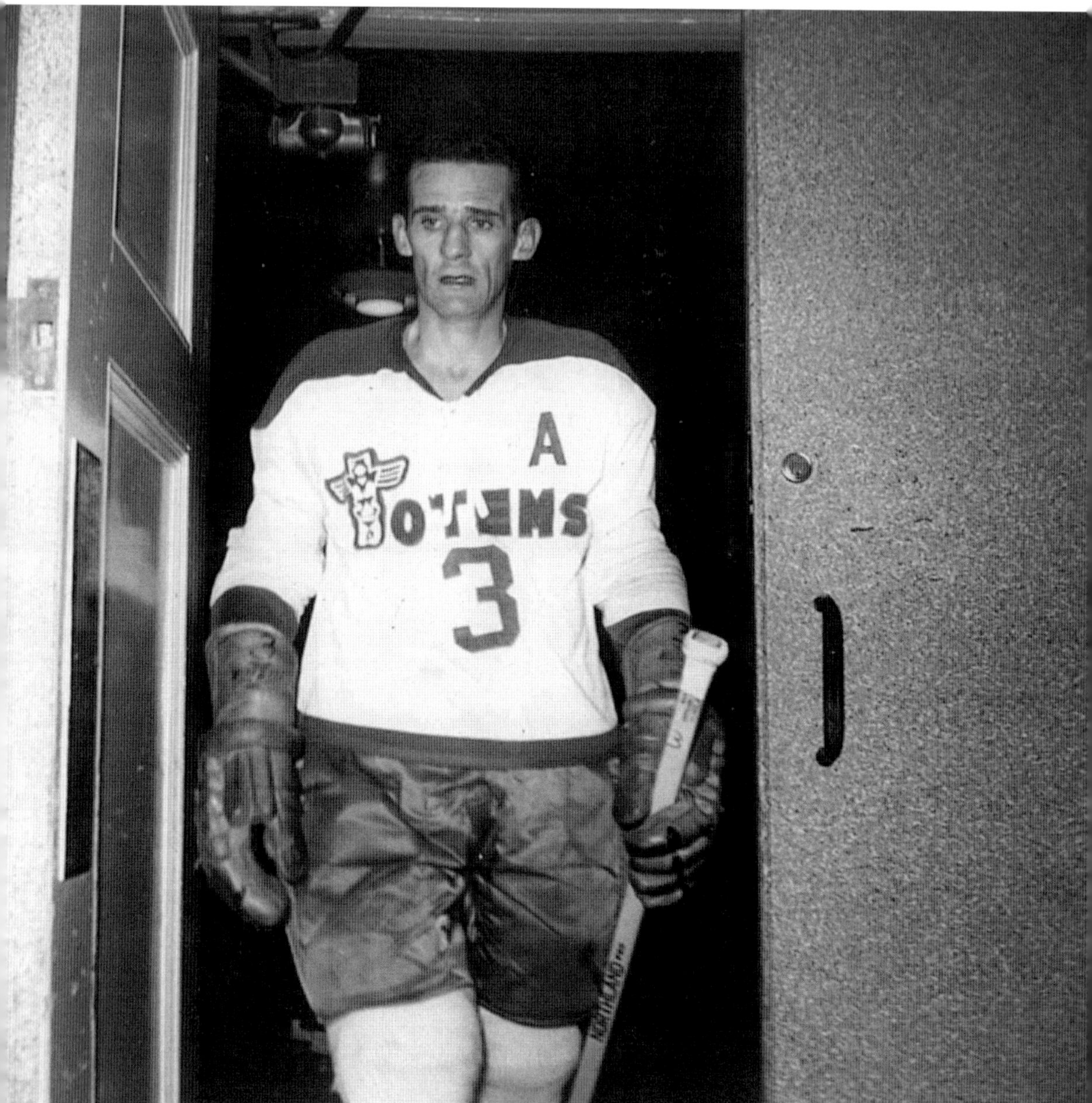

Gordie "Wedge" Sinclair was a fixture on the Seattle blue line for 11 seasons with the Americans and Totems between 1955 and 1966. While small of stature at five feet 10 inches tall and less than 150 pounds, he was nevertheless a force to be reckoned with. An excellent skater, Sinclair is fondly remembered by fans for his hip checks, arguably the most difficult type of body check and one at which he excelled. He was also an excellent puck handler and passer, earning 30 or more assists in nine of his 11 Seattle seasons. His 358 regular season assists are the third most by any Seattle player. He left the Totems following the 1965–1966 season, just missing out on the team's pair of championships in 1967 and 1968. He finished his professional career skating for the San Diego Gulls from 1966 to 1970, where he continued to be productive and put up two more 30-plus–assist seasons. (Courtesy of Dave Eskenazi.)

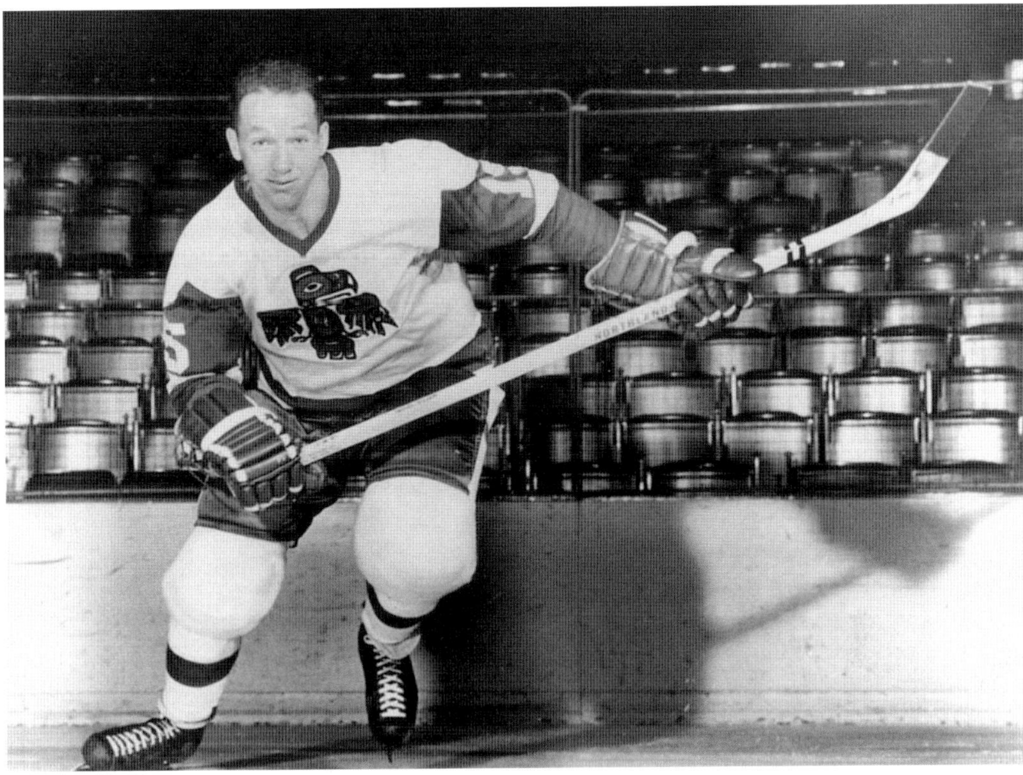

Howie Hughes had a long professional hockey career, though one that never saw him stay in the same place for very long. Between 1961 and 1975, he played four seasons for the Totems but never remained in Seattle for consecutive years. His longest period with the same team was the three seasons he spent in the NHL with Los Angeles, from 1967 to 1970.

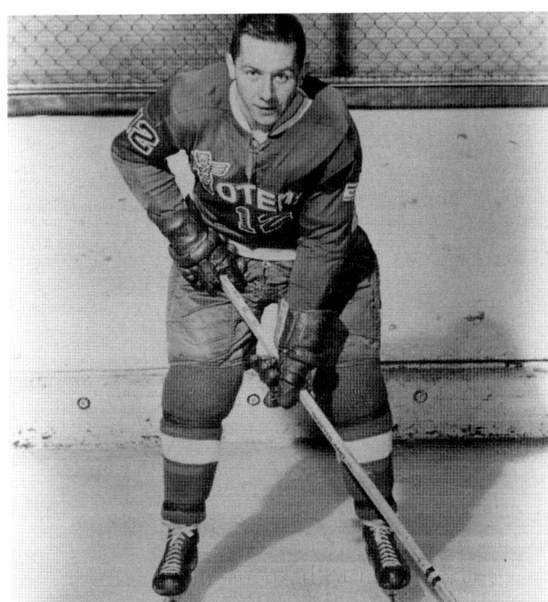

Barney Krake's promising career was hampered by injuries during his two seasons in Seattle. A shoulder injury kept him out of the 1962 playoffs, and that same injury along with one to his hand from a slashing incident limited him to 56 regular season and four playoff games the following year. (Courtesy of Dave Eskenazi.)

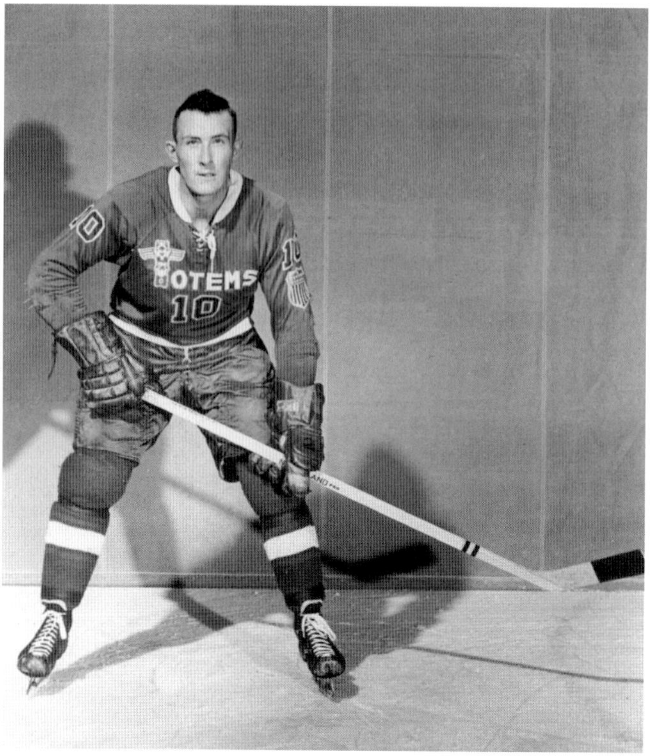

At the age of 22, left winger Laurie Langrell arrived in Seattle for training camp in 1961 with high hopes, coming off a 38-goal season in the IHL the year before. His tenure with the Totems was short-lived, however, as he only appeared in five games before returning to his former league, where he scored 25 goals with Minneapolis. (Courtesy of Dave Eskenazi.)

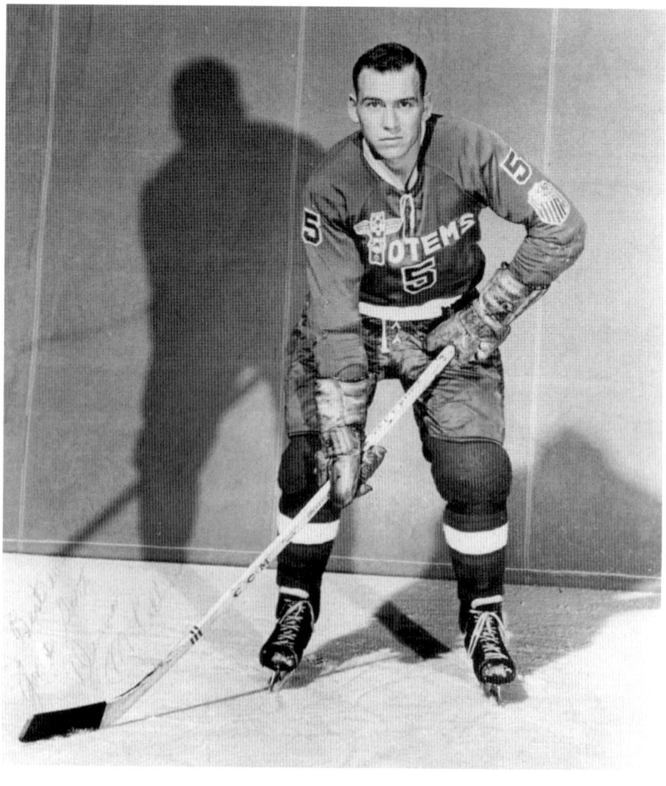

Dunc McCallum was a young, 21-year-old defenseman when he joined the Totems for his only Seattle season in 1961–1962, showing some toughness with 82 penalty minutes. While he did not last in Seattle, he had a successful professional career that included 187 regular season games in the NHL and another 100 games in the WHA.

Al Millar appeared in 87 games with the Totems during the marathon 1962–1963 campaign. A scheduling conflict forced the Totems to play the entire 1963 WHL Finals on the road in San Francisco, and the series went the full seven games, with four going into overtime, including the Totems loss in game seven. Millar livened up the series by fighting with Al Nicholson in the second game.

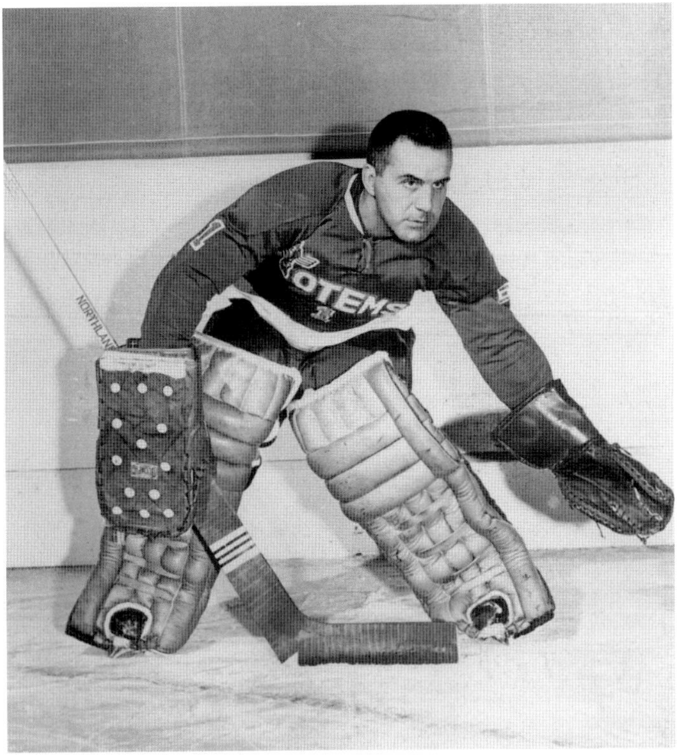

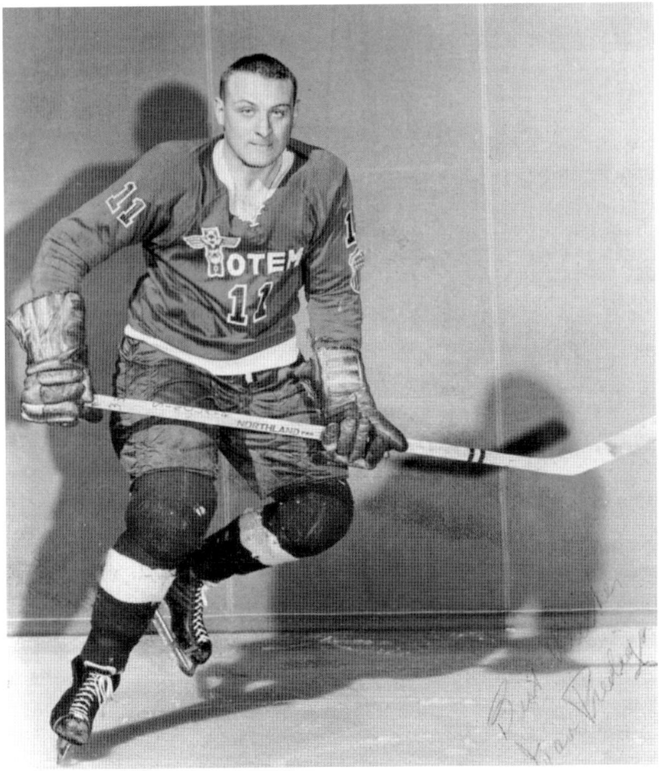

Ivan "The Terrible" Prediger was a tough defenseman from Neilburg, Saskatchewan. He joined the Totems in 1961 as a 20-year-old, getting into 61 games and picking up 68 penalty minutes. Early the following season, he was struck in the head by a puck during practice and only played in three games for the Totems, who then traded him to Omaha in the IHL.

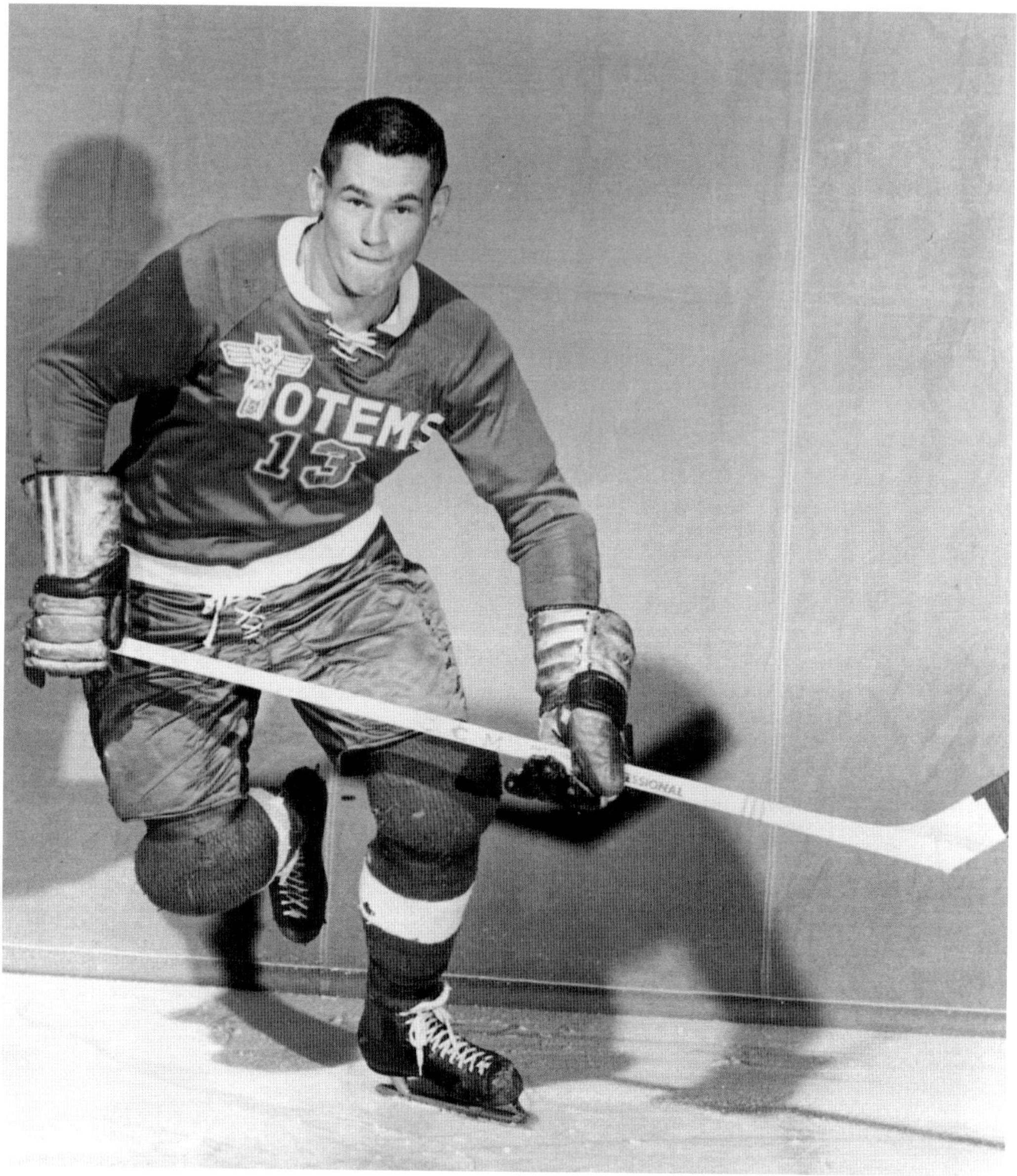

Don Ward's 691 regular season games in Seattle, all with the Totems, place him fifth on the all-time list for most games played in the city. At six foot two inches tall and 200 pounds, he was a large defenseman for his day and one known for his physical play. Already a veteran of 34 NHL games with Chicago and Boston prior to his 1961 arrival in Seattle, Ward quickly made his presence felt offensively with 30 points and defensively with 91 penalty minutes. His 1,110 regular-season career penalty minutes in Seattle is a record by a wide margin, and he had five 100-plus–minute seasons during his tenure with the Totems. The physical play took its toll, and Ward suffered from both back and knee injuries over the course of his career, finally calling it quits when he broke his leg in a game against San Diego in 1972 (though he did play 13 games in the EHL the following season). He won two WHL championships with the Totems.

Wayne Hall was transferred to the Totems in 1962 as part of their working agreement with the New York Rangers. The Rangers owned Hall's rights, and he played four games with the NHL club in 1960–1961. He missed five weeks with torn knee ligaments early in the 1962–1963 season, his only campaign in Seattle. (Courtesy of Dave Eskenazi.)

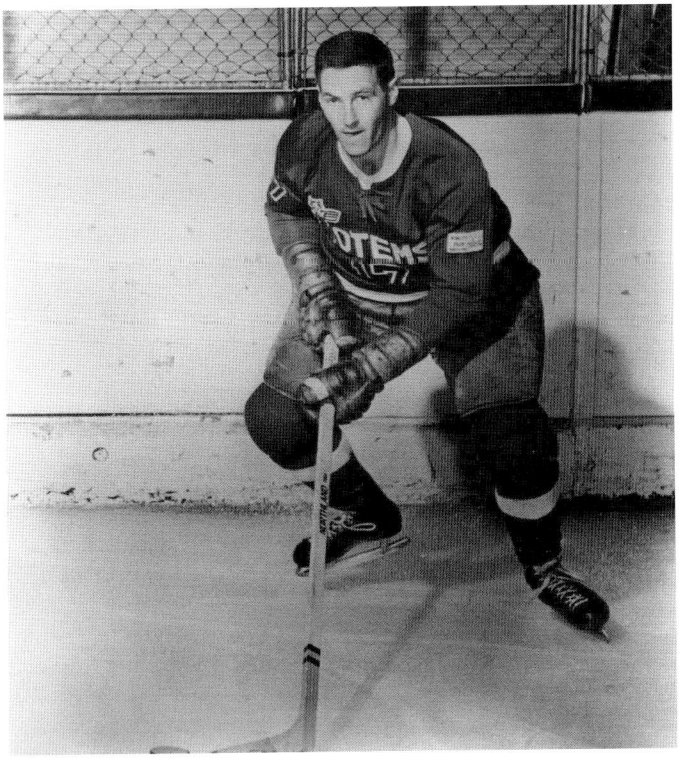

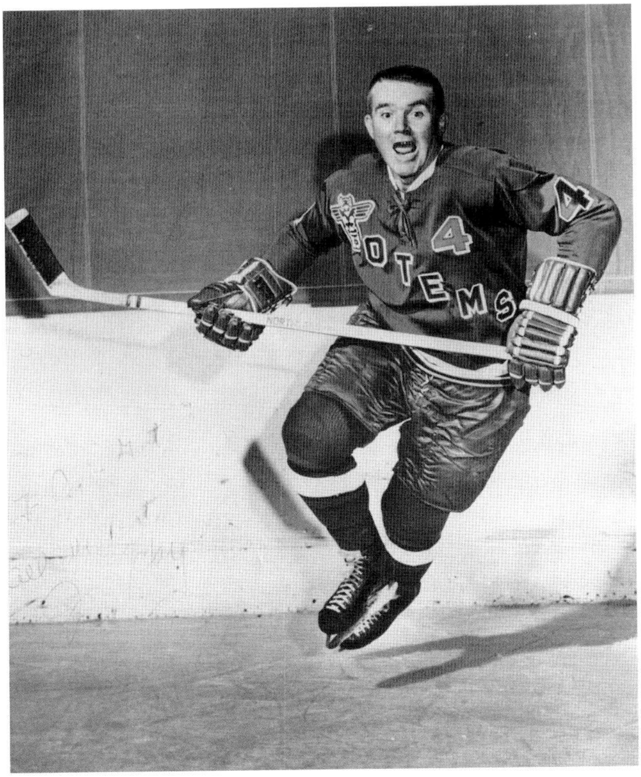

Jim "Red Eye" Hay was one of those players one hated if he played for another team but respected when he skated for one's own. The rough defenseman's career spanned across four decades, including a two-year stop in Seattle from 1962 to 1964, though local fans probably remember him most for the five seasons he spent with their archrivals, the Portland Buckaroos, in the mid-to-late 1960s.

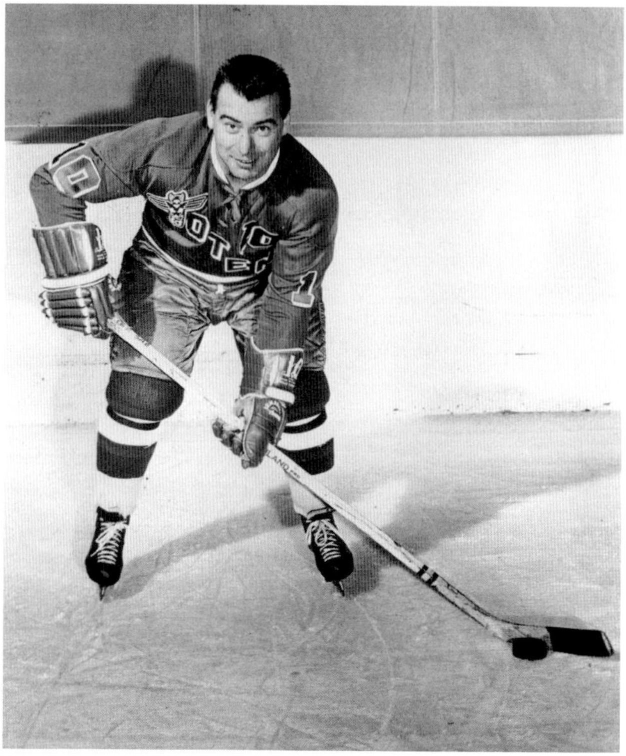

The Totems acquired veteran winger Bob Sabourin in an early season trade in 1962. In his first game in Seattle he was boarded by Leo Labine, the spark that ignited a huge bench-clearing brawl. A shoulder separation that same season limited his playing time, but he was back in shape for the playoffs and scored eight goals and eight assists in the postseason.

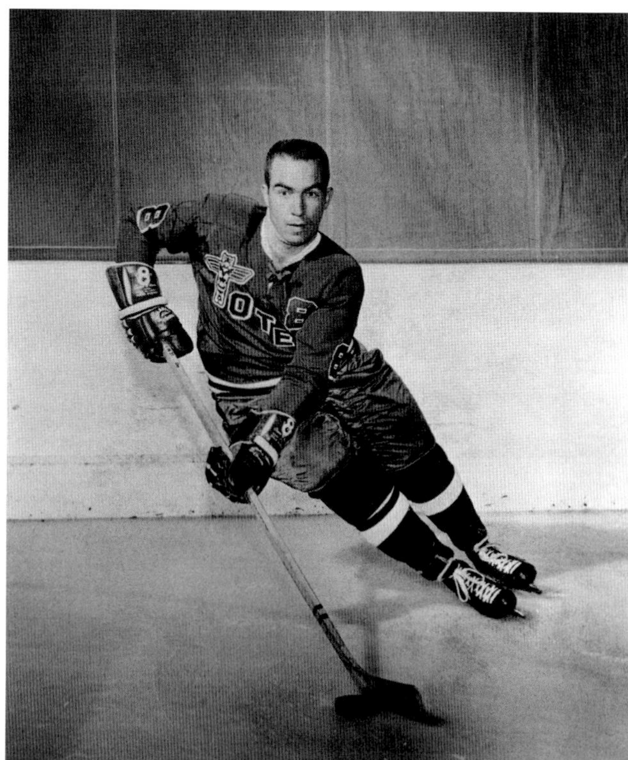

Center Bev Bell first appeared in Seattle with the Americans in 1955–1956, earning 14 goals and 28 points. He then had five productive years in Spokane, four of which saw him score 20-plus goals, before returning to Seattle in 1963–1964. During his one season with the Totems, he picked up 16 goals and 20 assists.

Jean-Marie Cossette firmly established his reputation as a goal scorer in the QHL and AHL prior to arriving in Seattle in 1963. He continued to produce offensively with the Totems, scoring 42 goals during his two seasons with the club from 1963 to 1965. Unfortunately, his period in Seattle was during a brief downturn, and the team could not capitalize on his skills.

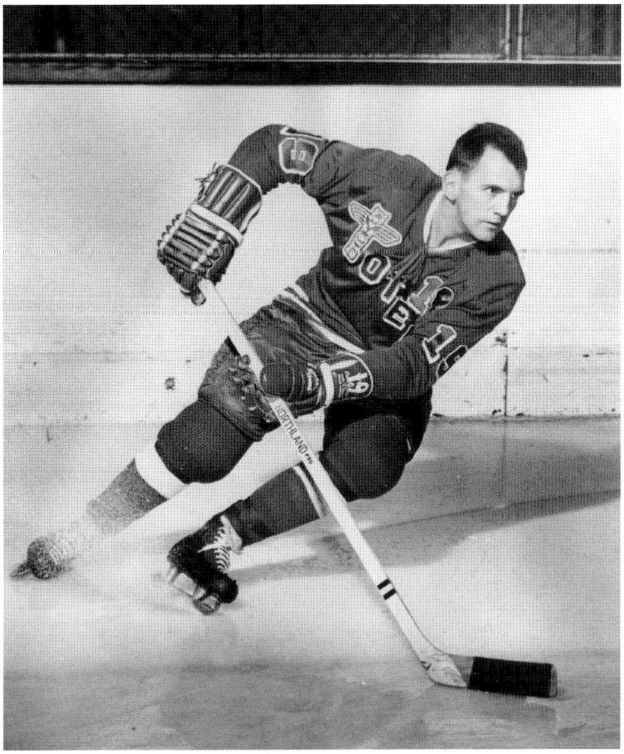

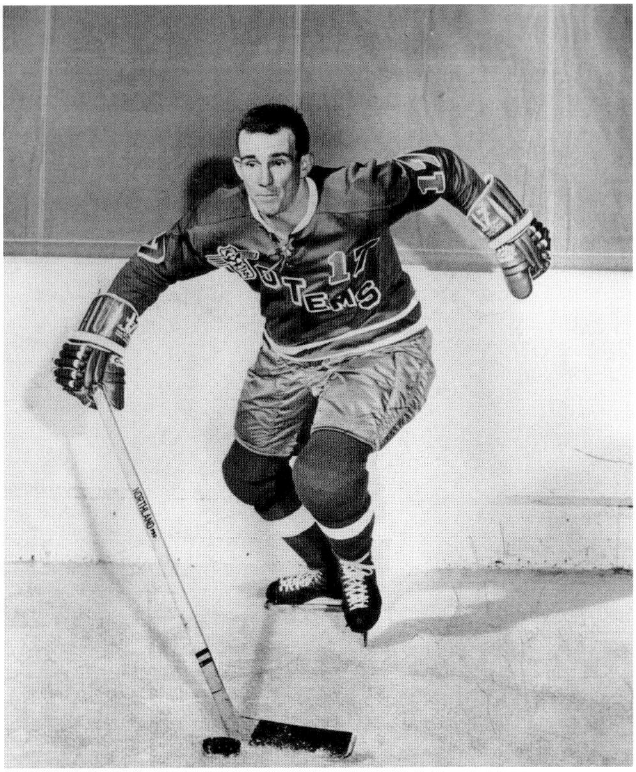

Larry Hale patrolled the blue line for the Totems from 1963 to 1968, winning two championships with the club. While a decent-sized player at six-foot, one-inch tall and 185 pounds, he was actually the smallest defenseman on the Totems infamous Jolly Green Giants blue line of 1966–1967. He was steady, not taking needless penalties, and contributed an average of 21 points per season.

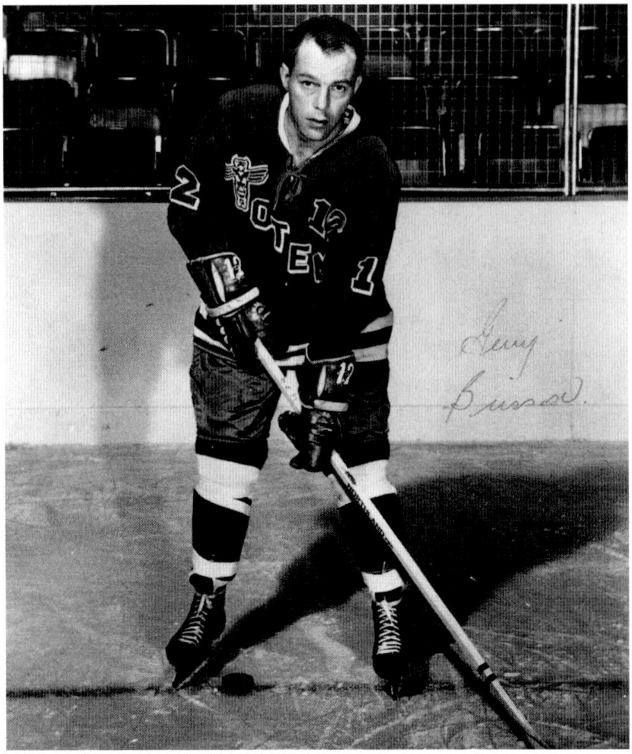

Gerry Brisson was an established goal-scoring threat in the WHL prior to arriving in Seattle in 1964, netting 44 goals with Spokane in 1961–1962. His 19 goals and 19 assists with the Totems in 1964–1965 were respectable, but the club still traded him to San Francisco early in the following season after he separated his shoulder in training camp.

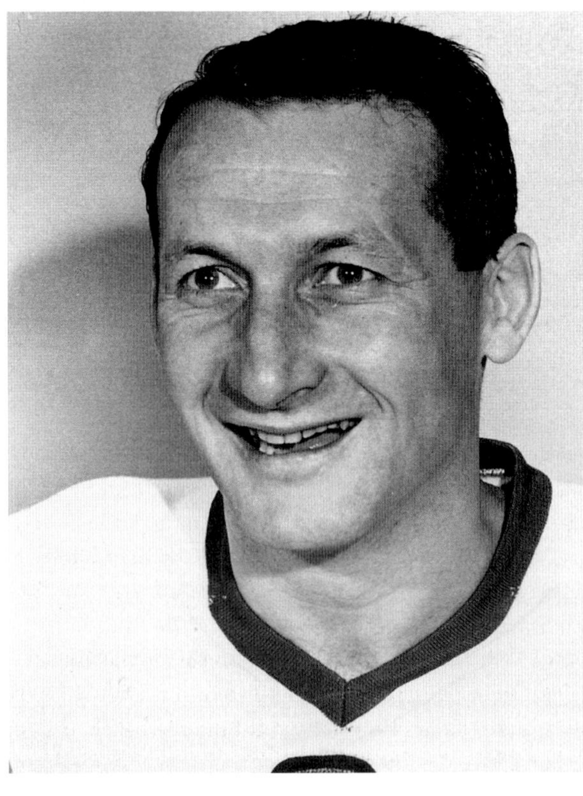

Bill Dineen already had five NHL and six AHL seasons under his belt prior to arriving in Seattle in 1964. He proved to be a key offensive contributor to the Totems, with four consecutive 20-plus goal efforts during his five full seasons in Seattle. His 28 regular-season goals led the 1967–1968 championship squad.

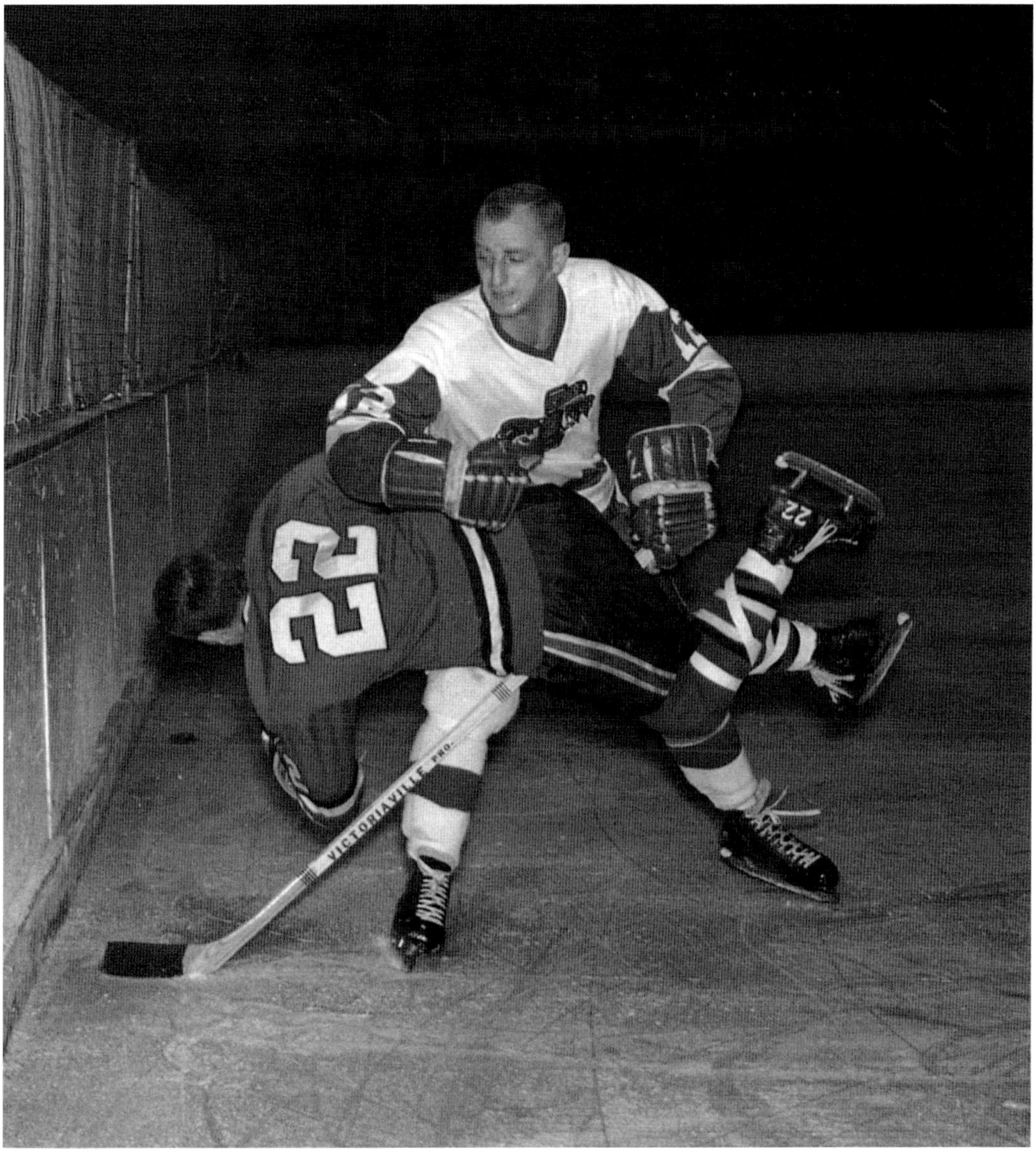

Chuck Holmes seemed an unlikely fan favorite when he came to Seattle in 1966, as many fans still remembered an incident in which he struck a female fan with his stick in January 1960 while skating for Edmonton. The crowd was so incensed after the incident that Holmes did not come out of the locker room for the third period on the recommendation of the police. All was forgiven, however, surely helped by a pair of 20-plus–goal seasons in 1967–1969. Other bizarre events punctuated his time in Seattle, such as Holmes pinning San Francisco Seals owner Barry van Gerbig up against a wall in the tunnel during the intermission of a road game in 1967 and later knocking Don Schock unconscious after Schock hit him with a high stick in 1970. He was also part of the Totems' improbable comeback from a 6-2 third-period deficit against Portland in game two of the 1968 WHL Finals, scoring the tying goal with 19 seconds remaining. Holmes later stepped behind the bench and coached the Totems in 1971–1972. (Photograph by Bob Carver.)

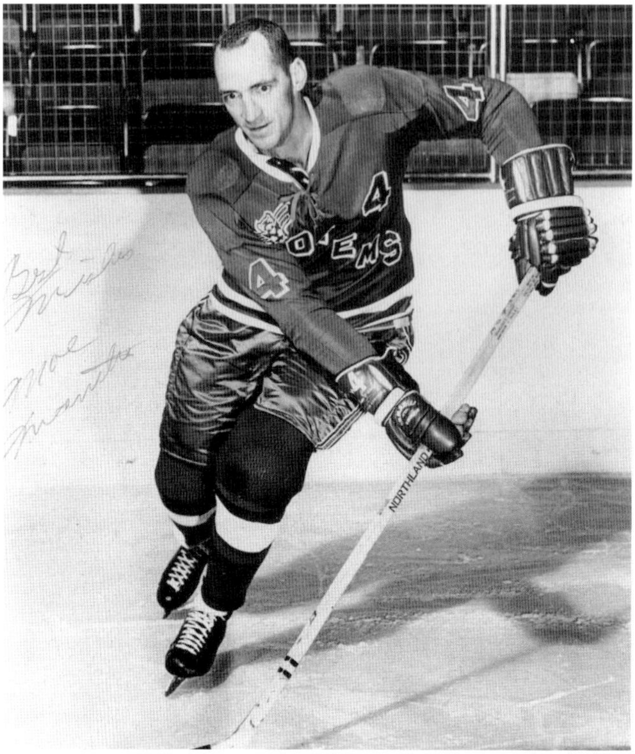

Mo Mantha probably does not have fond memories of the 1964–1965 season, his only in Seattle. A broken cheekbone caused him to miss 13 games, and the following year general manager Keith Allen criticized him for showing up at training camp out of shape, prompting Allen to trade Mantha to Vancouver.

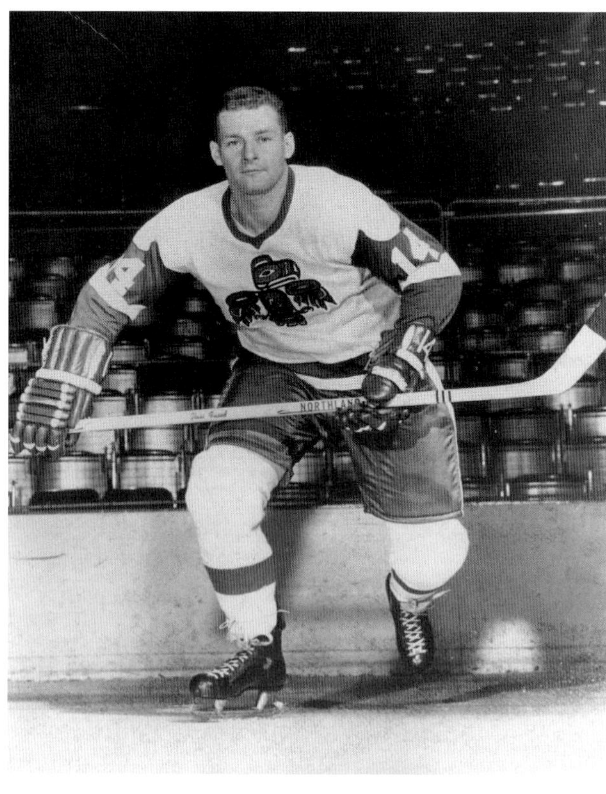

Left winger Don Chiz played five seasons with the Totems from 1965 to 1970, earning two championships with the club. He gained the approval of the Seattle fans during his first year with his overtime game-winning goal against Portland on March 11, 1966, giving the Totems a win and ending a frustrating 15-game losing streak against the Buckaroos.

Forward Earl Heiskala led the Totems in penalty minutes in all three of his full seasons with the team from 1965 to 1968, but lest one think he was just a fighter, he also scored 52 goals during that period. His play did not go unnoticed by Totems general manager Keith Allen, who made sure to acquire Heiskala's rights after joining the front office of the NHL-expansion Philadelphia Flyers.

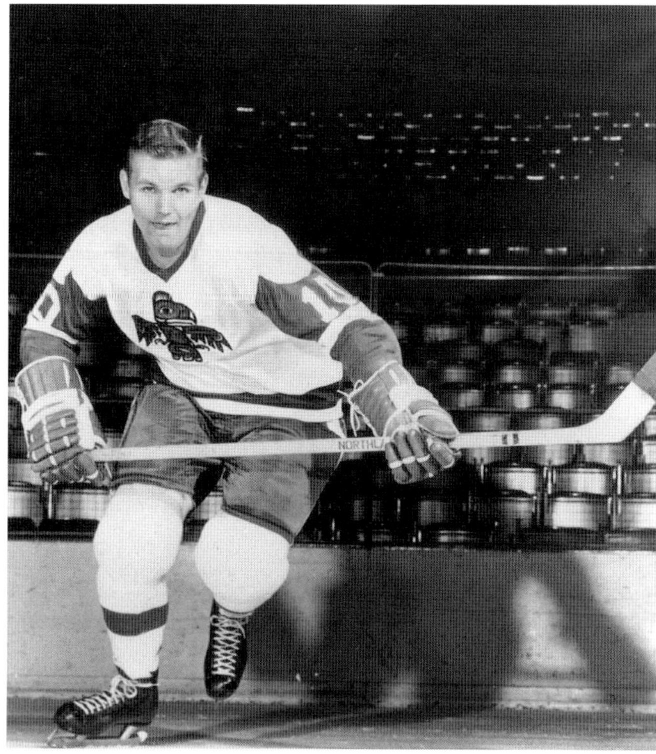

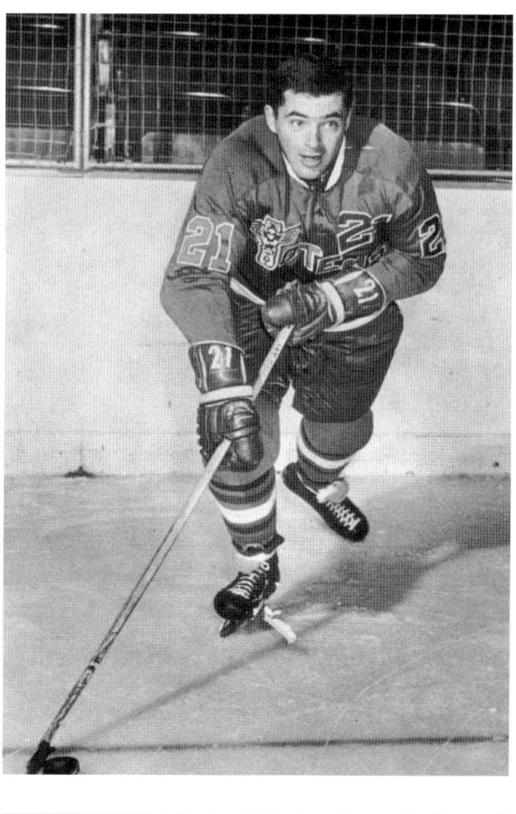

A goal-scoring threat in the junior leagues and in college with the University of North Dakota, Gerry Kell had a hard time making the transition to the pros. Kell started the 1965–1966 season with the Totems, but after being held to just on goal in 18 games he was sent to finish out the season with the Houston Apollos.

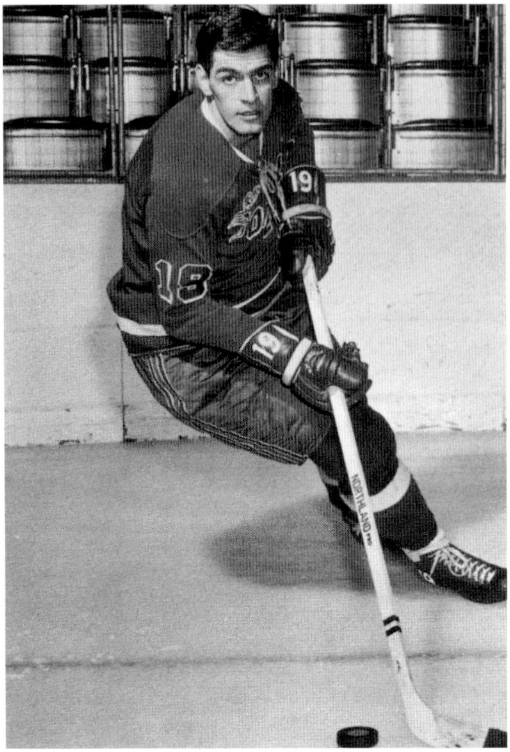

Center Larry Lund certainly had the scoring touch throughout his WHL career. He scored 81 goals during his four seasons in Seattle, leading the team in 1966–1967 with 34 in the regular season and five more in the playoffs to help the Totems to the first of their two back-to-back titles. He went on to play six seasons with Houston in the WHA.

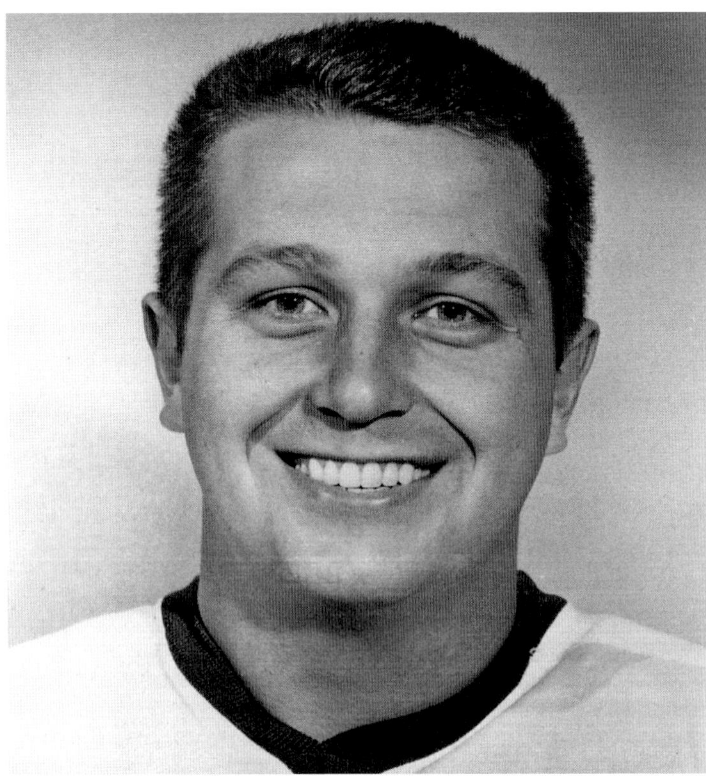

Jim Armstrong's three-year tenure as backup goaltender for the Totems came at the perfect time, allowing him to win back-to-back championships in 1967 and 1968. Though he was never the primary netminder, Armstrong still saw a lot of ice time and played 99 games between the pipes. A frightening neck injury in 1969 left him temporarily paralyzed, but he recovered fully and returned to hockey the following year.

Defenseman Don Fedun had trouble breaking into the lineup in 1966–1967, filled as it was by larger and much more experienced players. He only skated in seven games that season but was expected to be a starter in 1967–1968. Unfortunately, he only played 28 games that campaign and did not appear in the playoffs. (Courtesy of Dave Eskenazi.)

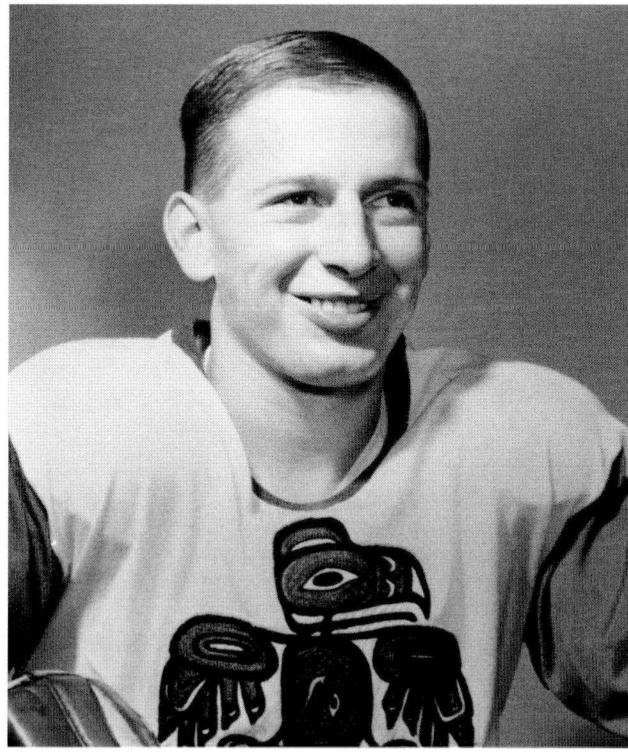

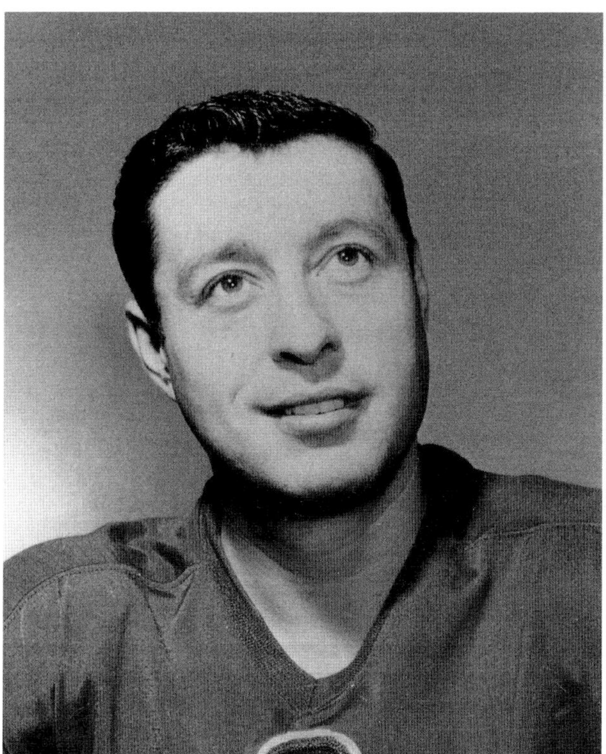

The Totems acquired veteran Jean Gauthier from the Montreal Canadiens for 1966–1967, and the big defenseman made his presence felt during his only season in Seattle. Not only was he a physical presence, but he also scored 31 points to make him the highest-scoring defenseman on the club. He contributed a goal and three assists during the 1967 playoffs.

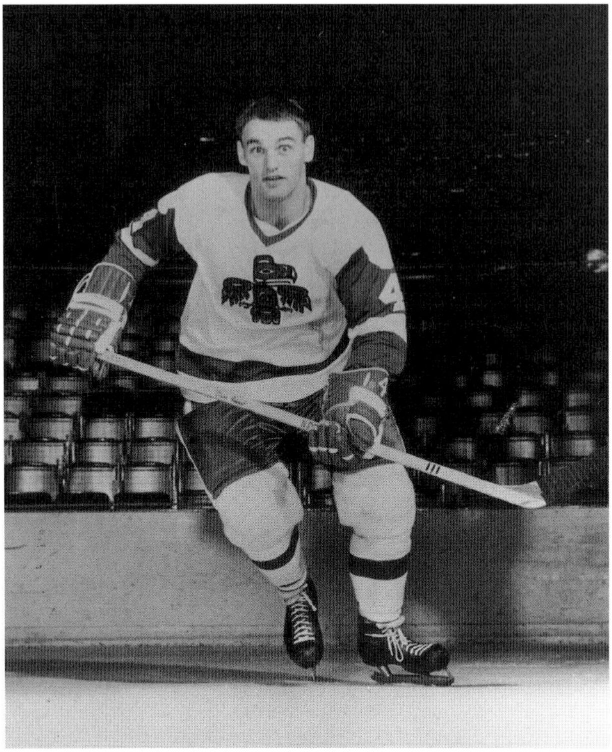

Bob Lemieux was another of the 1966–1967 Jolly Green Giants who only played that one season in Seattle. While Jean Gauthier led the defense in total scoring, Lemieux led the group in goals with 10 during the regular season and another pair in the playoffs. He also made sure to use his size as needed, earning 117 penalty minutes that year.

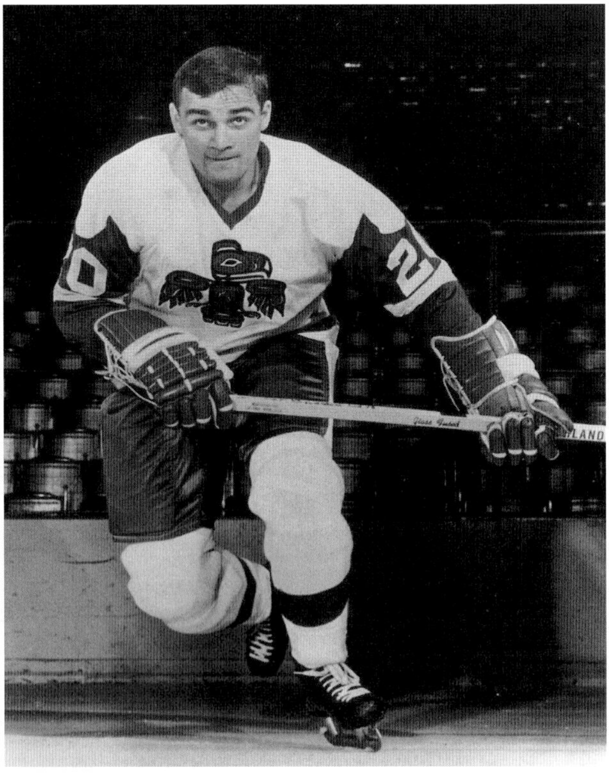

Dave Parenteau, like a number of others, was transferred to Seattle for 1966–1967 then gone the following season. The left winger saw somewhat limited duty, appearing in 38 games and scoring three goals and seven assists. He did not see ice time during the playoffs. Later in his career in the IHL and EHL, he regained the scoring touch he had shown in the juniors.

Another of the "just passing through" players on the 1966–1967 team was hard-hitting defenseman Noel Picard. His 135 penalty minutes were second most on the team, but he also showed a good touch with 27 assists. He came alive offensively in the 1967 WHL Finals, scoring the game-winner in game two and assisting on the winners in games one and three.

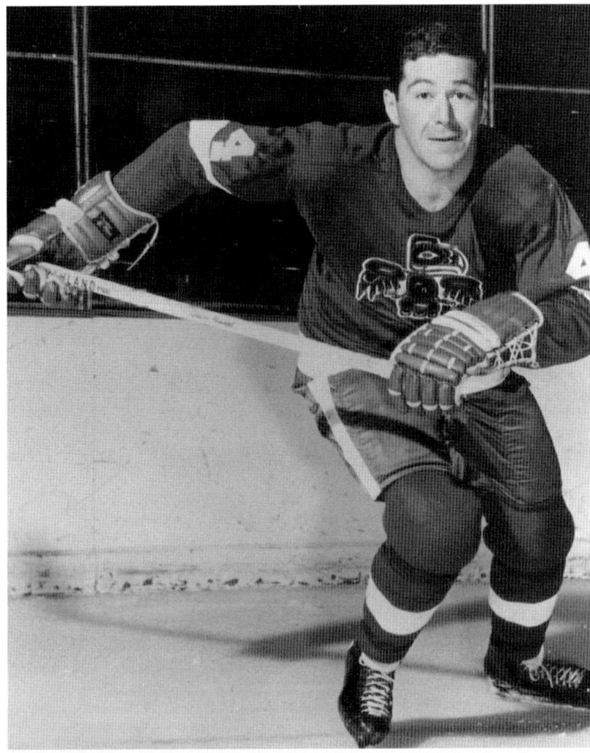

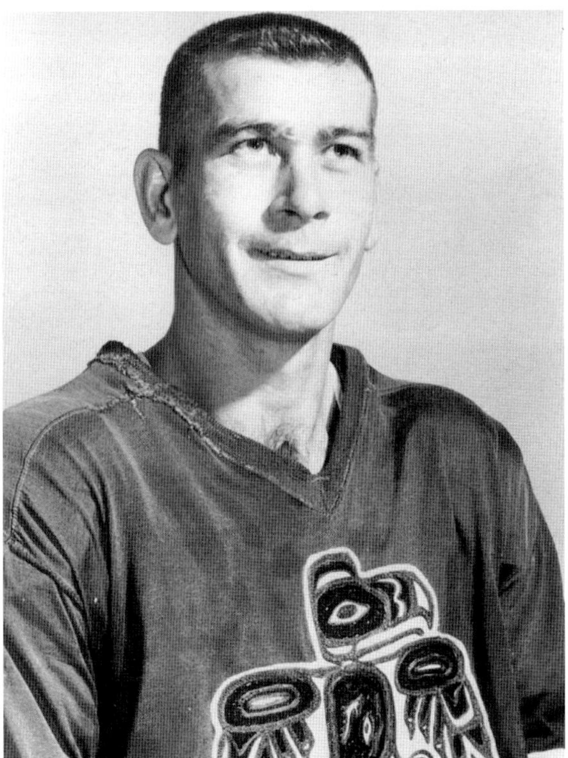

Keith Allen's move to the front office in Philadelphia ensured a relationship between the Totems and the Flyers, one that paid off almost immediately with the transfer of high-scoring center Bob Courcy to Seattle in 1967–1968. Courcy led the Totems over the next two years with a pair of 40-plus goal efforts, making him one of only four Totems to reach 40 goals in a season. (Courtesy of Dave Eskenazi.)

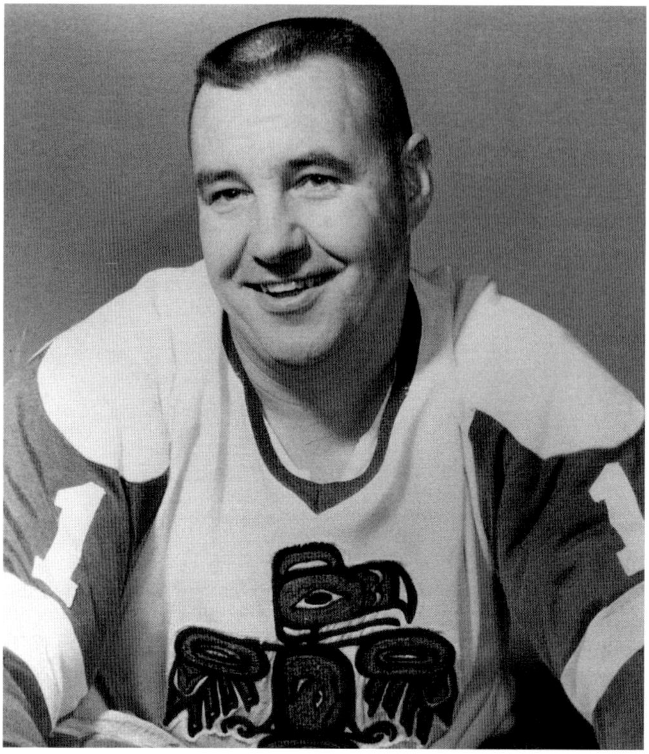

During the summer of 1967, the Totems made a surprise move and traded starting goaltenders with Portland, sending Jim McLeod south and acquiring the older Don Head. The move paid off, as the Totems won their second straight WHL title in 1968 behind Head's 8-1 playoff record and 2.17 goals against average. (Courtesy of Dave Eskenazi.)

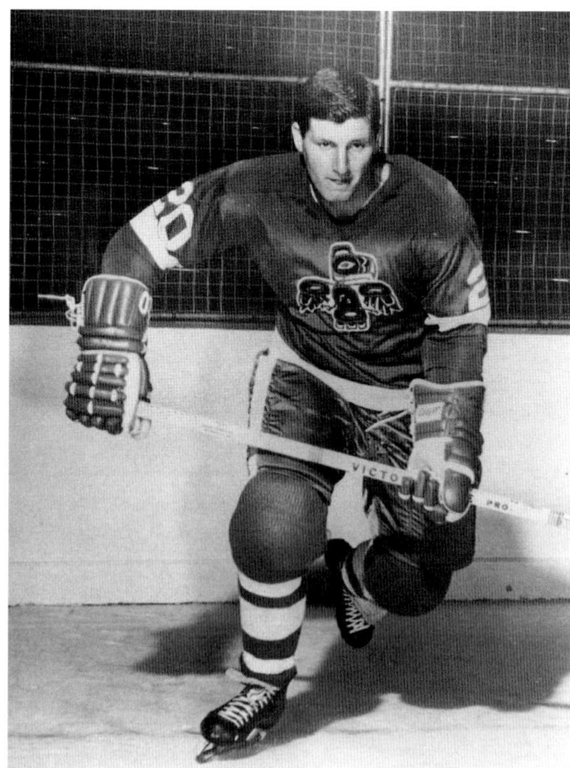

Gary Kilpatrick was a tough defenseman from Victoria, British Columbia. He joined the Totems in 1967–1968 and earned 81 penalty minutes in just 55 games. The following season, he led the Totems with 136 penalty minutes while also posting one of the best offensive years of his career, with three goals and 29 assists. (Courtesy of Dave Eskenazi.)

Dick Mortenson showed a lot of offensive talent in the juniors when he scored 53 goals and 93 points with Edmonton in 1967–1968, but he could not replicate that performance at the next level. Over the course of three seasons (1970–1973) in Seattle, he only scored 19 goals on some struggling Totems teams.

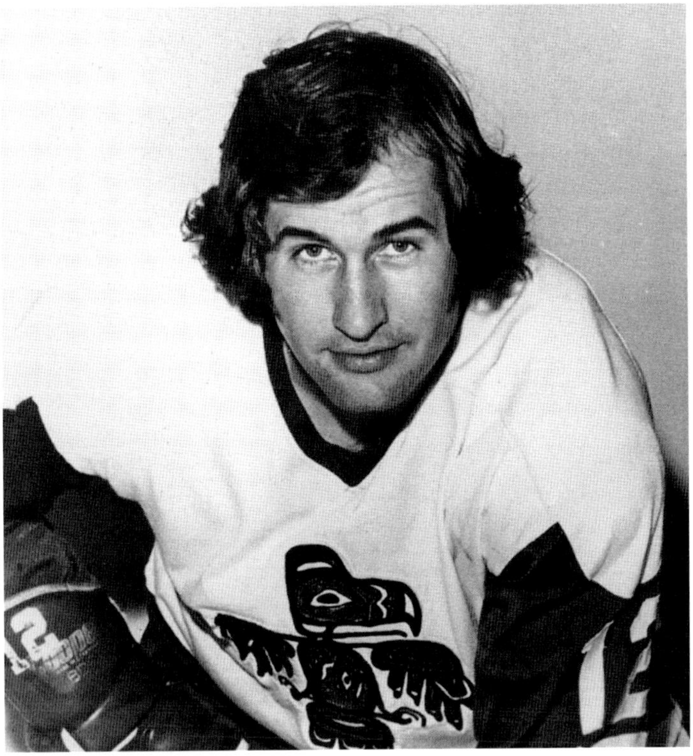

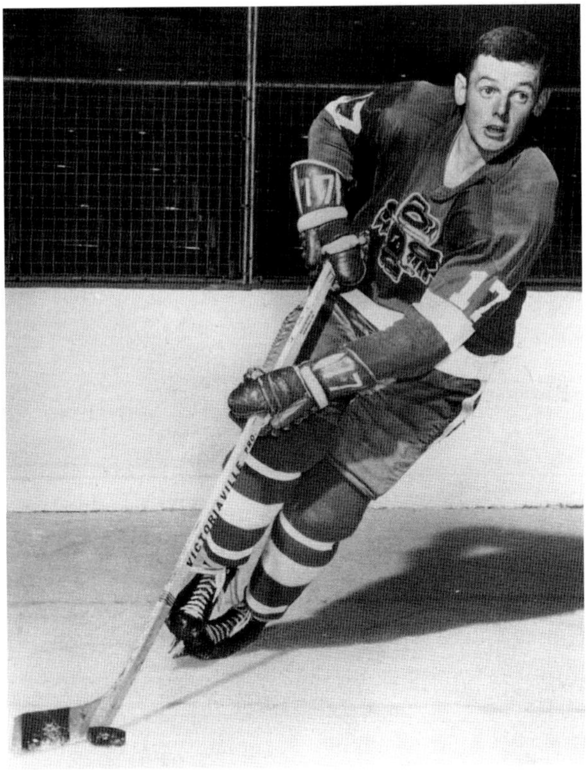

Jack Michie earned WHL Rookie of the Year honors in 1968–1969, his first season with the Totems. The 23-year-old winger scored 19 goals and 28 assists and spent some time on Guyle Fielder's line. After three successful seasons, his scoring touch left him during the Totems' dismal 1971–1972 campaign, in which he scored a meager seven goals.

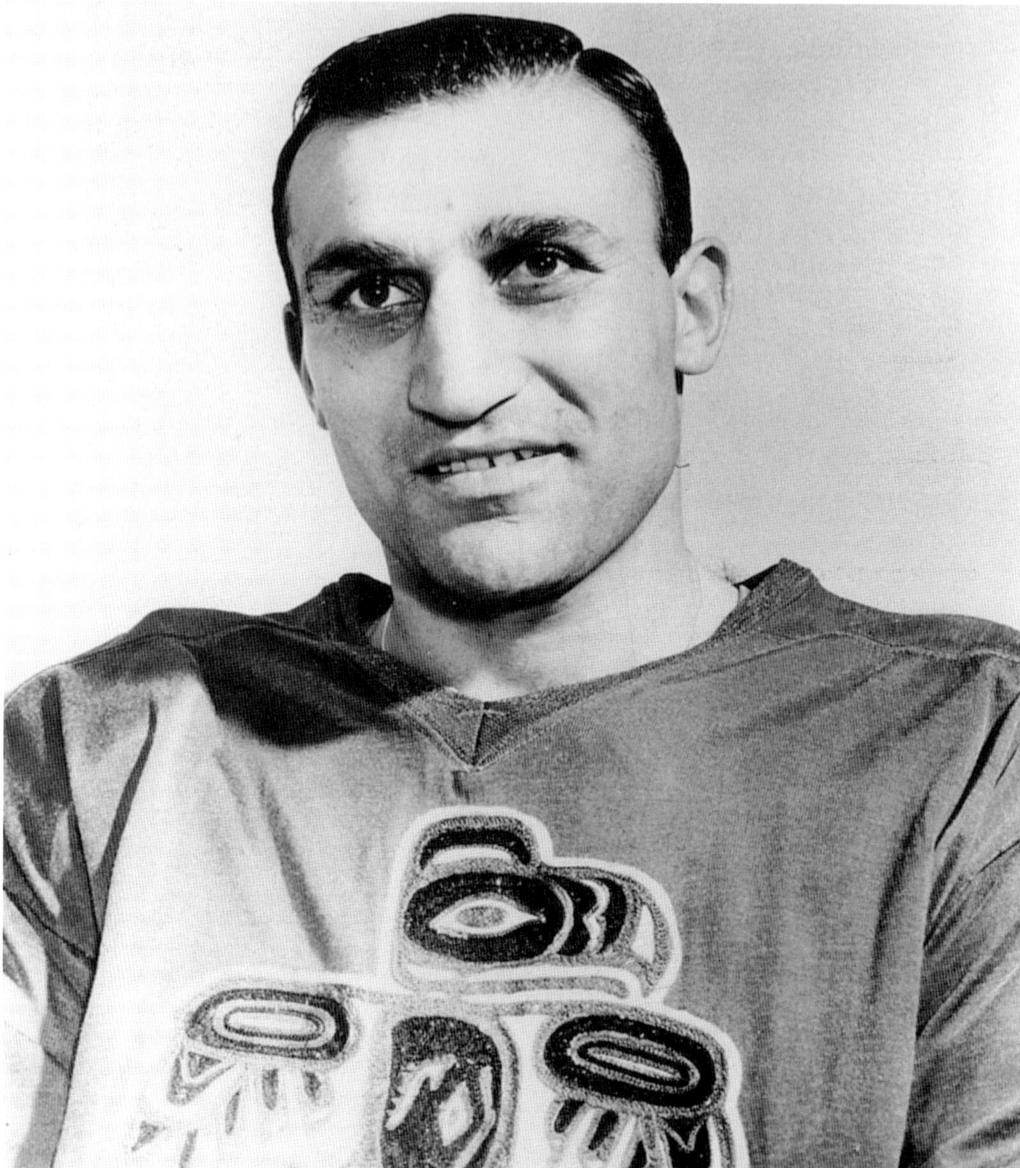

Defenseman John Hanna was already a veteran of 13 professional seasons before arriving in Seattle in 1968 as part of the Totems' working arrangement with the Philadelphia Flyers, serving as compensation for the Flyers signing Earl Heiskala. He was known for putting up some decent offensive numbers but truly blossomed in Seattle, due in large part to being extensively utilized on the power play. His 25 goals in 1968–1969 more than doubled his previous best effort, setting the team record for most goals in a season by a defenseman. He earned numerous accolades during his four seasons in Seattle, including the Leader Cup as WHL MVP in 1969, two Hal Laycoe Cups (1969 and 1971) as the league's top defenseman, and twice named a First Team All-Star (1969 and 1971). Following his playing days, Hanna and a number of other Canadian professional players found themselves in a legal dispute with the IRS over their US tax obligations.

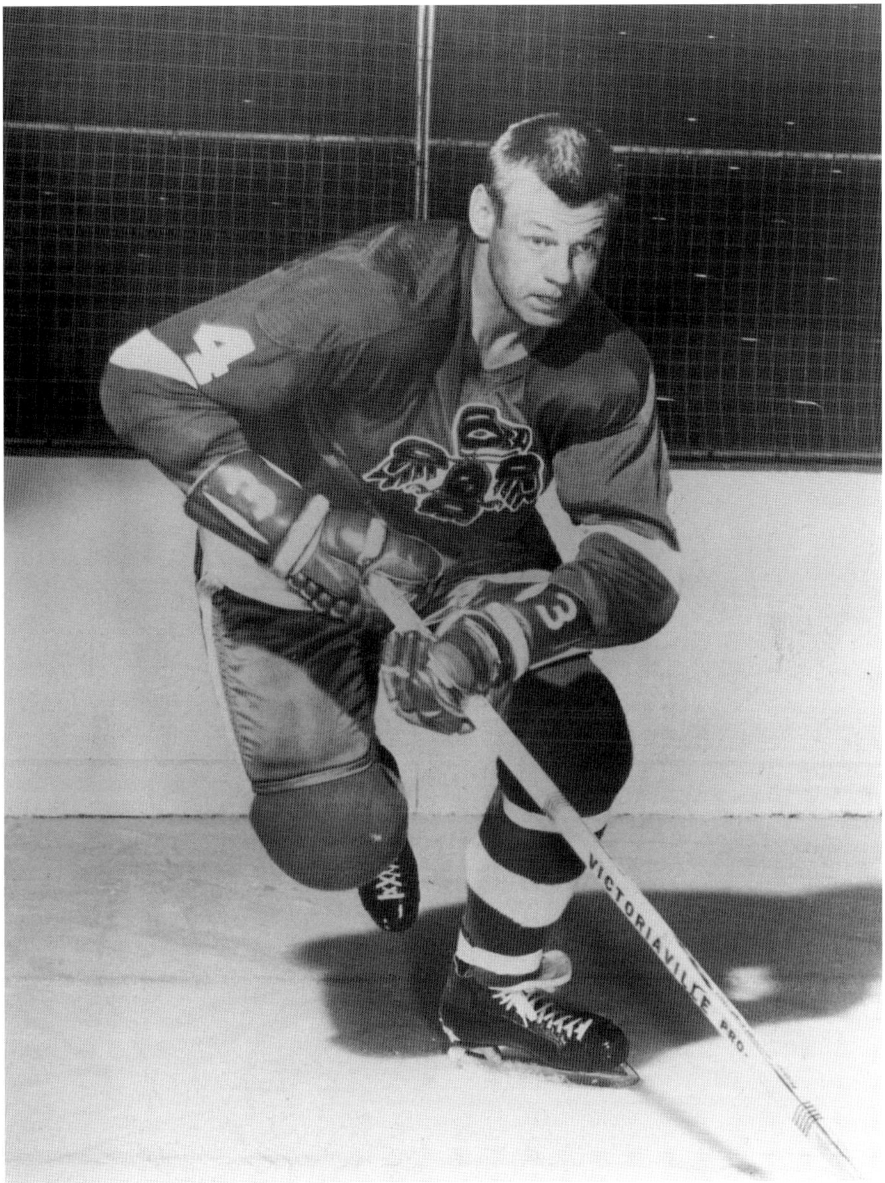

Based on the numbers, it would be fair to assume that defenseman Ray Larose had a relatively uneventful three seasons in Seattle from 1967 to 1970. He averaged 21 points and 76 penalty minutes per year—pretty standard fare for the time. But Larose was part of two important events, one infamous, the other noteworthy. On October 27, 1969, Larose got into a fight with Denver Spur John Schella with 15 seconds remaining in the game. The fight riled up the fans, and as the clock ticked down, Larry Mavety tried to climb the fence behind the Spur bench to get at members of the crowd who allegedly spit on the Denver players. A more positive moment occurred on April 6, 1970, when the Totems had their only ever one-game playoff after finishing the regular season tied with Phoenix for fourth place and the last playoff spot. Larose's third-period goal, only his fourth of the season, was the game winner for Seattle and propelled them into their last playoff appearance. (Courtesy of Dave Eskenazi.)

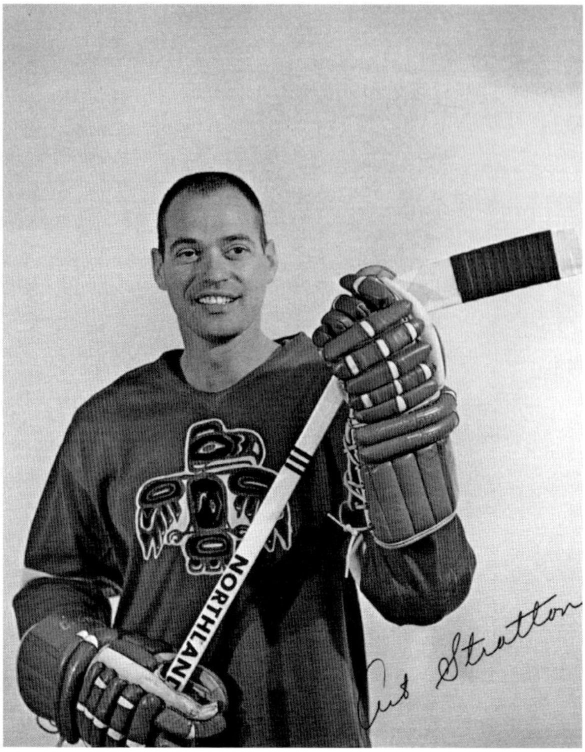

Despite a successful NHL campaign in 1967–1968 that saw him score 16 goals and 41 points, Art Stratton found himself in Seattle in 1968 as part of the compensation for the Flyers signing of Earl Heiskala. Stratton spent three full seasons and part of a fourth with the Totems, leading the club in assists in 1969–1970 with 55 helpers.

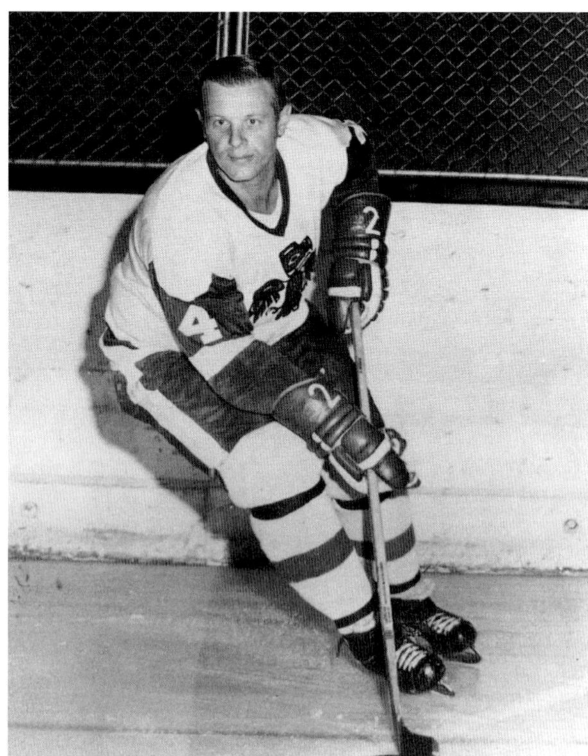

Seattle was the last stop in defenseman Ron Ingram's professional hockey career, one that included 114 NHL games with Chicago, Detroit, and New York. He was a consistent performer for the Totems in 1969–1970, appearing in all 72 regular-season games, but a knee injury kept him out of the postseason. (Courtesy of Dave Eskenazi.)

Gerry Meehan split time in the NHL and WHL in 1968–1969, but he was not quite ready for the big time. He was sent to Seattle for the 1969–1970 campaign, and that is where he showed his skills, picking up 23 goals and 53 points. He was with Buffalo in the NHL the following season and never looked back. (Courtesy of Dave Eskenazi.)

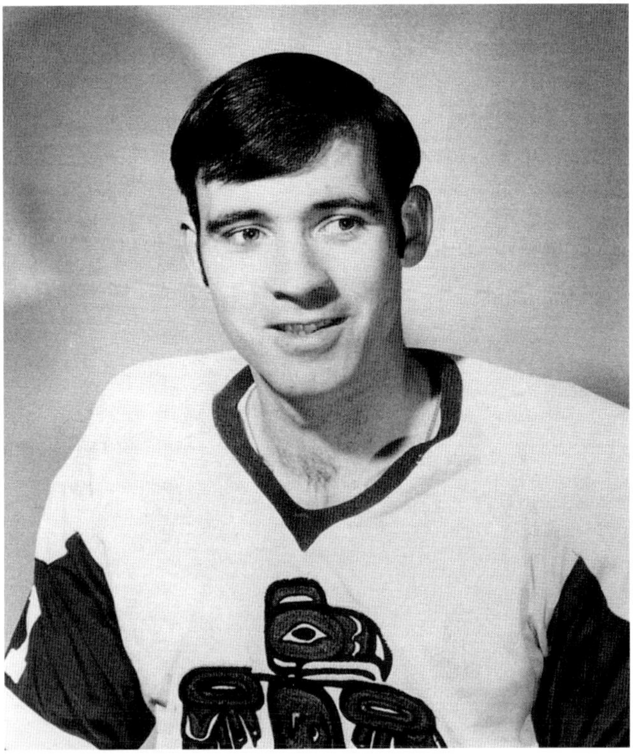

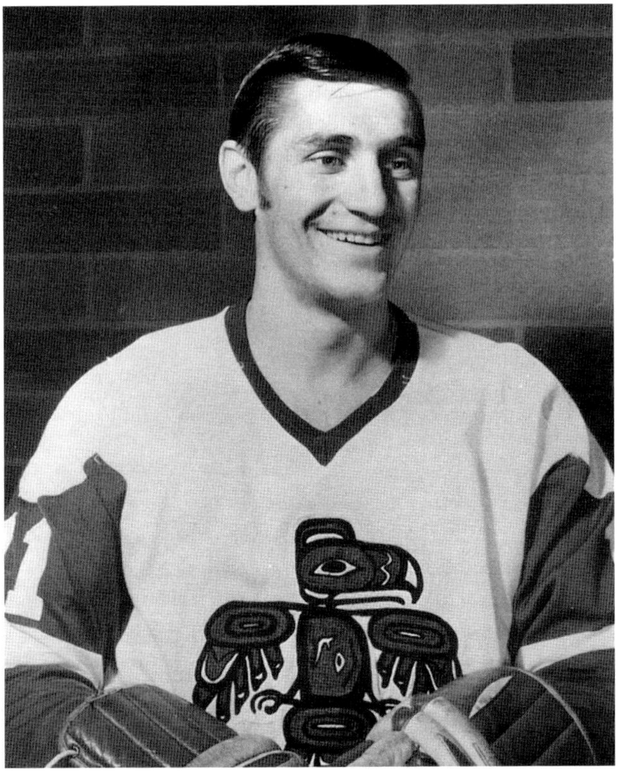

Guyle Fielder wanted to come out of retirement to play for the WHL-expansion Salt Lake City Golden Eagles in 1969–1970. The Totems still held Fielder's rights, but they agreed to transfer him to Salt Lake in exchange for experienced winger Bobby Schmautz. Schmautz played parts of two seasons in Seattle before moving on to Vancouver of the NHL. (Courtesy of Dave Eskenazi.)

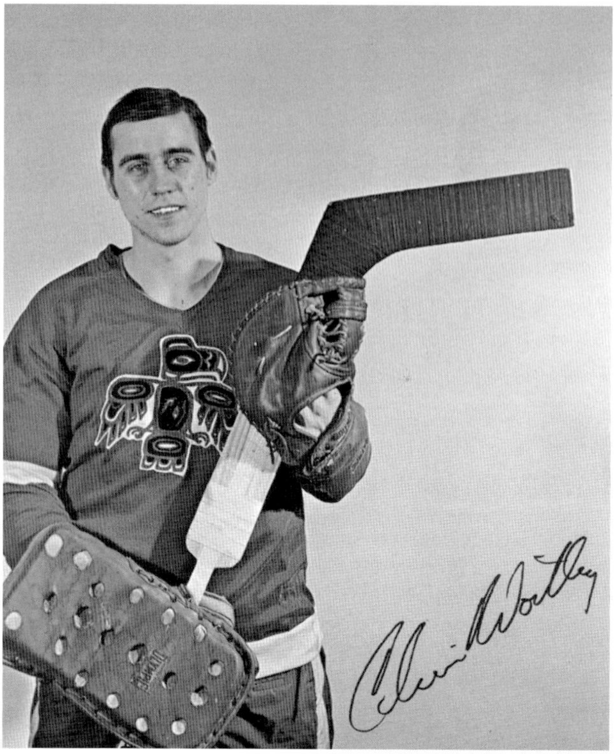

Totems goaltender Don Head cracked three ribs in the second game of the 1969–1970 season, sending the front office into a panic. Fortunately, the NHL's Oakland Seals were seeking a home for goaltending prospect Chris Worthy and loaned him to Seattle. Worthy proved adequate if not stellar, posting a 14-14-3 record. He later played in both the NHL and WHA.

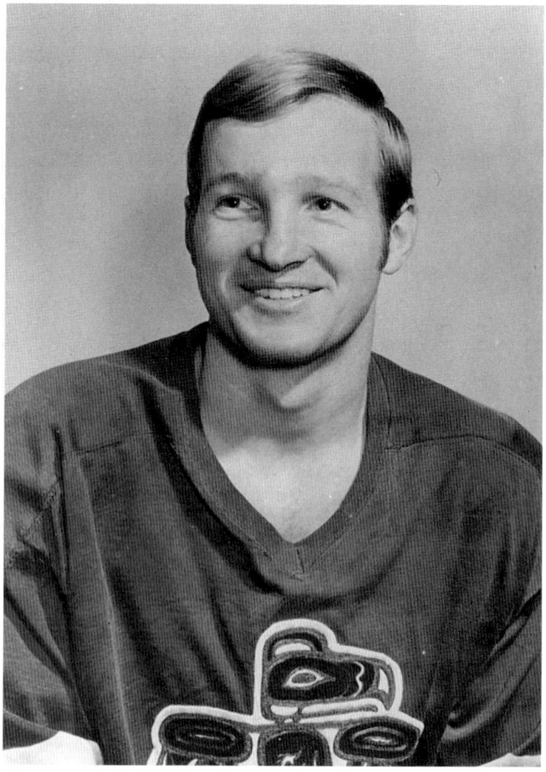

Ron Boehm was a 24-year-old prospect for the Oakland Seals when he was assigned to Seattle in 1970–1971. Unfortunately for the Totems, he had an off year offensively, only scoring 10 goals and 36 assists. He spent the following three years with Boston in the AHL, where he had a bit more success, but never made it back to the NHL. (Courtesy of Dave Eskenazi.)

Among the seven members of the 1970 AHL champion Buffalo Bisons acquired by the Totems for 1970–1971 was left winger Bob Jones. While Jones's numbers did not quite match those he had posted in Buffalo, his 60 points that season tied him for the team lead with defenseman John Hanna. (Courtesy of Dave Eskenazi.)

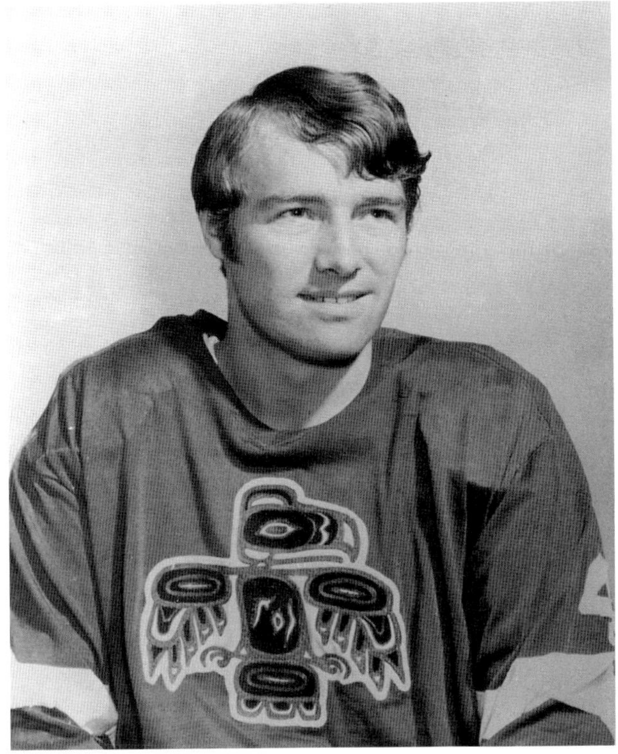

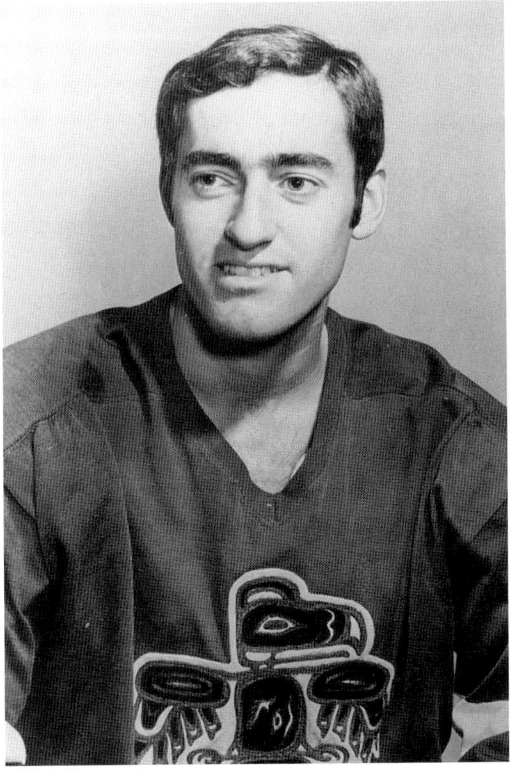

Brothers Gordon (shown) and Sheldon Kannegiesser joined the Totems for the 1970–1971 season, having patrolled the blue line together for the Kansas City Blues the year before. The Totems decided to keep Gordon and shipped Sheldon off to Omaha of the AHL. While Gordon played adequately for Seattle, perhaps the Totems should have kept his brother, who went on to play in 366 NHL games. (Courtesy of Dave Eskenazi.)

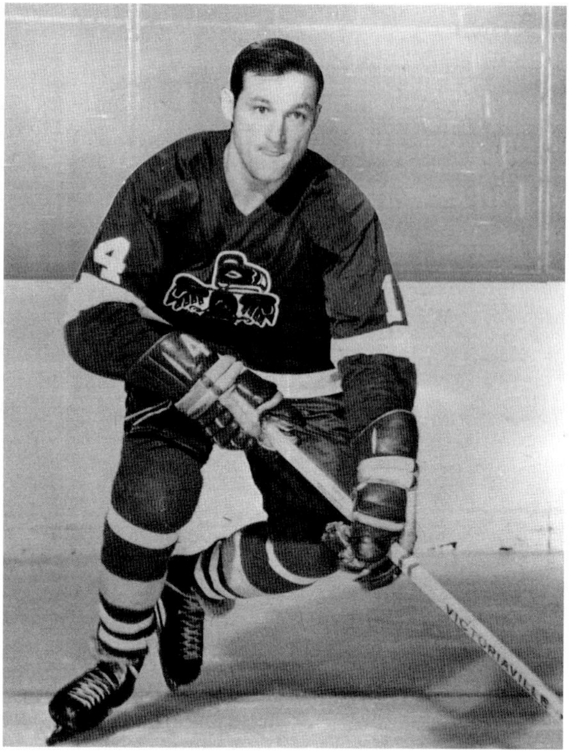

Center Billy Knibbs was another of the former Buffalo Bisons players to come to Seattle in 1970–1971. Though he had a productive first half of the season, with 14 goals and 31 points, he was shipped off to Omaha to make way for a couple of forwards in the Vancouver farm system, Ed Hatoum and Jim Wiste. (Courtesy of Dave Eskenazi.)

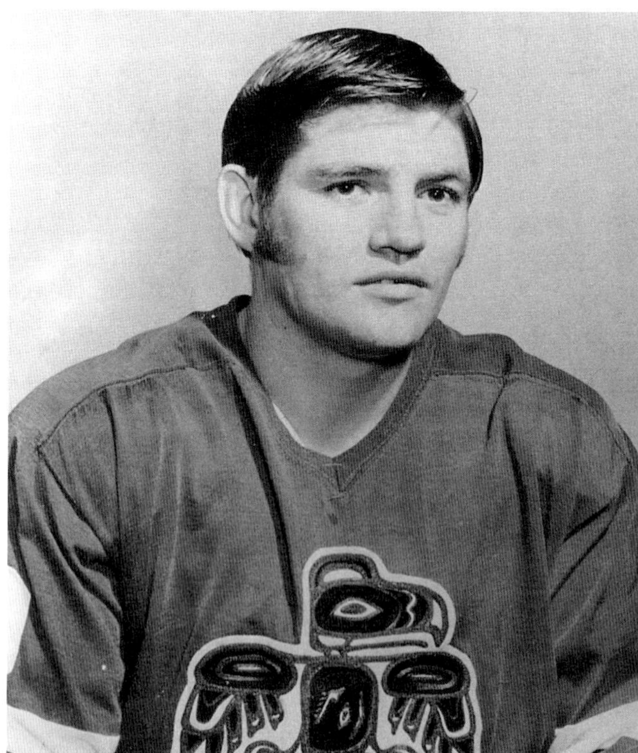

Defenseman Randy Legge may not have been big at five foot 11 inches tall and 185 pounds, but he made up for it with hard work. He had a reputation for racking up a lot of penalty minutes, a trend that continued during his only season in Seattle, when he led the Totems with 150 minutes in 1970–1971, almost double the total of the next closest player. (Courtesy of Dave Eskenazi.)

Rookie goaltender George Surmay was guaranteed to get plenty of ice time as Don Head's backup during the 1970–1971. The 37-year-old Head incurred a lot of injuries, including one during the preseason that allowed Surmay to play in the Totems first two home games. He went 13-14-3 in 34 appearances during his only season in Seattle. (Courtesy of Dave Eskenazi.)

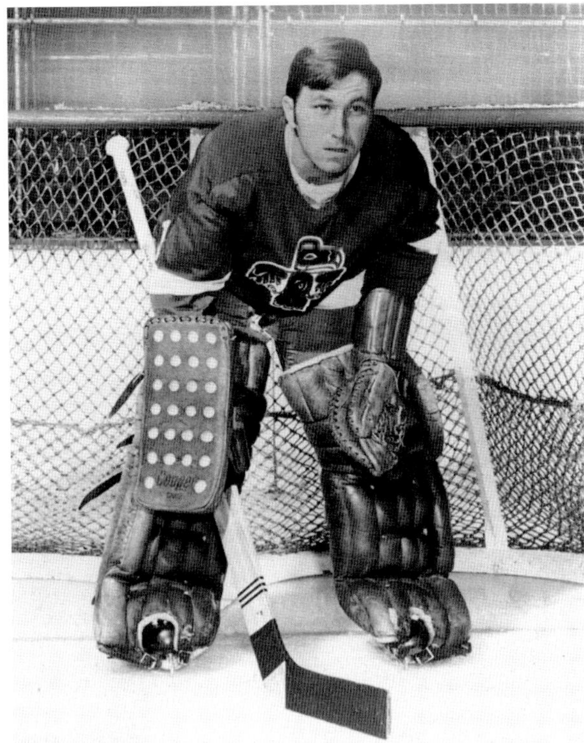

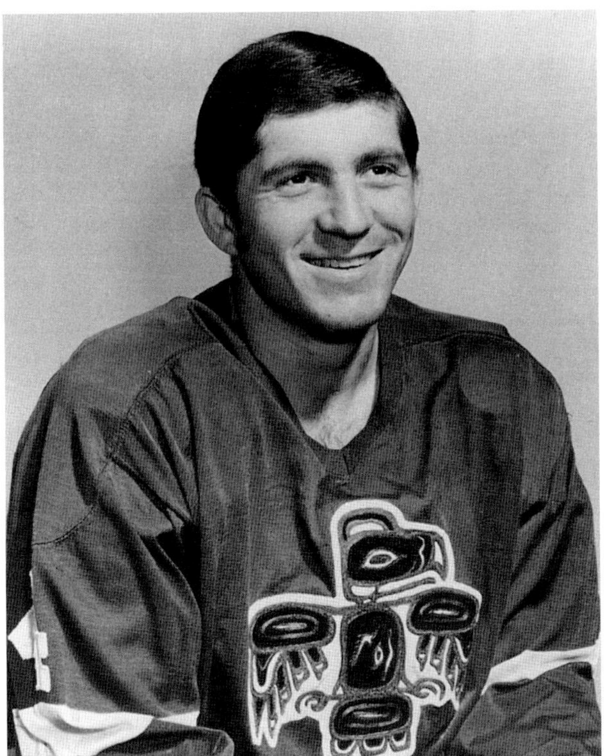

Left winger Gary Veneruzzo was another member of the 1969–1970 AHL champion Buffalo Bisons who made his way to Seattle for the 1970–1971 season. His 27 goals led an anemic Totems offense that managed only 223 goals in 72 games. Veneruzzo played one more year in the WHL before enjoying a five-year stint in the WHA. (Courtesy of Dave Eskenazi.)

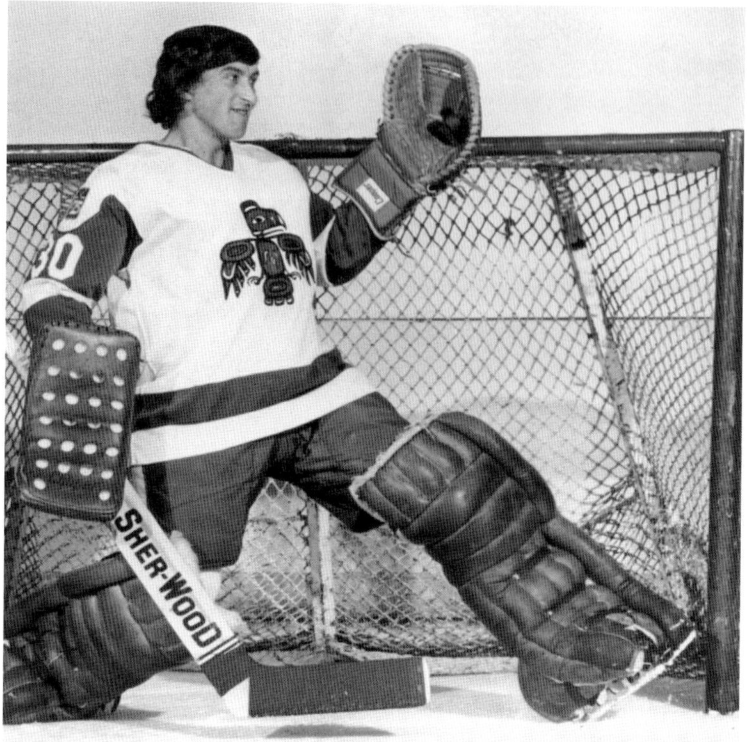

Goaltender Bruce Bullock helped usher in the final era of Totems hockey, playing with the club in its last four seasons, from 1971 to 1975. Despite only playing for losing teams, he still posted a respectable 46-53-10 record in Seattle. His 22-20-3 record in 1973–1974 was the first winning season by a Totems netminder since 1968–1969. He was also fortunate enough to appear in both games the Totems played against Russia.

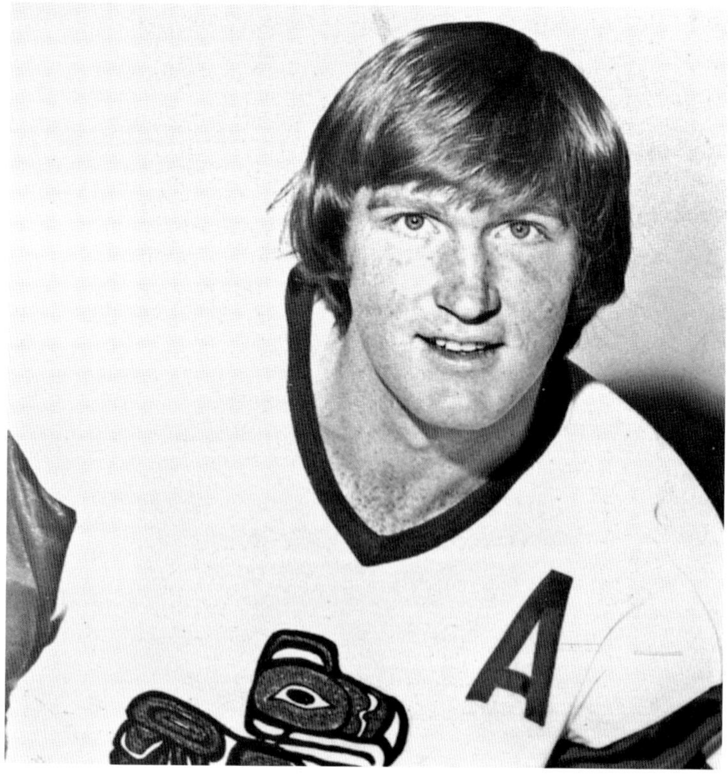

Dave Dunn was a valuable two-way defenseman for the Totems from 1971 to 1973. One of only a half-dozen players to return to Seattle following the disastrous 1971–1972 campaign, Dunn proved his worth by not only leading the team in penalty minutes with 147 but also finishing third in scoring with 19 goals and 56 assists to earn the Laycoe Cup as the league's top defenseman.

Randy Miller may be best remembered by Seattle fans not for his 19 goals and 38 points with the Totems in 1971–1972, but instead for his collision with Totems goalie Jim Armstrong in March 1969, when Miller was playing with the Denver Spurs. Miller ran into Armstrong at the end of a breakaway, knocking the goaltender back into the goalpost and temporarily paralyzing him.

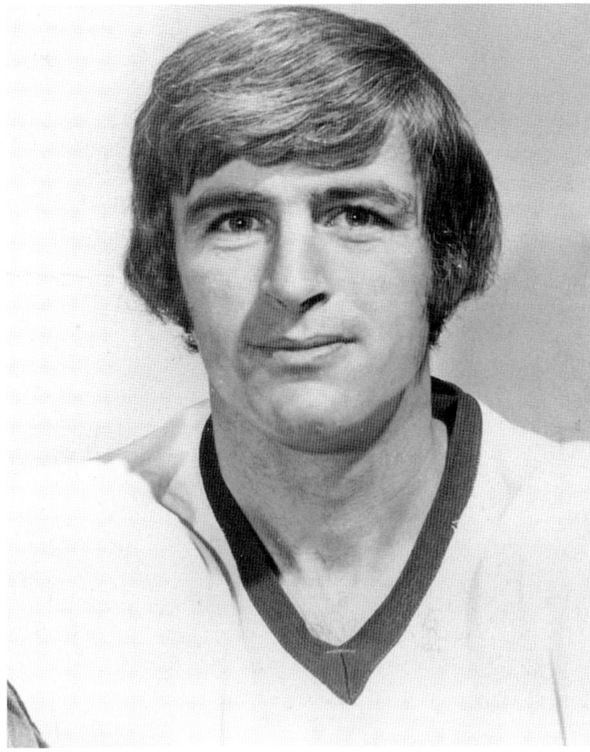

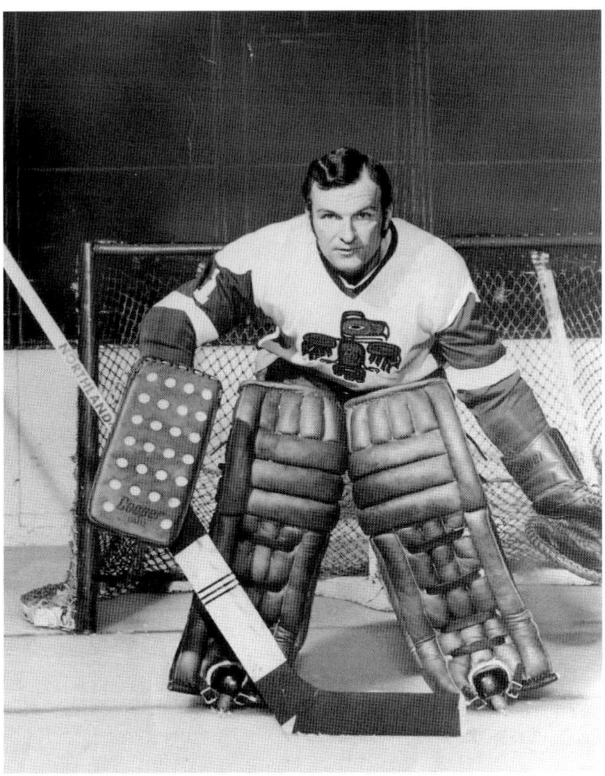

Goaltender Jack Norris was already 29 years old and had appeared in 58 NHL games when he was transferred to Seattle for the 1971–1972 season. Even a netminder with his experience could only do so much to help the Totems, and he posted a staggering 5-28-5 record. Despite those numbers, he was called up to the WHA the following year, his first of four at that level.

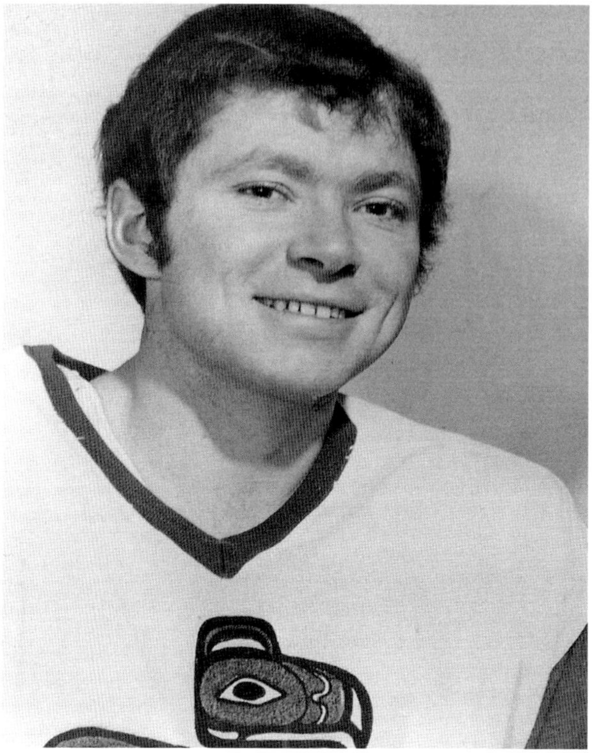

Center Al Rycroft put up some impressive numbers during his professional career, including 50 goals in only 48 games with Syracuse in 1972–1973 and 38 goals in 53 games with Macon the following year. Unfortunately, he had the misfortune of coming to Seattle during the worst season in franchise history and only contributed three goals in 24 games.

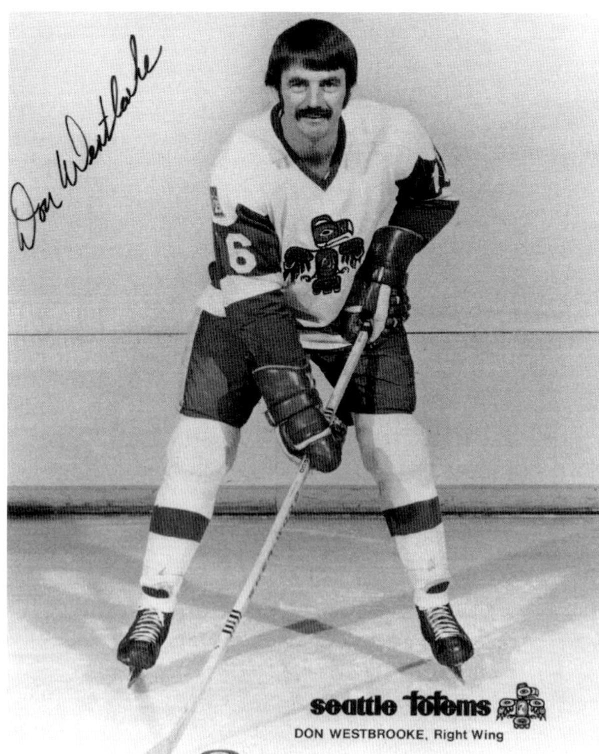

Don Westbrooke was one of the few bright spots for the Totems in the 1970s. He joined the club during the awful 1971–1972 season and led the team with 23 goals despite only playing 48 games. He was arguably the most successful Totem against the Russians, with three goals and two assists in two games.

Hal Willis was another of the long list of players who were in and out of Seattle for just part of the epically bad 1971–1972 season, but the defenseman made his presence felt by leading the team with an impressive 155 penalty minutes in only 42 games. Willis, like so many WHLers, eventually found his way to the WHA, appearing in 92 games with New York and Los Angeles.

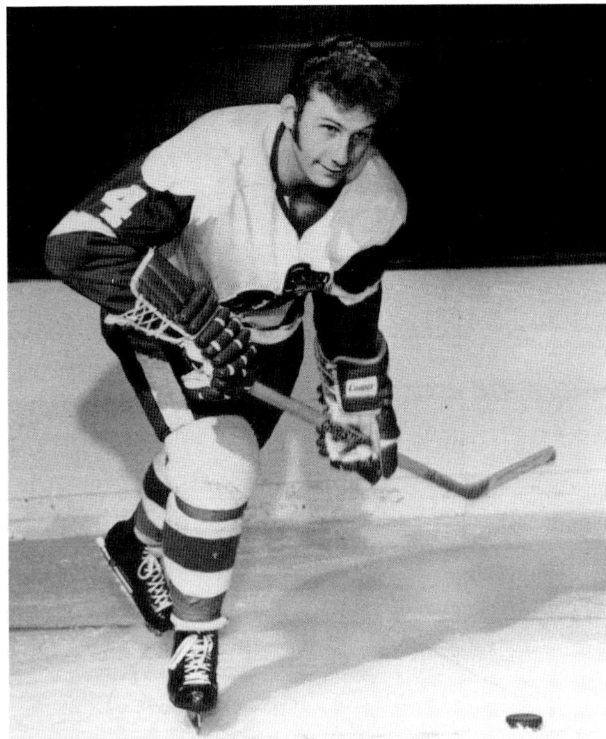

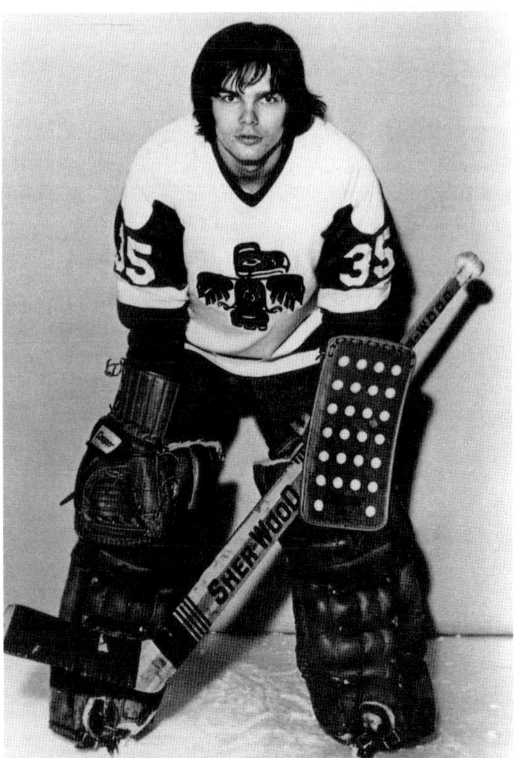

Dan Brady was part of the goaltending duo who backstopped the Totems from 1972 to 1975. He came to Seattle straight out of Boston University, where he led the Terriers to back-to-back NCAA championships in 1971 and 1972. Success was harder to come by with the Totems, and Brady went 39-58-15 in Seattle.

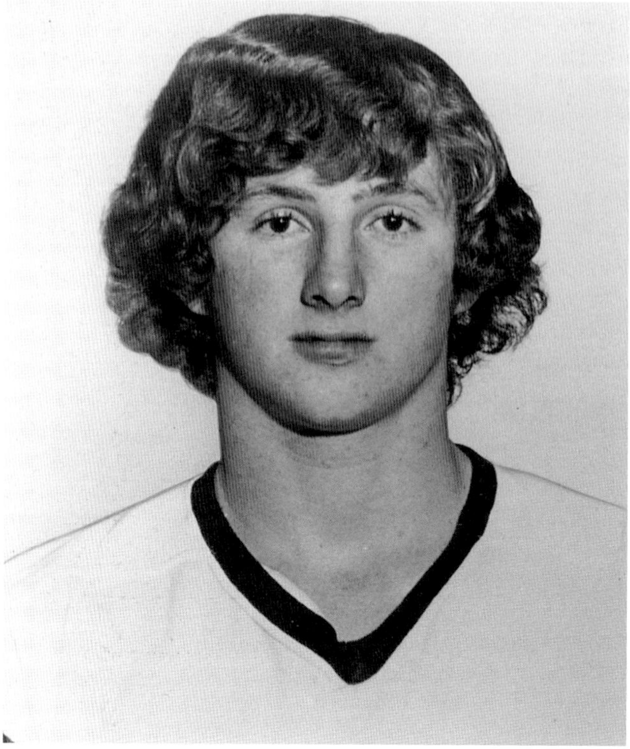

Ron Homenuke was a second-generation Seattle hockey player when he joined the Totems for the 1972–1973 season. His uncle George was a forward with the Ironmen and Bombers from 1951 to 1953, scoring 101 points. Ron did not have the same scoring touch, netting 21 goals during his two seasons in Seattle, though he did make it into one NHL game with Vancouver. (Courtesy of Dave Eskenazi.)

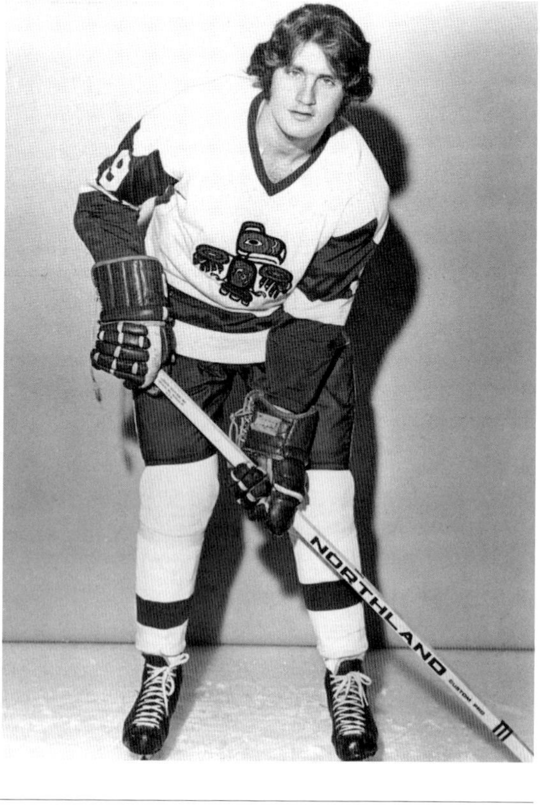

Young Barry Wilcox split time between Seattle and the NHL Vancouver Canucks in 1972–1973, and the Totems had high hopes for him going into the 1973–1974 season. Unexpectedly, he broke his arm during training camp, and to make matters worse, it did not heal properly, so it had to be broken and set again. He was back in Seattle in 1974–1975 but out of professional hockey by 1976.

Defenseman Dennis McCord was only 20 years old when he skated with the Totems against the Russians for the first time in 1972, and despite the 9-4 trouncing came away unimpressed, noting, "They weren't as good as I thought they were going to be." McCord was a solid two-way player for Seattle from 1972 to 1974, but a pair of knee injuries limited him to 26 games in 1974–1975.

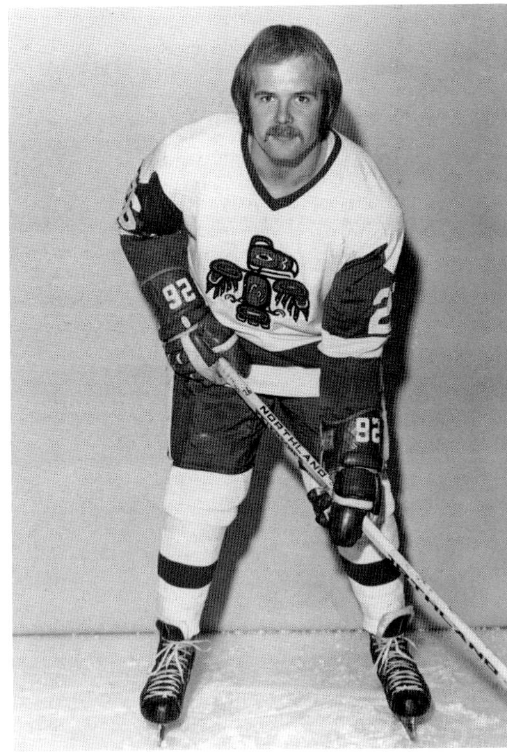

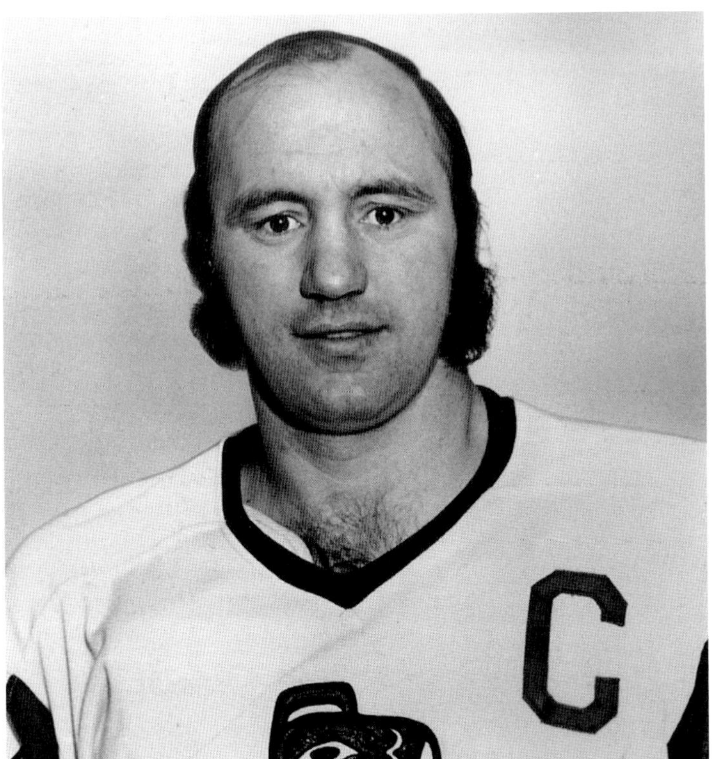

Defenseman Larry McNabb was already a 12-year professional-hockey veteran by time he arrived in Seattle for the 1972–1973 season, and he was well known to the local fans for his rough play. Despite being 33 years old, he still played a physical game, racking up 124 penalty minutes, the second most on the team.

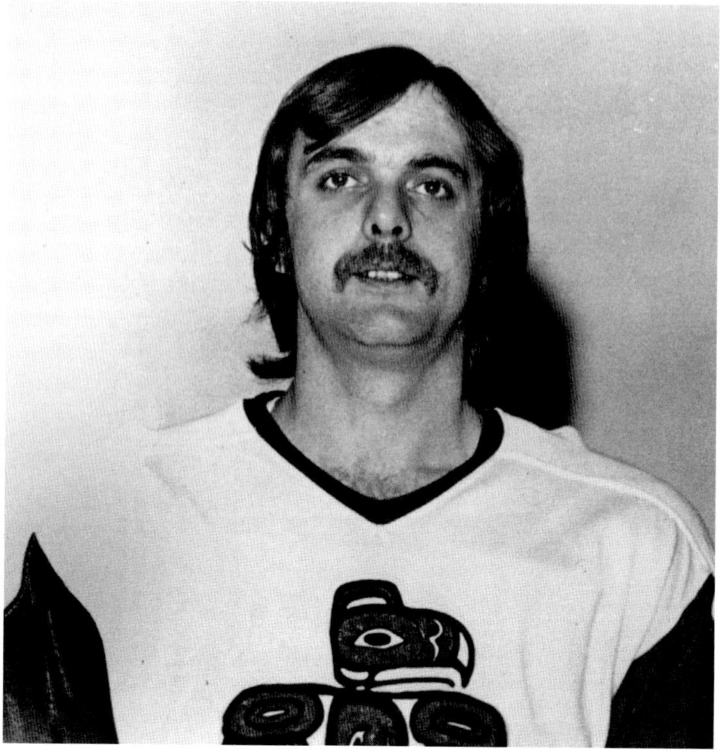

Rob Walton made the most out of his one year in Seattle, leading the WHL in assists (61) and points (101) in 1972–1973. Walton is one of only two Seattle professionals to score 100 or more points in a season, the other being Guyle Fielder, who accomplished the feat four times. He was promoted to the WHA the following year.

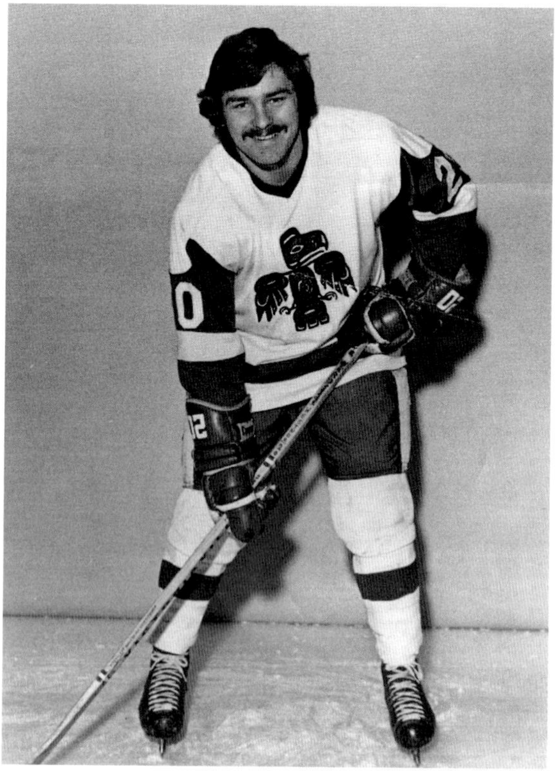

Dave Westner came to Seattle straight from Cornell University, where he won a NCAA championship in 1970 and lost in the finals to new teammate Dan Brady's Boston University in 1972. Westner posted respectable numbers with the Totems from 1972 to 1975 and picked up two goals and two assists in the 8-4 win over Russia in 1974.

Defenseman Dave Amadio was at the end of a long professional career when he joined Seattle in 1973, and that experience earned him a lot of respect with his teammates—he was team captain during his first and only season with the Totems. Despite a lackluster offensive year by his standards (19 points), he did pick up an assist in the win against Russia.

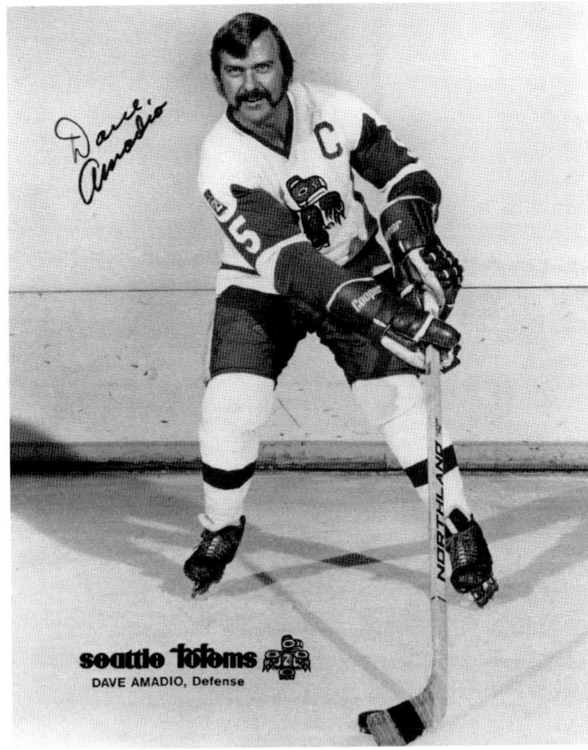

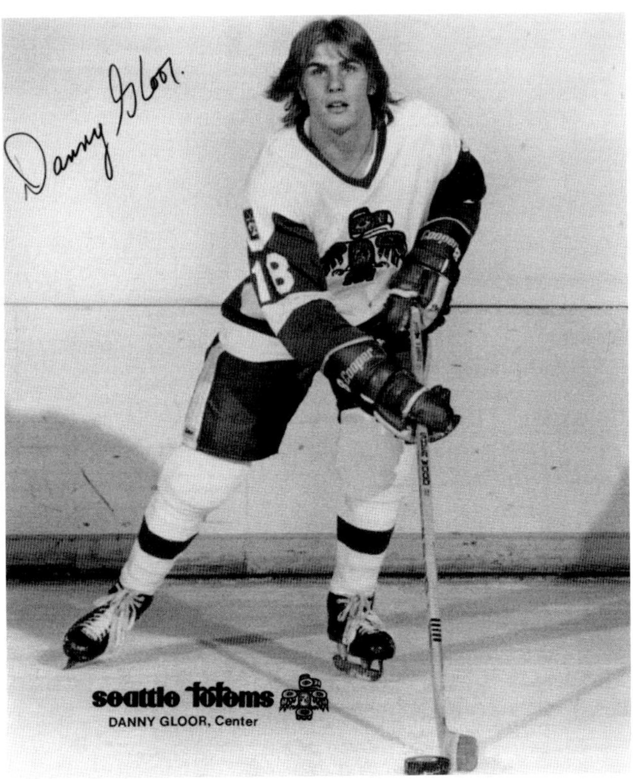

Though just 21 years old, Danny Gloor made a big splash in his first season in Seattle, leading the team in every offensive category with 36 goals, 48 assists, and 84 points in 1973–1974. An early-season leg injury the following year hampered his efforts, though he still put up a respectable 57 points.

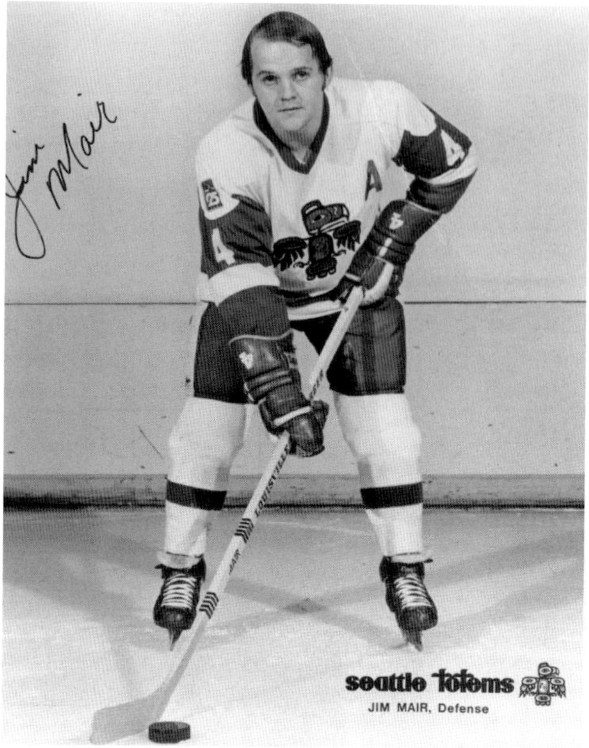

Jim Mair was one of two veteran defenseman brought to Seattle in 1973–1974 (the other being Dave Amadio) to be a stabilizing influence on a club that included much of the Vancouver Canucks' young talent. He made the most of the opportunity and was called up to Vancouver for a handful of appearances while with the Totems, helping out the Canucks in eight games over that two-year span.

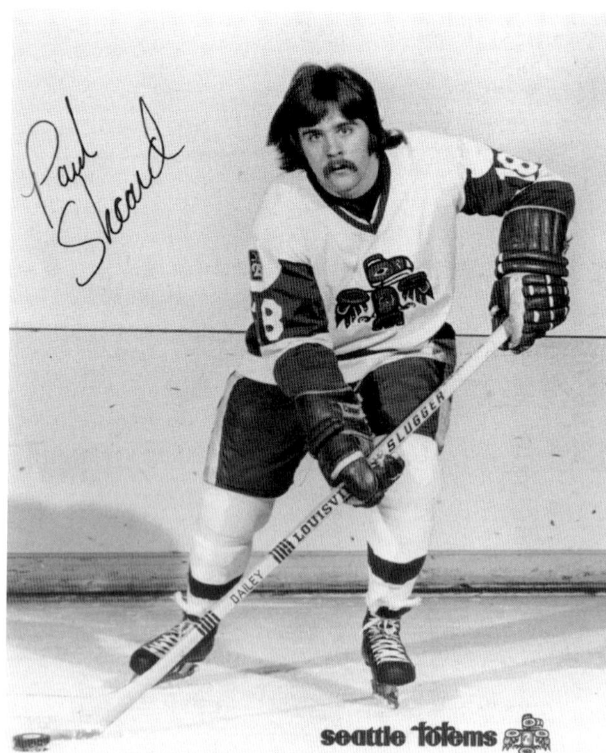

Winger Paul Sheard made the jump to the WHL straight from the juniors following three solid offensive years in Ottawa. He earned 43 points during his first season as a professional in 1973–1974, though after only a handful of games in 1974–1975, found himself transferred to the North American Hockey League.

Dave Wisener was another Boston University product and a member of their 1972 NCAA championship squad. He had two good seasons with the Totems from 1973 to 1975 and an impressive four-assist game against the Russians in 1974. He left the professional game in 1975, but that did not keep him off the ice, as he won the Hardy Cup with the 1976–1977 Campbellton Tigers.

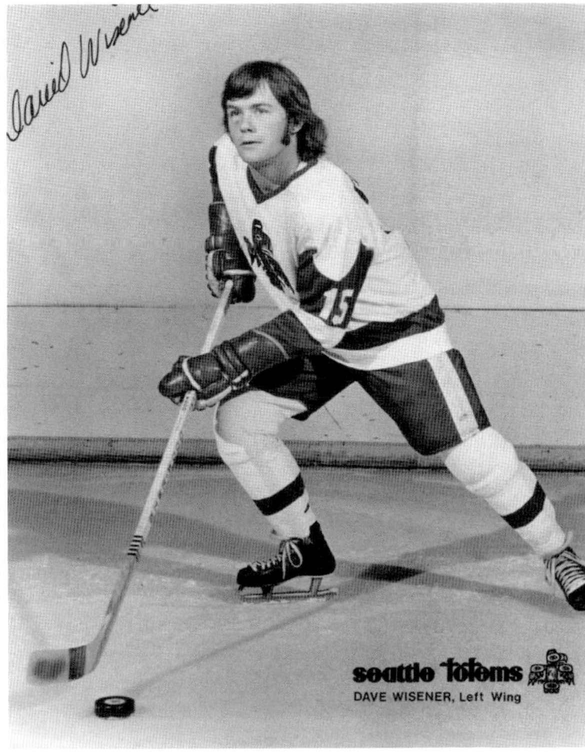

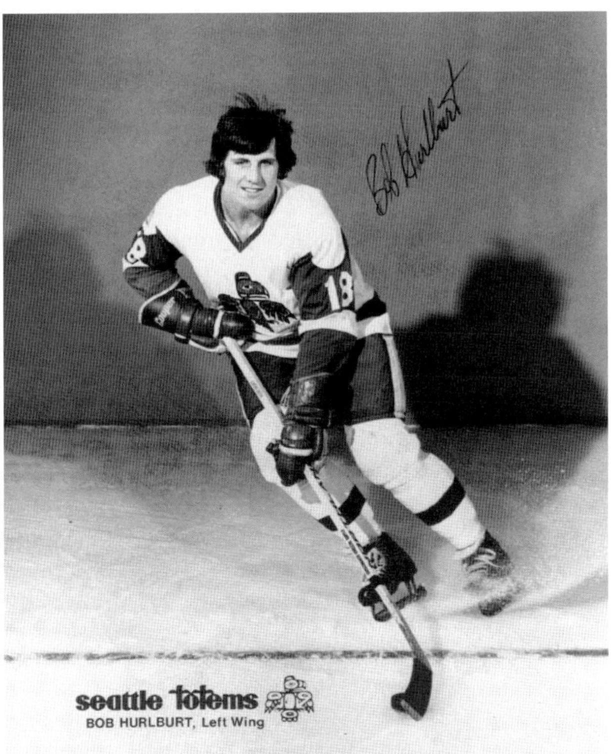

Left winger Bob Hurlburt was only with the Totems in their last season, the 1974–1975 CHL campaign. His 39 points and 68 penalty minutes earned him his shot for a "cup of coffee" in the NHL, getting into one game with the Canucks that year, his only NHL experience. (Courtesy of Dave Eskenazi.)

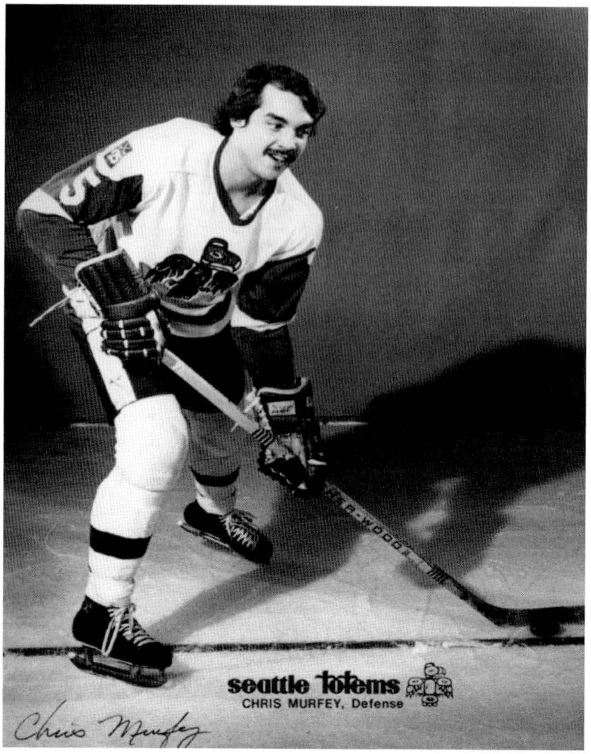

Being a farm team for the Vancouver Canucks meant that the Totems received a lot of young players making their first jump to the pros. Chris Murfey was one such skater, coming to Seattle fresh off a college hockey career with Michigan State University. He earned an impressive 33 assists as a rookie defenseman in Seattle. (Courtesy of Dave Eskenazi.)

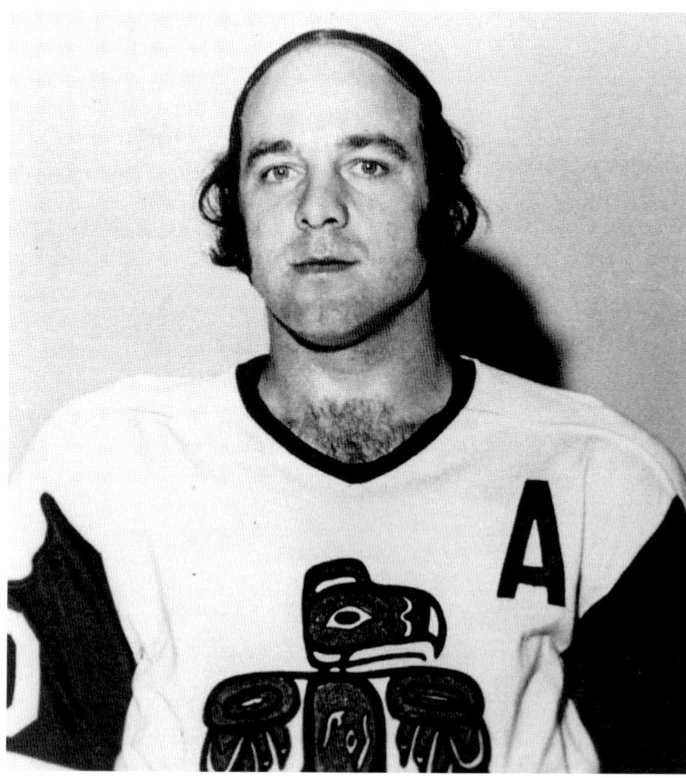

The Vancouver Canucks did the Totems a huge favor when they assigned left wing Danny Seguin to Seattle. He scored 95 goals over the course of three seasons, leading the CHL with 37 in 1974–1975. He also holds the distinction of being the last Totem to score a goal on home ice with his second period effort in a 6-2 win over Salt Lake City on March 29, 1975.

BIBLIOGRAPHY

Coleman, Charles L. *The Trail of the Stanley Cup, Volume 1, 1893–1926 inc.* Dubuque, IA: Kendall/Hunt Publishing Co., 1964.

hockeydb.com

Obermeyer, Jeff. *Emerald Ice: Hockey in Seattle from 1915 to 1975*. Seattle, WA: self-published, 2007.

———. *Hockey in Seattle*. Charleston, SC: Arcadia Publishing, 2004.

Scott, Jon C. *Ice Warriors: The Pacific Coast/Western Hockey League, 1948–1974*. Surrey, BC: Heritage House Publishing Company Ltd., 2008.

seattlehockey.net

seattletotems.org

Whitehead, Eric. *The Patricks: Hockey's Royal Family*. Toronto, ON: Doubleday Canada Ltd., 1980.